LEFT-WING MELANCHOLIA

NEW DIRECTIONS IN CRITICAL THEORY

New Directions in Critical Theory presents outstanding classic and contemporary texts in the tradition of critical social theory, broadly construed. The series aims to renew and advance the program of critical social theory, with a particular focus on theorizing contemporary struggles around gender, race, sexuality, class, and globalization and their complex interconnections.

LEFT-WING MELANCHOLIA

MARXISM, HISTORY, AND MEMORY

ENZO TRAVERSO

COLUMBIA UNIVERSITY PRESS   *New York*

COLUMBIA UNIVERSITY PRESS

PUBLISHERS SINCE 1893

NEW YORK   CHICHESTER, WEST SUSSEX

cup.columbia.edu

Library of Congress Cataloging-in-Publication Data

Names: Traverso, Enzo, author.

Title: Left-wing melancholia: Marxism, history and memory / Enzo Traverso.

Description: New York: Columbia University Press, 2016. | Series: New directions in critical theory | Includes bibliographical references and index.

Identifiers: LCCN 2016023862 | ISBN 978-0-231-17943-0 (pbk.) | ISBN 978-0-231-17942-3 (cloth) | ISBN 978-0-231-54301-9 (e-book)

Subjects: LCSH: Communism—History. | Memory. | Melancholy (Philosophy) | History—Philosophy.

Classification: LCC HX40 .T6365 2016 | DDC 335.4—dc23

LC record available at https://lccn.gov/2016023862

COVER DESIGN: Jenny Carrow

FOR MICHAEL LÖWY

CONTENTS

LIST OF ILLUSTRATIONS

PREFACE

THE aim of this book is to investigate the melancholic dimension of left-wing culture in the past century. The left I will deal with is not defined in merely *topological* terms (the parties on the left of the political and institutional space), according to the conventional viewpoint of political science, but rather in *ontological* terms: as movements that struggled to change the world by putting the principle of equality at the center of their agenda. Its culture is heterogeneous and open, insofar as it includes not only a multitude of political currents but also a plurality of intellectual and aesthetic tendencies. This is why I decided to analyze theories and testimonies (the political and philosophical ideas deposited in books, articles, letters) without excluding images (from propaganda posters to paintings and movies). Of course, I devote an important place to Marxism, which was the dominant expression of most revolutionary movements in the twentieth century. In other words, this book would like to approach left-wing culture as a combination of theories and experiences, ideas and feelings, passions and utopias. The memory of the left is a huge, prismatic continent made of conquests and defeats, while melancholy is a feeling, a state of the soul and a field of emotions. Thus, focusing on left-wing melancholy necessarily means going beyond ideas and concepts.

At the beginning of the 1980s, the rise of memory in the field of the humanities coincided with the crisis of Marxism, which was absent from the "memorial moment" characteristic of the turn of the twenty-first century. The Marxist vision of history implied a memorial prescription: we had to inscribe the events of the past in our historical consciousness in order to project ourselves into the future. It was a "strategic" memory of past emancipatory struggles, a future-oriented memory. Today, the end of communism has broken this dialectic between past and future, and the eclipse of utopias engendered by our "presentist" time has almost extinguished Marxist memory. The tension between past and future becomes a kind of "negative," mutilated dialectic. In such a context, we rediscover a melancholic vision of history as remembrance (*Eingedenken*) of the vanquished—Walter Benjamin was its most significant interpreter—that belongs to a hidden Marxist tradition. This book tries to analyze this mutation, this transition from utopia to memory.

For more than a century, the radical left drew its inspiration from Marx's famous eleventh thesis on Feuerbach: until now, philosophers have only interpreted the world, but the point is to change it. When, after 1989, we became "spiritually roofless" and were forced to recognize the failure of all the past attempts to transform the world, the ideas themselves with which we had tried to interpret the world were put into question. And when, a decade later, new movements appeared proclaiming that "another world is possible," they had to redefine their own intellectual and political identities. More precisely, they had to reinvent themselves—both their theories and their practices—in a world without a visible, thinkable, or imaginable future. They could not "invent a tradition," like other generations of "orphans" had done before them. This shift from an age of fire and blood that, in spite of all its defeats, remained decipherable to a new time of global threats without a foreseeable outcome takes on a melancholic taste. This melancholia, however, does not mean a retreat into a closed universe of suffering and remembering; it is rather a constellation of emotions and feelings that envelop a historical transition, the only way in which the search for new ideas and projects can coexist with the sorrow and mourning for a lost realm of revolutionary experiences. Neither regressive nor impotent, this left-wing melancholia should not evade the burden of the past. It is a melancholy criticism that, while being open to the struggles in the present, does not avoid self-criticism about its own past failures; it is the melancholy criticism of a left that is not resigned to the world order sketched by neoliberalism but that cannot refurbish its intellectual armory without identifying empathetically with the vanquished of history, a large multitude inexorably joined, at the end of the twentieth century, by an entire generation—or its remains—of defeated leftists. In order to be fruitful, however, this melancholia needs to become recognizable, after having been removed during the previous decades, when storming heaven appeared the best way to mourn our lost comrades.

Thus, the ambition of this book is to rethink the history of socialism and Marxism through the prism of melancholy. In exploring such a past both familiar and "unknown" (insofar as it was repressed), I will try to connect intellectual debates with cultural forms. The traces of left-wing melancholia can be recognized and captured much easier in the multiple expressions of socialist imagination than in doctrinal productions and theoretical controversies; furthermore, the latter reveal new meanings when they are reconsidered through the collective imagination that accompanied them. Therefore, this book shifts alternately from concepts to images, without establishing any hierarchy between them, assuming them as equally important in molding and expressing the culture of the left. It wishes to connect them and to grasp their resonances, showing what many classical Marxist works share with paintings, photographs, and movies. In short, I will work with multiple sources, analyzing them as "thought-images" (*Denkbilder*), according to Benjamin's concept. My purpose is not to build a monument or write an epitaph; it is to explore a multiform and at times contradictory memory landscape. Differently from currently dominant humanitarianism that sacralizes the memory of *victims*, and mostly neglects or rejects their commitments, left melancholy has always focused on the *vanquished*. It perceives the tragedies and the lost battles of the past as a burden and a debt, which are also a promise of redemption.

The seven chapters that compose this book excavate this melancholy constellation from different perspectives: by sketching the features of a left-wing culture of defeat (chapter 1), by depicting a Marxist conception of memory (chapter 2), by extracting a vision of mourning from paintings and movies (chapter 3), and by investigating the tension between ecstasy and sorrow that shapes the history of revolutionary Bohemia (chapter 4). Some chapters focus on particular figures that epitomize different forms of left-wing melancholia. From Marx to Benjamin, passing through Gustave Courbet and young Trotsky exiled in Vienna, the attempt of "winning the energies of intoxication for revolution"—thus Benjamin on Surrealism—merged in a peculiar osmosis with the despair of defeat and the pariah existence of aesthetic and political outsiders. The last three chapters deal with productive, conflicting, belated, or missed encounters between Marxist thinkers, revealing the paths through which left melancholia took shape. On the one hand, Benjamin's melancholia tried to articulate a new vision of history as catastrophe with a messianic reinterpretation of Marxism as political agency and possible redemption; on the other hand, Adorno's sorrow—"melancholy science," in his own words—simply adopted a contemplative posture of dialectical criticism resigned to the advent of universal reification (chapter 5). Breaking away from a Eurocentric, Hegelian, and Marxist vision of the West as world's destiny, C. L. R. James looked at the signals of a growing revolt against colonialism, whereas Adorno stoically contemplated the ruins produced by the "self-destruction of reason" (chapter 6). Finally, this book retraces the incandescent intellectual encounter between the French philosopher Daniel Bensaïd and Walter Benjamin, a fruitful and creative "meeting" that reveals a resonance between two crucial turning points of the twentieth century—1940 and 1990—through a vision of history based on the idea of remembrance (chapter 7). After the fall of the Berlin Wall, the remaining rebels of the 1960s and 1970s met a vision of history engendered by the defeats of the 1930s, an encounter that took place under the sign of political melancholy.

Paris; Ithaca, NY, December 2015

ACKNOWLEDGMENTS

SOME chapters of this book have been already published, in a shorter version, in different languages. The ideas developed in the introduction have been presented and discussed first at Cornell University in 2011, under the auspices of the Mellon Lectures, then at the Institute Nicos Poulantzas of Athens in 2014. I would like to remember with affection Stavros Kostantakopoulos, who recently passed away, and who had introduced me on this occasion. The key concepts of chapter 2 appeared in French, in a much shorter version, in "Marxisme et mémoire: De la téléologie à la mélancolie," *Le Portique* 32 (2013), which was later translated into Spanish. A first version of chapter 4 appeared as "Bohemia, Exile and Revolution: Notes on Marx, Benjamin and Trotsky," in *Historical Materialism* 10, no. 1 (2002). Some ideas of chapter 5 were originally included in a small article titled "Marx et l'Occident," *Europe: Revue littéraire mensuelle* 89, no. 988–89 (2011). Chapter 6 appeared in a short version as the introduction to *Correspondance Adorno-Benjamin, 1928–1940* (Paris: La Fabrique, 2002), then it was included in my book *La pensée dispersé* (Paris: Lignes, 2004) as well as in its Italian and Spanish translations (Verona: Ombre Corte, 2004; and Mexico: UNAM, 2004). A

German version, "Eine Freundschaft im Exil: Der Briefwechsel zwischen Adorno und Benjamin," appeared in a collected book on intellectual exile edited by Elfi Müller, *Fluchtlinien des Exils* (Münster: Unrast, 2004). I sketched some ideas of chapter 7 in my preface to the second edition of Daniel Bensaid, *Walter Benjamin: Sentinelle messianique* (Paris: Les Prairies ordinaries, 2010), as well as in "Daniel Bensaid Between Marx and Benjamin," *Historical Materialism* 24, no. 3 (2016). All these texts have been rethought, expanded, and rewritten in order to be included in the present book, where they take on a new dimension sometimes absent in their original form.

This book results from the graduate seminar "Left Melancholy" that I taught at Cornell University in the fall 2014. I would like to thank the numerous graduate students who attended it for their questions, critical observations, and suggestions, which contributed to enrich and clarify my thoughts on this topic. Some chapters have been discussed in seminars and lectures held in different universities in Europe, Latin America, and the United States. Without these moments of critical discussion, this book could not have been written. Thus, I am deeply indebted to all the colleagues and friends who made them possible and wish to thank them: Noël Barbe at the EHESS of Paris, Enrico Donaggio and Diego Guzzi at the Istituto Antonicelli of Turin, Eli Müller at Jour Fixe of Berlin, Natalie Melas and Paul Fleming at Cornell University of Ithaca, NY, Horacio Tarcus at the CeDinCi of Buenos Aires, Esther Cohen at the UNAM of Mexico and Fernando Matamoros at the Universidad de Puebla, Mexico. Federico Finchelstein and Eli Zaretsky, from the New School for Social Research, formulated many fruitful critical remarks on the manuscript and made extremely valuable suggestions. My interest in melancholy probably began with a book written by Michael Löwy and Robert Sayre at the beginning of the 1990s, *Révolte et mélancolie* (Paris: Payot, 1992), translated into English as *Romanticism Against the Tide of Modernity* (Durham: Duke University Press, 2001), which introduced me to the melancholic dimension of revolutionary thought. This is only one of my numerous intellectual debts to Michael, who, I hope, will perceive a resonance with his own writings in the pages of this book. Moreover, I wish to mention with gratitude Nicolas Bujalski, my research assistant at Cornell, who entirely revised the manuscript, trying to give an elegant form to my poor English. The pictures related to Portbou could not have been included without the precious help of Jordi Font Agulló, director of the Museu Memorial del Exili (MUMO), La Jonquera, who quickly fulfilled my request, and Sophie Bensaïd provided the photographs of Daniel for this book: I am grateful to both of them. At Columbia University Press, this book benefited enormously from the criticism and advices of two anonymous readers, as well as from Robert Demke's careful editing of the manuscript; my editors Wendy Lochner and Christine Dunbar supported it from the beginning, and Amy R. Allen agreed to include it in her wonderful series, alongside many authors whom I enormously admire: many thanks to all of them.

LEFT-WING MELANCHOLIA

HAUNTING PASTS WITHOUT UTOPIAS

In the century-long struggle between socialism and barbarism, the latter is a length ahead of the former. We enter the twenty-first century with less hope than our ancestors at the edge of the twentieth.

—DANIEL BENSAÏD, *JEANNE DE GUERRE LASSE* (1991)

HISTORICAL TURN

In 1967, reconstructing the long trajectory of the uses of Cicero's sentence *historia magistra vitae*, Reinhart Koselleck stressed its exhaustion at the end of the eighteenth century, when the birth of the modern idea of progress replaced the old, cyclical vision of history. The past ceased to appear as an immense reservoir of experiences from which human beings could draw moral and political lessons. Since the French Revolution, the future had to be invented rather than extracted from bygone events. The human mind, Koselleck observed quoting Tocqueville, "wandered in obscurity" and the lessons of history became mysterious or useless.[1] The end of the twentieth century, nevertheless, seemed to rehabilitate Cicero rhetorical formula. Liberal democracy took the form of a secular theodicy that, at the epilogue of a century of violence, incorporated the lessons of totalitarianism. On the one hand, historians pointed out the innumerable changes that occurred in a turbulent age; on the other hand, philosophers announced the "end of history." Fukuyama's optimistic Hegelianism has been criticized,[2] but the world that emerged from the end of the Cold War and the collapse of communism was desperately uniform. Neoliberalism invaded the stage; never, since the Reformation, had a single ideology established such a pervasive, global hegemony.[3]

The year 1989 stresses a break, a *momentum* that closes an epoch and opens a new one. The international success of Eric Hobsbawm's *Age of Extremes* (1994) lies, first of all, in its capability of inscribing into a broader historical perspective the hugely shared perception of the end of a cycle, of an epoch, and, finally, of a century.[4] For its unexpected and disruptive character, the fall of the Berlin Wall immediately took the dimension of an *event*, an epochal turn exceeding its causes, opening new scenarios, suddenly projecting the world into an unpredictable constellation. Like every great political event, it modified the perception of the past and engendered a new historical imagination. The collapse of State Socialism aroused a wave of enthusiasm and, for a short moment, great expectations of a possible democratic socialism. Very quickly, however, people realized that it was an entire representation of the twentieth century that had fallen apart. People on the left—a multitude of currents including many anti-Stalinist tendencies—felt uncanny. Christa Wolf, the most famous dissident writer of the former GDR, described this strange feeling in her autobiographical account *City of Angels*: she had become spiritually homeless, an exile from a country that no longer existed.[5] Beside the official, already discredited "monumental history" of communism, there was a different historical narrative, created by the October Revolution, in which many other epochal events had been inscribed, from the Spanish Civil War to the Cuban Revolution and May '68. According to this approach, the twentieth century had experienced a symbiotic link between barbarism and revolution. After the shock of November 1989, however, this narrative vanished, buried under the debris of the Berlin Wall. The dialectic of the twentieth century was broken. Instead of liberating new revolutionary energies, the downfall of State Socialism seemed to have exhausted the historical trajectory of socialism itself. The entire history of communism was reduced to its totalitarian dimension, which appeared as a collective, transmissible memory. Of course, this narrative was not invented in 1989; it had existed since 1917, but now it became a shared historical consciousness, a dominant and uncontested representation of the past. After having entered the twentieth century as a promise of liberation, communism exited as a symbol of alienation and oppression. The images of the demolition of the Berlin Wall appear, a posteriori, as a reversal of Eisenstein's *October*: the film of revolution had been definitely "rewound." In fact, when State Socialism broke down, the communist hope was already exhausted. In 1989, their superposition engendered a transmissible narrative of both of them, subsuming revolution under the narrative of totalitarianism.

Reinhart Koselleck defined as a *Sattelzeit*—a "saddle time," a time of passage—the period going from the crisis of the Old Regime to the Restoration. In this cataclysmic era of transition, a new form of sovereignty based on the idea of nation emerged and, for a short moment, erased the European dynastic regimes, when a society of orders was replaced by a society of individuals. Words changed their meanings and a new conception of history as a "singular collective," including both a "complex of events" and a meaningful narrative (a kind of "historical science"), finally appeared.[6] Does the concept of *Sattelzeit* help us to understand the transformations of contemporary world? We may suggest that, *toutes proportions gardées*, the years from the end of the 1970s to September 11, 2001, witnessed a transition whose result was a radical change of our general landmarks, of our political and intellectual landscape. In other words, the fall of the Berlin Wall symbolizes a transition in which old and new forms merged together. It was not a simple revival of the old anticommunist rhetoric. During this quarter of a century, market and competition—the cornerstones of the neoliberal lexicon—became the "natural" foundations of post-totalitarian societies. They colonized our imagination and shaped a new anthropological habitus, as the dominant values of a new "life conduct" (*Lebensführung*) in front of which the old Protestant asceticism of a bourgeois class ethically oriented—according to Max Weber's classical portrait—seems an archeological vestige.[7] The extremities of such *Sattelzeit* are utopia and memory. This is the political and epistemic framework of the new century opened by the end of Cold War.

In 1989, the "velvet revolutions" seemed to go back to 1789, short-circuiting two centuries of struggle for socialism. Freedom and political representation appeared as their only horizon, according to a model of classical liberalism: 1789 opposed to 1793 as well as to 1917, or even 1776 opposed to 1789 (freedom against equality).[8] Historically, revolutions have been factories of utopias; they have forged new imaginaries and new ideas, and have aroused expectancies and hopes. But that did not occur with the so-called velvet revolutions. On the contrary, they frustrated any previous dream and paralyzed cultural production. A brilliant essayist and playwright like Vaclav Havel became a pale, sad copy of a Western statesman once elected President of the Czech Republic. The writers of Eastern Germany were extraordinarily fruitful and imaginative when, submitted to the suffocating control of the STASI, they created allegorical novels stimulating the art of reading between the lines. Nothing comparable appeared after the *Wende.* In Poland, the turn of 1989 engendered a nationalist wave and the deaths of Jacek Kuron and Krizstof Kieslowski sealed the end of a period of critical culture. Instead of projecting themselves into the future, these revolutions created societies obsessed by the past. Museums and patrimonial institutions devoted to recovering national pasts kidnapped by Soviet communism simultaneously appeared all over the countries of Central Europe.

More recently, the Arab revolutions of 2011 have quickly reached a similar deadlock. Before being stopped by bloody civil wars in Libya and Syria, they destroyed two hated dictatorships in Tunisia and Egypt but did not know how to replace them. Their memory was made of defeats: socialism, pan-Arabism, Third Worldism, and also Islamic fundamentalism (which did not inspire the revolutionary youth). Admirably self-organized, these revolutions showed an astonishing lack of leadership and appeared strategically disoriented, but their limits did not lie in their leaders or in their social forces: they are the limits of our epoch. Such uprisings and mass movements are burdened with the defeats of the revolutions of the twentieth century, which are an overwhelming heaviness paralyzing the utopic imagination.

This historical change inevitably affected feminism. Revolutionary feminism had deeply put into question many assumptions of classical socialism—notably its implicit identification of universalism with male vision and agency—but it shared an idea of emancipation projected into the future. Feminism stressed a conception of revolution as global liberation that transcended class exploitation toward a complete reconfiguration of gender relationships and forms of human life. It redefined communism as a society of equals in which not only class but also gender hierarchies were abolished, and in which equality implied the recognition of differences. Its utopian imaginary announced a world in which kinship, sexual division of labor, and the relationship between public and private were completely reconfigured. In the wake of feminism, socialist revolution also meant *sexual revolution*, the end of bodily alienation and the accomplishment of repressed desires. Socialism did not merely designate a radical change of social structures but also the creation of new forms of life. Feminist struggles were often experienced as emancipatory practices that anticipated the future and prefigured a liberated community. In capitalist society, they claimed gender recognition and equal rights; within the left, they criticized the paradigm of virility that shaped a militarized conception of revolution inherited from nineteenth-century socialism and reinforced by Bolshevism during the Russian Civil War; among women, they created a new subjective consciousness. It is this ensemble of experiences and practices that was mourned after the end of revolutionary feminism. The collapse of communism was accompanied—or rather preceded—by the exhaustion of feminist struggles and utopias, which engendered their peculiar forms of melancholia. Like (and inside) the left, feminism mourned its own loss, a loss that combined both the vanished dream of a liberated future and the finished experiences of practical transformation. In the post–Cold War era, liberal democracy and free-market societies proclaimed the victory of feminism with the accomplishment of juridical equality and individual self-determination (the saga of business-women). The fall of feminist utopias engendered a variety of regressive "identity politics" and, in the academy, the growth of women studies. In spite of their significant scholarly accomplishments, the latter ceased to consider sex and race as markers of historical oppression (against which feminism struggled) and transformed them into unvaried, hypostatized—Rosi Braidotti called them "metaphysical"[9]—categories, adapted to a commodified recognition of gender otherness. According to Wendy Brown, that meant that gender was regarded "as something that can be bent, proliferated, troubled, re-signified, morphed, theatricalized, parodied, deployed, resisted, imitated, regulated . . . but not emancipated."[10]

END OF UTOPIAS

Thus, the twentieth-first century is born as a time shaped by a general eclipse of utopias. This is a major difference that distinguishes it from the two previous centuries. Opening the nineteenth century, the French Revolution defined the horizon of a new age in which politics, culture, and society were deeply transformed. The year 1789 created a new concept of revolution—no more a rotation, according to its original astronomical meaning, but a rupture and a radical innovation[11]—and laid the basis for the birth of socialism, which developed with the growth of industrial society. Demolishing the European dynastic order—the "persistence" of the Old Regime—the Great War birthed the twentieth century, but this cataclysm also engendered the Russian Revolution. October 1917 immediately appeared as a great and at the same time tragic event that, during a bloody civil war, created an authoritarian dictatorship that rapidly transformed into a form of totalitarianism. Simultaneously, the Russian Revolution aroused a hope of emancipation that mobilized millions of men and women throughout the world. The trajectory of Soviet communism—its ascension, its apogee at the end of the Second World War, and then its decline—deeply shaped the history of the twentieth century. The twenty-first century, on the contrary, opens with the collapse of this utopia.[12]

François Furet drew this conclusion at the end of *The Passing of an Illusion*, with a "resignation" to capitalism that many reviewers delightedly emphasized: "The idea of another society has become almost impossible to conceive of, and no one in the world today is offering any advice on the subject or even trying to formulate a new concept. Here we are, condemned to live in the world as it is."[13] Without sharing the satisfaction of the French historian, the Marxist philosopher Frederic Jameson formulated a similar diagnostic, observing that the end of the world is easier to imagine nowadays than the end of capitalism.[14] The utopia of a new, different model of society appears as a dangerous, potentially totalitarian desire. In short, the turn of the twenty-first century coincided with the transition from the "principle of hope" to the "principle of responsibility."[15] The "principle of hope" inspired the battles of the passed century, from Petrograd in 1917 to Managua in 1979, passing through Barcelona in 1936 and Paris and Prague in 1968. It haunted also its most terrible moments and encouraged resistance movements in Nazi Europe. The "principle of responsibility" appeared when the future darkened, when we discovered that revolutions had generated totalitarian monsters, when ecology made us aware of the dangers menacing the planet and we began to think about the kind of world we will give to future generations. Using the famous conceptual couple elaborated by

Reinhart Koselleck, we could formulate this diagnostic in the following way: communism is no more a point of intersection between a "space of experience" and a "horizon of expectation."[16] The expectation disappeared, whereas experience has taken the form of a field of ruins.

The German philosopher Ernst Bloch distinguished between the chimeric, Promethean dreams haunting the imagination of a society historically unable to realize them (the abstract, compensatory utopias, such as the aircrafts imagined in the technologically primitive societies arising from the Middle Ages), and the anticipatory hopes inspiring a revolutionary transformation of the present (the concrete utopias, such as socialism in the twentieth century).[17] Today, we could observe the vanishing of the former and the metamorphosis of the latter. On the one hand, taking varied forms, from science fiction to ecology studies, the dystopias of a future nightmare made of environmental catastrophes replaced the dream of a liberated humanity—a dangerous dream of the age of totalitarianism—and confined the social imagination into the narrow boundaries of the present. On the other hand, the concrete utopias of collective emancipation turned into individualized drives for the inexhaustible consumption of commodities. Dismissing the "warm stream" of collective emancipation, neoliberalism introduced the "cold stream" of economic reason. Thus, utopias are destroyed by their *privatization* into a reified world.[18]

According to Koselleck, the present gives its meaning to the past. At the same time, the latter offers to the actors of history a collection of experiences from which they can formulate their own expectations. In other words, past and future interact, related by a symbiotic link. Instead of being two rigorously separated continents, they are connected by a dynamic, creative relationship. At the beginning of the twenty-first century, nevertheless, this dialectic of historical time seems exhausted. The utopias of the past century have disappeared, leaving a present charged with memory but unable to project itself into the future. There is no visible "horizon of expectation." Utopia seems a category of the past—the future imagined in a bygone time—because it no longer belongs to the present of our societies. History itself appears as a landscape of ruins, a living legacy of pain.

Some historians, such as François Hartog, characterize the regime of historicity that emerged in the 1990s as *presentism*: a diluted and expanded present absorbing and dissolving in itself both past and future.[19] "Presentism" has a double dimension. On the one hand, it is the past reified by a culture industry that destroys all transmitted experience; on the other hand, it is the future abolished by the time of neoliberalism: not the "tyranny of the clocks" described by Norbert Elias but the dictatorship of the stock exchange, a time of permanent acceleration— borrowing the words of Koselleck—without a "prognostic structure."[20] Twenty-five years ago, the fall of real socialism paralyzed and prohibited the utopian imagination, generating for a while new eschatological visions of capitalism as the "insuperable horizon" of human societies. This time is over, but no new utopias have yet appeared. Thus, "presentism" becomes a suspended time between an unmasterable past and a denied future, between a "past that won't go away"[21] and a future that cannot be invented or predicted (except in terms of catastrophe).

In recent times, "presentism" has become, far beyond a historical diagnostic, a sort of manifesto for some left intellectuals. One of them is the former situationist art historian T. J. Clark, who, claiming a sort of Nietzschean, disenchanted reformism, suggests a realist politics that would renounce any utopia. "There will be no future," he assesses, "only a present in which the left (always embattled and marginalized, always—proudly—a thing of the past) struggles to assemble the 'material for a society' Nietzsche thought had vanished from the earth. And this is a recipe for politics, not quietism—a left that can look the world in the face."[22] In such an assessment, the boundary between recognition of the objective situation and resignation to defeat as an ineluctable destiny of the left almost disappears.

The twenty-first century engendered a new kind of disillusionment. After the "disenchantment of the world" announced by Max Weber one century ago, when he defined modernity as the dehumanized age of instrumental rationality, we have experienced a second disenchantment brought by the failure of its alternatives. This historical impasse is the result of a paralyzed dialectic: instead of a negation of the negation— the socialist transcendence of capitalism according to the Hegelian (and Marxian) idea of *Aufhebung*—we observed the reinforcement and the extension of capitalism through the demolition of its enemies. Blochian hope of human becoming—the "not yet" (*noch-nicht*)—is abandoned in favor of an eternal present.[23] Of course, the failure of real socialism is not the only source of this historical change. Socialist utopia was deeply linked to a workers' memory that disappeared during the last crucial decades. The fall of communism coincided with the end of Fordism, that is, the model of industrial capitalism that had dominated the twentieth century. The introduction of flexible, mobile, and precarious work as well as the penetration of individualist models of competition among salary men eroded traditional forms of sociability and solidarity. The advent of new forms of production and the dislocation of the old system of big factories with enormous concentration of labor forces had many consequences: on the one hand, it deeply affected the traditional left, putting into question its social and political identity; on the other hand, it disarticulated the social frameworks of the left's memory, whose continuity was irremediably broken. The European workers movement lost both its social basis and its culture.

Simultaneously, the decade of the 1990s was marked by the crisis of the traditional "party model." Mass political parties—which had been the dominant form of political life after the Second World War and whose paradigm were the left parties (both communist and social-democratic) —disappeared or declined. Comprising hundreds of thousands, sometimes millions, of members, and deeply rooted in civil societies, they had been a major vector of the formation and transmission of a collective political memory. The new "catchall" parties that replaced them are electoral machines without strong political identities. Socially decomposed, class memory vanished in a context where laboring men and women had lost any public visibility; it became a kind of "Marrano" memory, that is, a hidden memory (exactly as Holocaust memory was just after the war) and the European left lost both its social bases and its culture. The failure of real socialism was followed by an ideological offensive of conservatism, not by a strategic balance sheet of the left.

The obsession with the past that is shaping our time results from this eclipse of utopias: a world without utopias inevitably looks back. The emergence of memory in the public space of Western societies is a consequence of this change. We entered the twenty-first century without revolutions, without Bastilles or Winter Palace assaults, but we got a shocking, hideous ersatz on September 11 with the attacks on the Twin Towers and the Pentagon, which spread terror instead of hope. Deprived of its horizon of expectation, the twentieth century appears to our retrospective gaze as an age of wars and genocides. A previously discreet and modest figure bursts on the center of the stage: the *victim*.[24] Mostly anonymous and silent, victims invade the podium and dominate our vision of history. Thanks to the quality and the influence of their literary works, the witnesses of the Nazi camps and Stalin's gulags became the icons of this century of victims. Capturing this *Zeitgeist*, Tony Judt concluded his fresco of postwar Europe with a chapter devoted to the memory of the continent emblematically titled: "From the House of the Dead."[25]

This empathy toward victims illuminates the twentieth century with a new light, introducing in history a figure that, in spite of his omnipresence, always remained in the shadow. Henceforth, the past seems the landscape contemplated by Benjamin's Angel of History: a field of ruins incessantly accumulating toward the skies. Yet, the new *Zeitgeist* is exactly antipodal to the messianism of the German-Jewish philosopher: there is no "now-time" (*Jetztzeit*) resonating with the past in order to accomplish the hopes of the vanquished and to assure their redemption.[26] The memory of the Gulag erased that of revolution, the memory of the Holocaust replaced that of antifascism, and the memory of slavery eclipsed that of anticolonialism: the remembrance of the victims seems unable to coexist with the recollection of their hopes, of their struggles, of their conquests and their defeats. Several observers wrote as early as 1990 that it was, once again, "midnight in the century." According to the Mexican historian Adolfo Gilly, the neoliberal offensive tried "to eradicate the idea itself of socialism in the mind and the dreams of human beings."[27]

The turn of 1989 produced a clash between history and memory, merging two concepts that, from Maurice Halbwachs to Paul Ricoeur and Aleida Assmann, scholars had rigorously separated throughout the twentieth century. "Historical memory" exists: it is the memory of a past that definitely appears as closed and has entered into history. In other words, it results from the collision between memory and history that shapes our time, a crossroads between different temporalities, the mirror of a past at the same time still living in our minds and archived. The writing of the history of the twentieth century is a balance between both temporalities. On the one hand, its actors achieved—as witnesses—a status of source for the historians; on the other hand, scholars work on a matter that constantly interrogates their lived experience, destabilizing their own status. Books such as *Age of Extremes* by the Marxist Eric Hobsbawm and *The Passing of an Illusion* by the conservative François Furet are in many aspects antipodal, but their interpretations of the twentieth century carry on a recollection of its events that takes often a similar autobiographical form.

In his posthumous book *History: The Last Things Before the Last* (1969), Siegfried Kracauer suggested the metaphor of exile for describing the historian's journey. In his eyes, the historian is, like an exile or a "stranger" (*Fremde*), a figure of *extraterritoriality*.[28] He is divided between two worlds: the world where he lives and the world he tries to explore. He is suspended between them because, in spite of his effort to penetrate the mental universe of the actors of the past, his analytical tools and hermeneutic categories are formulated in his own time. This temporal gap implies both traps—first of all anachronism—and advantages, because it allows a retrospective explanation that is not submitted to the cultural, political, and also psychological constraints belonging to the context in which the subjects of history act. It is precisely from this gap that historical narratives and representations of the past originate. The metaphor of exile is undoubtedly fruitful—exile remains one of the most fascinating experiences of modern intellectual history—but nowadays needs to be nuanced. Historians of the twentieth century—notably left-wing historians who investigate the history of communism and revolutions—are both "exiles" and "witnesses" because they are deeply involved in the events that constitute the object of their research. They do not explore a far and unknown past, and the difficulty of their task lies in taking distance with respect to a recent past, a past that they often have lived and observed and that still haunts their environment. Their empathetic relationship with the actors of the past permanently risks being disturbed by unexpected moments of "transfer" that break through to the surface in their workshop, awaking lived experience and subjectivity.[29] In other words, we live in a time in which historians write the history of memory, while civil societies carry on the living memory of a historical past. Thus, the exploration of the multiform planet of left culture results in an exercise of melancholy criticism, in a precarious equilibrium between history and memory.

THREE REALMS OF REVOLUTION

A common view among the radical left of the 1960s and the 1970s described world revolution as a process displayed in three distinct but correlated "sectors." A Marxist thinker of that time, the Belgian economist Ernest Mandel, scrutinized the dialectical links intertwining the anticapitalist movements of the West with the antibureaucratic revolts in the countries of "actually existing socialism" and the anti-imperialist revolutions spreading across the Third World.[30] Between the Cuban Revolution (1959) and the end of the Vietnam War (1975), this vision seemed, more than an abstract or doctrinal scheme, to be an objective description of reality. May '68 was the climax of a wave of radical movements shaking many countries in Western Europe, from the Italian "hot autumn" to the Portuguese Revolution and the end of Francoism in Spain. In Czechoslovakia, the Prague Spring openly defied Soviet rule, threatening a contagion in other "really socialist" countries. In Latin America, many guerrilla movements followed—mostly with tragic outcomes—the Cuban experience, but until the Chilean putsch of General Pinochet in 1973, socialism was an option for tomorrow rather than a vague dream projected into a far future. In Asia, the Vietcong inflicted a historical defeat upon the US imperial domination. The feeling of a growing convergence between these rebellious experiences, of a sort of synchronism among the "three sectors of world revolution," deeply shaped the youth, transforming the idea and practice of revolution. Probably for the first time in history, a global popular culture appeared that—far beyond ideologies and political texts—took the form of novels, songs, movies, hairstyles, and clothes. In Italy, a song of the movement Lotta continua, written in 1971 by Pino Masi, was titled "Hour of the Gun." Based on the melody of "Eve of Destruction" by P. F. Sloan and Barry McGuire (1965), it transformed this famous pacifist song into an appeal to insurrection and described a revolutionary world that was "exploding from Angola to Palestine." After enumerating the countries currently witnessing revolts—from Latin American guerrillas to Poland workers strikes and the US ghettos' uprisings—the song concluded with a rhetorical question: "And so: what more would you need, comrade, to understand / That the hour of the gun has sounded?"[31]

During these "street fighting years" of utopian strains, memory was not a cult object; it was rather incorporated into these struggles. Auschwitz played a significant role in the anticolonial commitment of many French activists and intellectuals. During the Vietnam War, the Nuremberg Trial became a model for the Russell Tribunal that in 1967 gathered many prominent intellectuals in Stockholm—from Jean-Paul Sartre to Isaac Deutscher, from Noam Chomsky to Peter Weiss—in order to denounce US war crimes. The comparison between Nazi violence and US imperialism was a commonplace of the antiwar movement.[32] Memory was mobilized in order to fight the executioners of the present, not to commemorate the victims of the past. In his intervention, Sartre qualified antiguerrilla warfare as "total genocide" and Günther Anders, a Jewish philosopher who had been an exile in the US, suggested the transfer of the tribunal to Auschwitz or Krakow, a highly symbolical location.[33] In the West as well as in the Third World, war memories were to be integrated into the political commitment of the present. As Michael Rothberg pertinently observed quoting Aimé Césaire, it was a sort of "boomerang effect" (*un choc en retour*).[34] In Europe, the struggle against imperialism was inscribed in the continuity of the resistance movements against Nazism; in the South, Nazism was perceived—since Aimé Césaire's *Discourse on Colonialism* (1950)—as a form of radical imperialism.

Nevertheless, a big change occurred during the 1980s. The revolutionary wave had its epilogue in Managua, in July 1979, which corresponded with the traumatic discovery of the Cambodian killing fields. In Europe, the Holocaust became the core of collective memory. Antifascism was marginalized in public recollections and the victims began to occupy the stage of a new memorial landscape. The legacy of the past was no longer interpreted as a collection of struggle's experiences and became a strong sense of duty in defense of human rights. Suddenly, three decades of the Cold War had been removed from collective memory. In France, May '68 became a purely cultural change, a kind of carnival in which, playing a revolutionary game, the youth pushed the society from Gaullism to modern forms of liberalism and individualism.[35] In Italy and Germany, the 1970s became the "years of lead" (*anni di piombo*), in which the revolt of a generation was reduced to the single dimension of terrorism.[36] In Germany, it became a commonplace to compare the radical left of the 1970s to the *Hitlerjugend*.[37] The repression of the "street fighting years" was also a form of expiation by a generation that repudiated its past experiences and took positions of responsibilities in governments and other powerful institutions. After the shipwreck of world revolution, its "three sectors" became the fields of three different victims' memories, three distinct places of mourning.

THREE MEMORIES

As Dan Diner suggested, the commemoration of the victory of May 8, 1945, is an interesting observatory for exploring this mutation of the memory landscape at the beginning of the twenty-first century.[38] Established as a national holiday in many countries, this anniversary does not have the same meaning for the Western world, Eastern Europe, and Northern Africa. Western Europe celebrates the unconditional surrender of the Third Reich to the Allied forces as an event of liberation, the starting point of an era of peace, freedom, democracy, and the reconciliation of a continent that had been involved in a fratricidal conflict. With the passing of time, Germans themselves adhered to this vision of the past, abandoning their old perception of the defeat of the Third Reich as a national humiliation that was followed first by the privation of their sovereignty and then by the division of their country into two enemy states. In 1985, the former president of the German Federal Republic Richard von Weiszäcker defined May 8, during a resounding talk, as "liberation day," and twenty years later chancellor Gerhard Schröder participated, side by side with Jacques Chirac, Tony Blair, Georges Bush, and Vladimir Putin, in the commemorations of the Allied landing in Normandy on June 6, 1944. Germany's adoption of a kind of "constitutional patriotism" strongly rooted in the West was definitely ratified.

In this context, the memory of the Holocaust plays the role of a *unifying narrative*. It is a relatively recent phenomenon—we could date it to the beginning of the 1980s—concluding a process of remembering that passed through different steps. At first, there was the silence of the postwar years, then the anamnesis of the 1960s and 1970s—provoked by the awakening of Jewish memory and a generational change—and finally the memory obsession of the last twenty years. After a long period of repression, the Holocaust returned to the surface in a European culture finally liberated from anti-Semitism (one of its major elements until the 1940s). All the countries of continental Europe were involved in this change, not only France, which has the largest Jewish community outside of Russia, but also Germany, where continuity with the Jewry of the years before the war was radically broken. In a rather paradoxical way, the place of the Holocaust in our representations of history seems to be growing as the event becomes more and more remote. Of course, this tendency is not irreversible and things could change with the death of the last survivors of the Nazi camps. Until now, however, it dominates the memorial space of the West—both Europe and the United States—where the Holocaust has become a kind of "civil religion" (that is, a secular belief, according to Rousseau, useful for unifying a given community).[39] The Holocaust allows for the sacralization of the foundational values of liberal democracies—pluralism, tolerance, and Rights of Man—whose defense takes the form of a secular liturgy of remembering.

It would be wrong to confuse *collective memory* and the *civil religion* of the Judeocide: the first is the presence of the past in today's world; the second is a politics of representation, education, and commemoration. Rooted into the formation of a transnational historical consciousness, the civil religion of the Holocaust is the product of state pedagogic efforts. Within the European Union, it tries to create the illusion of a supranational community built on ethical values: a virtuous appearance that conveniently conceals the enormous democratic vacuum of an institution founded, according to the terms of its abortive constitutional project, on a "highly competitive" market economy in which the only effective supranational sovereignty is embodied by the central bank.

Like every civil religion, the memory of the Holocaust has its ambiguities. In Germany, the creation of a memorial devoted to the murdered Jews (*Holocaust Mahnmal*) in the heart of Berlin fulfilled an identity change of historical dimension. The crimes of Nazism definitely belong to the German identity in the same way as the Reformation or *Aufklärung*. Germany ceased considering itself as an ethnic collective body and became a political community where the myth of blood and soil was replaced by a modern vision of citizenship. At the same time, the "duty to remember" the Holocaust was followed by a systematic destruction of the traces of the German Democratic Republic. The demolition of the Republic Palace (replaced by the reconstruction of the Hoenzollern castle) sharply contrasts with the methodical restoration of ancient synagogues, Jewish cemeteries, and all memory sites of the Third Reich. The memory of the GDR (as well as that of antifascism) had to be erased.[40]

In the age of the victims, the Holocaust becomes the paradigm of Western memory, the foundation upon which the remembrance of other ancient or recent forms of violence and crimes should be built. Thus, the propensity emerges to reduce history to a binary confrontation between executors and victims. This temptation does not concern exclusively the remembrance of genocides but also that of completely different historical experiences, for instance, the Spanish Civil War. Thirty years later, with a willingly "amnesic" transition to democracy, based upon the so-called pact of oblivion (*pacto de olvido*), the ghosts of Francoism come back.[41] The fear of falling again into violence generated the repression of the past—a repression that was neither imposed nor total, but effective—that accompanied the advent of democracy. Today, within the solid democracy in which a new generation was formed, the European integration of Spain has also taken a memorial dimension with some paradoxical consequences. In recent years, historians have extensively investigated the violence of the Civil War and have reconstituted the forms, the methods, and the ideology of the violence between 1936 and 1939, identifying and quantifying the victims on both sides. For the first time, the history of Franco's concentration camps was seriously investigated and described. In the public debate, nevertheless, this valuable work elucidating the past does not hinder a new interpretation in which the remembrance of the victims simply eclipses the meaning of history. According to this approach, the conflict between democracy and fascism—the way the Spanish Civil War was perceived in Europe during the 1930s—becomes a sequence of crimes against humanity. Some historians depict a Spanish "genocide," an eruption of violence in which there were only persecutors and victims.[42]

In Eastern Europe, on the opposite side, the end of the Second World War is not celebrated as a moment of liberation. Of course, in the Soviet Union—and today in Russia—the anniversary of German surrender was commemorated as the triumph of the "Great Patriotic War." In the countries that were occupied by the Red Army, however, this anniversary indicates the transition from one foreign occupation to another. The end of the Nazi nightmare coincided with the beginning of the long night of Soviet hibernation, a "kidnapping" through which Central Europe had been separated from the West:[43] its true "liberation" did not come until 1989. This explains the violent confrontations in Tallinn in the summer of 2006, in which Estonians came to grips with Russians around a monument devoted to the memory of the soldiers of the Red Army. For the Russians, this statue celebrates the Great Patriotic War; for the majority of Estonians, on the contrary, it is the symbol of many decades of Soviet oppression.[44]

Today, in the countries of the former Soviet bloc, the past is revisited almost exclusively through the prism of nationalism. In Poland, the Institute of National Remembrance was created in 1998, which, postulating a substantial continuity between Nazi occupation and Soviet domination, celebrates the history of the twentieth century as a long national martyrdom and totalitarian night. A similar vision of national history inspires the House of Terror in Budapest, a museum devoted to illustrating the "fight against the two cruelest systems of the twentieth century," which fortunately ended with "the victory of the forces of freedom and independence." In Kiev, the Parliament passed a law in 2006 defining the Soviet collectivization of agriculture and the famine of the 1930s as "genocide of the Ukrainian people." Depicting themselves as representatives of nation-victims, the governments of Central Europe leave a marginal place to the memory of the Holocaust, which appears as a kind of competitor and as an obstacle to a complete acknowledgment of their suffering. This contrast is paradoxical because the extermination of the Jews did take place in this part of the continent: it was there that the great majority of the victims lived and the Nazis created ghettos and death camps. The new members of the European Union often seem to consider the Holocaust as an object of diplomatic mourning. Exhuming an image forged by Heinrich Heine in order to depict the conversion of the Jews in nineteenth-century Germany, Tony Judt presented this compelled condolence as a "European entry ticket," that is, the price to pay for getting respectability and showing sensibility with regard to the human rights.[45]

During the 1990s, the war in Yugoslavia was a crossing point between Western and Eastern memories. The end of the Cold War, ten years after the death of Tito, produced an explosion of nationalisms that reactivated the memory of the Second World War, with its cortege of massacres, and mobilized the myths linked to a Balkan history made of imperial domination. In Croatia, Serbian nationalists fought the ghosts of Ante Pavelic and in Kosovo the symbols of Ottoman conquerors. On the other side, the European Union discovered the virtues of a military humanitarianism for which memory offered an excellent pretext. Bombing Serbian towns became a duty in order to redeem the victims of the Gulag, to not repeat the errors of Munich and the like. According to Jürgen Habermas, NATO bombs were a providential sign of the advent of a Kantian cosmopolitan right.[46]

In Northern Africa, the anniversary of May 9, 1945, evokes other events. On that day, French colonial forces opened fire on many thousands of Algerian nationalists who, celebrating the defeat of Nazism in the streets of Setif, refused to retire their flag. Military repression spread to other towns and villages and the conflict concluded with new demonstrations in which Algerian *indigènes* were compelled to submit themselves to the colonial authorities, bowing down in front of a French banner. The massacre resulted in between fifteen and forty-five thousand victims, according to French or Algerian sources.[47] Setif was the starting point for a wave of violence and military repression in French colonies, notably in Madagascar, where an insurrection was bloodily sedated in 1947. In May 2005, while the representatives of Western great powers celebrated the anniversary of the end of the Second World War, Algerian President Abdel Aziz Boutlefika officially asked for the recognition of the bloodbath of Setif, qualifying colonialism as "genocide" and claiming reparations from France.

Thus, the commemoration of the victory of May 8, 1945, is a condensation of entangled memories. Observed from a Western, Eastern, or postcolonial perspective, the history of the twentieth century takes a different aspect. The historical narratives intertwined by this anniversary are different, in spite of their shared tropism toward the victims of the past, which is the dominant feature of the globalization of memories in the early twenty-first century. Of course, they are not monolithic and incompatible memories and their pluralism could open fruitful spaces of coexistence, beyond closed national and cultural identities. Until now, however, their different focus—Holocaust, communism, and colonialism—illustrates the tendency to draw competitive rather than complementary "history lessons." The global memory of the beginning of the twenty-first century sketches a landscape of fragmented sufferings. New collective hopes have not yet risen above the horizon. Melancholy still floats in the air as the dominant feeling of a world burdened with its past, without a visible future. The West, the East, and the South: the former "three sectors" of world revolution have become three realms of wounded memories.

SPECTERS

In 1959, Theodor W. Adorno denounced the amnesia that, favored by a hypocritical use of the notion of "working through the past" (*Aufarbeitung der Vergangenheit*), had struck Western Germany (and Europe). This "highly suspect" formulation, he explained, did not mean "seriously working upon the past, that is, through a lucid consciousness breaking its power to fascinate." On the contrary, it meant rather "to close the books on the past and, if possible, even remove it from memory."[48] More than fifty years later, a similar amnesia affects our cultures, where entire dimensions of the past—antifascism, anticolonialism, feminism, socialism, and revolution—are buried under the official rhetoric of the "duty of memory."

In such a landscape of sorrow, the legacy of liberation struggles has become almost invisible, taking a ghostly form. As psychoanalysis explains, specters have posthumous existences, haunting our recollections of supposedly finished, exhausted, and archived experiences. They inhabit our minds as figures coming from the past, as etheric revenants separated from our bodily lives. Sketching a kind of ghostly typology, Giorgio Agamben points out a particular genre of specters, the "larval" specters, which "do not live alone but rather obstinately look for people who generated them through their bad conscience."[49] Stalinism generated these kinds of "larval" specters. Differently from other epochs of restoration, like France after June 1848 or after the Commune of 1871, the turn of 1989 could offer to the vanquished nothing but the memory of a disfigured socialism, the totalitarian caricature of an emancipated society. Not only was the prognostic memory of socialism paralyzed, but the mourning itself of the defeat was censured. The victims of violence and genocide occupy the stage of public memory, while the revolutionary experiences haunt our representations of the twentieth century as "larval" specters. Their vanquished actors lie in wait of redemption. They are no longer specters that announce a "presence to come," like for Burke in 1790 and Marx and Engels in 1847. As Derrida observed twenty years ago, they reveal rather "the persistence of a present past, the return of the dead which the worldwide work of mourning cannot get rid of."[50] The ghosts haunting Europe today are not the revolutions of the future but the defeated revolutions of the past.

We can always take comfort in the fact that revolutions are never "on time," that they come when nobody expects them. The Italian writer Erri De Luca provoked scandalized commentaries when he recently compared the legacy of the rebellious 1970s to the tragic destiny of Eurydice, the nymph of justice in Greek mythology: she could not be saved by her beloved husband, Orpheus, who in order to rescue her went down into Hades, the realm of the dead.[51] In this allegory, Erri De Luca describes the 1970s as a decade invaded by a "collective Orpheus" who, having fallen in love with justice, took arms for conquering it. It is significant that, differently from Marx, he does not compare revolution with an assault on Heaven but rather with a descent into the underworld. The conquest of Heaven and the journey through Hades are the poles of the transition I described above from utopia to memory, from the future to the past. Left-wing melancholy does not mean to abandon the idea of socialism or the hope for a better future; it means to rethink socialism in a time in which its memory is lost, hidden, and forgotten and needs to be redeemed. This melancholia does not mean lamenting a lost utopia, but rather rethinking a revolutionary project in a nonrevolutionary age. This is a fruitful melancholia that, one could say with Judith Butler, implies the "transformative effect of loss."[52]

One of the most significant examples of a fruitful work of mourning that, instead of paralyzing action, stimulates it in a self-reflexive and conscious way deals with the reactions of gay activists to the disruptive consequences of AIDS, a pandemic whose outbreak coincided with the fall of communism. In 1989, Douglas Crimp observed that, far from spreading passivity and favoring a retreat into a private sphere of suffering, this trauma inspired a new form of militancy, a militancy coming from mourning, which drew its strength from *within* melancholy and bereavement. For many gay activists who lived with a permanent feeling of loss and knew they soon would die and share the same destiny of the mourned, this was an incitement to act. Many dead were young people and the survivors felt alone, impotent, and deprived of their closest friends and lovers. Their lives changed. They needed to rebuild a destroyed community, reinvent friendship, pleasure, and sexual practices, feeling overwhelmed by threats and surrounded by a hostile, stigmatizing environment. Many of them were paralyzed by fear and internalized the stigma as a feeling of guilt, as the death drive transformed into self-aggression. The gay activism that reacted against this death drive in such tragic circumstances—to some extent comparable to the fall of communism—was inseparable from grief and mourning. Rather than escaping melancholia, it channeled it toward a fruitful work of reconstruction, creating medical centers, assuring psychological care, defending recently achieved rights, and rebuilding a network of associations. Act Up was the product of a fruitful, political melancholia. The meaning of this experience, concluded Douglas Crimp, could be summarized in a formula that mirrors very well the spirit of this book: "Militancy, of course, but mourning too: mourning *and* militancy."[53]

1 THE CULTURE OF DEFEAT

SHIPWRECK WITH SPECTATOR

THE history of socialism is a constellation of defeats that nourished it for almost two centuries. Instead of destroying its ideas and aspirations, these traumatic, tragic, often bloody defeats consolidated and legitimated them. Falling after a well-fought struggle gives dignity to the vanquished and can become a source of pride. Exiled and banished revolutionaries often knew misery and privations, certainly the sufferings of loss, but rarely isolation among the people surrounding them. They always occupied a place of honor within the left and socialist movements, from Heine, Marx, and Herzen in nineteenth-century Paris to the antifascist émigrés in twentieth-century New York. The defeat suffered by the left in 1989, however, was a different one: it did not occur after a battle and did not engender any pride; it ended a century and summarized in itself a cumulative sequence of downfalls that, suddenly gathered and condensed in a symbolic historical turn, appeared as overwhelming and unbearable. Such a defeat was so heavy that many of us preferred to escape rather than face it. It struck us like a boomerang whose strength was as great as the energy with which it had been launched one century earlier from Petrograd, Berlin, and Budapest and that had passed over the planet like a lightening bolt, from Beijing to Havana and Lisbon. What remains of this century of "storming heavens" is a mountain of ruins and we do not know how to start to rebuild, or if it is even worth doing. The melancholy that came out from such a historical defeat—it has lasted an entire generation—is probably the necessary premise for reacting, mourning, and preparing a new beginning. At first, the most widespread reaction was avoidance, showing an "inability to mourn" (*Unfahigkeit zu trauern*) like that described by Alexander and Margarete Mitscherlich in their famous essay from the 1960s devoted to postwar Western Germany.[1] Similarly to that search for pretexts to evade the legacy of National Socialism, communism has been suppressed in different ways: either changing names or "forgetting" it, building new mimetic identities or choosing between the innumerable outlets offered by the universal commodification of neoliberal capitalism. As in Germany, nevertheless, such a past will not pass and will inevitably come back, compelling us to face it.

Inherited from a century and resulting from a historical cycle in which revolution had taken the form of communism, this crepuscular melancholy could be compared to others that preceded it and composed a huge gallery of sorrow. The Mesoamerican civilizations destroyed by the horses, guns, and microbes that came with the ships of Cortés expressed themselves through a multitude of languages that no longer exist or remain today without speakers, like that evoked by Mario Vargas Llosa in his novel *The Storyteller*;[2] in a similar way, after the Holocaust, the Yiddish poets wrote with the language of a disappeared world: there is no doubt that melancholy has inspired a noble intellectual tradition. As many historians have highlighted, in the Renaissance it was held to be a Jewish sickness.[3] According to Fernando Cardoso, studied by Josef Hayim Yerushalmi as one of the most outstanding representatives of the Marrano culture that flourished in the seventeenth century between Inquisitorial Spain and the Italian ghettos, melancholy expressed first of all "the sadness and the fear born from the wounds of oppression and exile."[4] This was also the source that, three centuries later, pushed Erwin Panofsky, Raymond Klibansky, and Fritz Saxl, three scholars of the Warburg Institute who emigrated to America in the 1930s, to devote to Saturn and melancholy one of their most famous essays.[5] More often, this crepuscular melancholy of a lost past took a nostalgic taste, from the celebration of the Habsburg myth in the autobiographies and novels of Stefan Zweig and Joseph Roth to the grief for the British empire in the prose of Sir V. S. Naipaul. The paradigm of this conservative melancholy is doubtlessly Chateaubriand, the resigned and sublime narrator of the fall of the Old Regime. In 1802, he devoted a chapter of his *Genius of Christianity* to the migration of birds, comparing it to that of human beings. Exile prescribed by nature, observed the French writer, is highly different from that ordered by man. The bird does not leave alone but in a flock, bringing with it all the objects of its affection and knowing it will come back: "It returns, at last, to die on the spot which gave it birth. There it finds again the river, the tree, the nest, and the sun, of its forefathers." The exile, on the contrary, does not know whether one day he will see his home again or not, because "the proscription which has banished him from his country seems to have expelled him from the world."[6] A distinguished representative of the aristocratic emigration from which he had fought against the French Revolution, Chateaubriand wrote these words when he came to Paris after eight years of exile. He had understood, some decades before Tocqueville, that the revolutionary break was irreversible and the age of absolutism definitively over. But differently from Tocqueville, who was educated under the Restoration, he had lived the fall of the Old Regime as an actor, not as a distant spectator or a late commentator.

Chateaubriand very well deserves the metaphor of the shipwreck sharply analyzed by Hans Blumenberg in a famous essay,[7] whose starting point is the description of a sinking ship in the second book of Lucretius's *De Rerum Natura*: "Tis is sweet, when, down the mighty main, the winds roll up its waste of waters, from the land to watch another's laboring anguish far. Not that we joyously delight that man should thus been smitten, but because 'tis sweet to mark what evils we ourselves be spared."[8] Whereas Lucretius described the reaction of the spectator of a natural catastrophe, Blumenberg transfers his metaphor to history, giving the example of Goethe, who, in 1806, visited the devastated battlefield of Jena one day after Napoleon's victory. At the same time, he changes the metaphor itself through a quotation of Pascal's *Thoughts*, which announces the spirit of modern times: we are no longer spectators, we are "embarked" (*embarqués*)[9] and can neither escape nor contemplate from a distant, secure observatory, the calamities that surround us; we belong to and participate in them. The relief of those who escaped catastrophe and watched it from afar is a privilege unknown to us; we are shipwrecked ourselves; we have to avoid drowning and to rebuild our sunken ship. In other words, we cannot escape our defeat, or describe or analyze it from outside. Left-wing melancholy is what remains after the shipwreck; its spirit shapes the writings of many of its "survivors," drafted from their lifeboats after the storm.

The epistemic value of Blumenberg's metaphor nevertheless allows the shipwrecked, even the most "embarked" one, to adopt for a moment—ephemeral but crucial—a distant view of the downfall he has experienced. Like Proust in *The Guermantes Way*, who comes back to the house of his grandmother after a long absence and suddenly, in front of her portrait, feels that he sees an old woman as unknown to him as she had been to the photographer who framed her image, the melancholic vanquished can contemplate his defeat from an external observatory. Just for a moment, he can neutralize his emotional commitment to an exhausted experience and scrutinize it as the viewer of a photograph. Of course, an image cut from its familiar world is emotionally mutilated and "unredeemed" but it deserves an iconological approach, relieved of any subjective involvement or identification, and such an estrangement can be epistemologically fruitful. According to Siegfried Kracauer, "melancholy as an inner disposition not only makes elegiac objects seem attractive but carries still another, more important implication: it favors self-estrangement," which is a premise of critical understanding.[10] Instead of deepening a pathological attachment to a dead, engulfed past, this melancholic vision enables one to overcome a suffered trauma.

THE VANQUISHED LEFT

Reinhart Koselleck, the founder of conceptual history, posited the epistemological superiority of the vanquished in interpreting the past: "If history is made in the short run by the victors," he wrote, "historical gains in knowledge stem in the long run from the vanquished."[11] The victors inevitably fall into an apologetic vision of the past based on a providential scheme. Two eloquent examples of this self-satisfied historical reconstruction, he suggested, were Johann Gustav Droysen, the author of a monumental history of Prussia written between 1855 and

1884, the decades of the rise of Germany to the rank of *Weltmacht,* and François Guizot, who published his history of French civilization in 1830, the year in which the advent of the July Monarchy consecrated the triumph of his conservative liberalism. The vanquished, on the contrary, rethink the past with a sharp and critical regard: "The experience of being vanquished contains an epistemological potential that transcends its cause."[12] According to Koselleck, the most striking example of this second posture was Karl Marx, who extensively wrote on the revolutions of the nineteenth century through the point of view of the defeated proletarian classes. His empathy with the vanquished was all the more deep and strong in that he felt himself an exiled socialist and a marginal intellectual.[13] Quite astonishingly, in his article Koselleck did not quote Walter Benjamin, for whom the empathetic gaze toward the victors—epitomized by the positivistic French historian Fustel de Coulanges—was precisely "the method which historical materialism has broken with."[14] A large current of Marxist historiography—from British "history from below" to Indian "subaltern studies"—has adopted this fruitful methodological approach. Edward P. Thompson described the Industrial Revolution from the point of view of the English laboring classes; Ranajit Guha reinterpreted the history of colonial India looking for the "small voices" of the oppressed peasants, moving away from both the British colonizers and the Indian assimilated elites.[15]

Koselleck borrowed this dichotomy between victors and vanquished from Carl Schmitt, one of his mentors. In a small text written at the end of the war, when he was imprisoned by the Soviet and American armies occupying Germany, Schmitt depicted Tocqueville as vanquished, emphasizing an essential link between this status and his vision of the past.[16] The experience of defeat forged the sharpness of his critical insight and transformed him into the most important historian of the nineteenth century. Contrary to the liberal canonization of Tocqueville as the harbinger of modern democracy, Schmitt regarded him as a lucid conservative, aware of belonging to a defeated class. Tocqueville wrote his works on the French Revolution as a representative of aristocracy, a social group eclipsed by the ineluctable advent of democracy.[17] He had extensively analyzed this historical change in his books on America and all his texts were inspired by a deep, complete resignation to the irreversible process of democratic transformation. Tocqueville, Schmitt suggested, was a vanquished conservative who had renounced the *Katechon.*[18]

Meaning "resistance"—a force that withholds, retains, or brakes—this theological concept appears in Paul's Letters to the Thessalonians as the most powerful obstacle to the advent of the Antichrist, that is, an era of impiety and decadence.[19] Until the Second World War, Schmitt's political theology remained attached to the idea of *Katechon*. In the tradition of Joseph de Maistre and Donoso Cortés, he depicted Hitler as a kind of secular *Katechon* opposed to Bolshevism (the modern embodiment of the Antichrist). In 1946, however, Schmitt himself felt vanquished. A resigned vanquished, insofar as he had lost any illusion toward fascism.

Overturning Schmitt's perspective, Koselleck applied it to Marx. In his wake, we could easily establish a parallel between Schmitt (or Tocqueville) and several Marxist thinkers, particularly many members of the Frankfurt School. Walter Benjamin himself suggested such a reversal in his theses "On the Concept of History," where, adopting the point of view of "a historian schooled in Marx," he wrote the following cryptic passage: "The Messiah comes not only as the redeemer; he comes as the victor over the Antichrist."[20] Differently from Benjamin, Theodor W. Adorno no longer believed in revolution and, like Tocqueville, wrote as a vanquished without a *Katechon*. Similarly to the French historian, an aristocrat who had never lived under the Old Regime, Adorno wasn't a Bolshevik; the former had not believed in Maistre's Restoration, and the latter had no confidence in Lenin and Trotsky. Adorno was not attracted by revolution and was stoically resigned to the ineluctable advent of totalitarianism (that is, in his vision, universal reification, whatever its political form would be). In his writings, the negative dialectic of history only deserves contemplative criticism, without redemption. There is no social or political alternative to domination and even aesthetic creation can only testify to the wounds inflicted upon humanity by the eclipse of civilization.[21] Progress was illusion; instrumental reason had exhausted all the emancipatory potentialities of the Enlightenment and critical thought could no longer inspire political action.

Guizot's definition of Tocqueville—"a vanquished who accepts his defeat"[22]—might be valuable in order to depict Auguste Blanqui, the legendary figure of nineteenth-century socialism, at the end of his life. In 1872, one year after the bloodily repression of the Paris Commune, an event he had observed from his prison in the fortress of Toreau, he wrote his most enigmatic text, *Eternity According to the Stars*. At the end of a long and sometimes naïve meditation on the finiteness of the universe in spite of its apparent immensity, he described both the cosmos and history as a perpetual repetition of the same structure, imprisoning human beings in a kind of ineluctable hell. After presenting progress as misconception and affirming his distrust of human agency, he implicitly evoked the eternal repetition of defeat. This immutable character of nature and life meant the uninterrupted reproduction of barbarism. Emancipation was illusory and his own life seemed engulfed in the shipwreck of the revolutions in which he had been tirelessly involved. Rediscovering a cyclical vision of history, he retreated into melancholy and abandoned any hope in the future. The last words of his text sound like a desperate admission of failure:

> What a noisy humanity, infatuated with its greatness, believing itself to be the universe and living in its prison as in the vast immensity, only to soon sink along with the globe that, in the most profound disdain, has carried the burden of its pride. The same monotony and the same apathy [*immobilisme*] even in the foreign stars [*les astres étrangers*]. The universe is repeated without end; it's stomping its hoofs in the same place [*piaffe sur place*]. Eternity imperturbably plays the same representations over and over, ad infinitum.[23]

This obscure text fascinated Walter Benjamin, who read it in a tragic-historical conjuncture, after the German-Soviet Pact of 1939, the outbreak of the Second World War, and the capitulation of France, the country where he lived in exile. Written ten years before *Thus Spoke Zarathustra*, Blanqui's book was a powerful vision of "eternal recurrence" as a fatalistic downfall that is striking for its Nietzschean accents. "This resignation without hope is the last word of the great revolutionary," Benjamin observed, concluding that the charismatic leader of the nineteenth-century French revolutions had finally renounced challenging the established order: "the terrible indictment he pronounces against society takes the form of an unqualified submission to its results."[24] Revolt against domination had proved to be a vain effort. As Miguel Abensour has suggested, Benjamin himself stayed in the middle of Blanqui's magnetic field, torn between melancholy and revolution (or perhaps seeking a dialectical link between them).[25]

Blanqui was a fighter and a revolutionary thinker. In his recollections, Tocqueville sketched his portrait with extremely despising words, revealing a kind of physical disgust. In his eyes, the chief of the Parisian barricades only deserved the greatest contempt. In more recent years, a Marxist historian with a Tocquevillian flavor was Eric J. Hobsbawm. For him, the twentieth century had been the century of communism, a historical experience he interpreted, similarly to his aristocratic predecessor, as vanquished. A comparison with François Furet, a self-proclaimed Tocquevillian historian of both the French Revolution and communism, is inevitable. They deeply despised each other. In an article written for the French journal *Le Débat*, Hobsbawm defined *The Passing of an Illusion* as a "late product of the Cold War," whereas Furet considered *Age of Extremes* the vestige of an ideology condemned by history.[26] Among them, Furet claimed the legacy of Tocqueville's ideas, but the most Tocquevillian in style was certainly Hobsbawm. The French historian wrote with the arrogance of the victor, his British colleague with a pencil sharpened by the awareness of defeat.[27] Whereas Furet's book dealt with the rise and fall of communism, Hobsbawm paid attention to the crisis and rebirth of capitalism. Crippled in 1914 with the Great War, defied by the Russian Revolution, and weakened by the Great Depression of 1929, capitalism had been able to recover in the postwar decades and won in 1990. *The Passing of an Illusion* celebrates the triumph of capitalism and liberal democracy; *Age of Extremes* tells a tragedy.[28] According to Hobsbawm, communism has been brutal but it could not have been different. It collapsed because of its own contradictions and it was condemned to fail from the beginning. Nevertheless, it played a necessary historical role because it saved civilization and finally capitalism itself. Its vocation was sacrificial:

> It is one of the ironies of this strange century that the most lasting results of the October revolution, whose objective was the global overthrow of capitalism, was to save its antagonist, both in war and in peace—that is to say, by providing it with the incentive, fear, to reform itself after the Second World War, and, by establishing the popularity of economic planning, furnishing it with some of the procedures for its reform.[29]

During the Second World War, communism saved a humanity threatened by National Socialism, which would not have been defeated without the resistance of the USSR. After the economic crisis of 1929, the Russian Revolution appeared as a global alternative and compelled the capitalist system to reform itself. Keynesianism would not be understandable without the USSR facing the capitalist crisis. Both the New Deal and the welfare state experiences of postwar decades had been conceived and accomplished as capitalist answers to the communist challenge. Such a threat, nevertheless, saved capitalism. Hobsbawm abandoned the old Marxist teleological vision of history insofar as he no longer believed in the socialist achievement of human history. Furet developed a satisfied liberal teleology, presenting capitalism and market democracy as the end of history.

However, Hobsbawm's attempt to historicize communism was both apologetic and melancholic. He depicted the foundation of the Communist International in 1919 as a mistake because it irreversibly split the international socialist movement. Soviet communism could not succeed, because of its illusory premises. Its authoritarian features, clearly revealed under Stalinism (forced collectivization with catastrophic results, concentration camps, bureaucratization, and an extreme rigidity of the political system), finally paralyzed the USSR. Quoting Plekhanov, the Menshevik philosopher opposed to Lenin, Hobsbawm admitted that socialism in backward Russia could not be but "a Chinese empire colored red."[30] He recognized the atrocities of Stalin, presenting him as an "autocrat of exceptional, some might say unique, ferocity, ruthlessness and lack of scruple," but he immediately added that in the primitive conditions of Tsarist Russia it would have been impossible to modernize and industrialize the country without authoritarianism and violence.[31] In his eyes, "the tragedy of the October revolution was precisely that it could only produce this kind of ruthless, brutal, command socialism."[32] According to Hobsbawm, the impact of the Russian Revolution was bigger and deeper than that of the French Revolution, its ancestor that similarly spread over the planet a universal message. As he wrote in his autobiography, "the dream of the October revolution," which had represented for his generation "the hope of the world," always inhabited him.[33] In the conflict between Progress and Reaction that shaped the history of the twentieth century, he concluded, communism had been on the good side, as a radical movement belonging to the tradition of Enlightenment. Such a binary vision of the conflicts running through the past century can appear rather simplistic—in his eyes, fascism could not have resulted from the "dialectic of the Enlightenment"—but allowed him to inscribe the trajectory of communism into a providential vision of history. He was vanquished, aware of his defeat, but his fight was neither useless nor wrong.

Faithful to himself, Hobsbawm remained a Marxist historian, even if a Marxist without a socialist telos (communism had played the role of a *Katechon* against fascism, but had been unable to overthrow capitalism). Perhaps it is precisely this vanquished, spectral Marx, amputated of his revolutionary dimension, who, at the beginning of the 1990s, attracted Jacques Derrida. Marxism did not fascinate him when it inspired actual revolutions all over the world; it became acceptable to him only as an empty messianic hope or, in his own words, an *eskhaton* without a telos.[34]

DIALECTIC OF DEFEAT

A famous Brecht poem tells the story of the tailor of Ulm who, in 1592, wished to fly like a bird and constructed a rudimentary machine with two wings. Defending the natural (and religious) order of things, the bishop sentenced that men cannot fly and dared the tailor to prove the contrary. The tailor threw himself from the window of the cathedral with his rustic wings and crashed to the ground. The bishop won his challenge—natural order could not be changed—but several century later men were able to fly. The tailor of Ulm was not so foolish; he only had a too-precocious imagination. Today, his ridiculous failure can be viewed as the attempt of a forerunner.

Remembering this poem of Brecht in his last, melancholically lucid book, Lucio Magri suggested that communism might experience a similar destiny.[35] It failed in the twentieth century but we cannot exclude the possibility that its utopia will be accomplished in the future. In the long run, human societies cannot exist without utopias. This assessment sounds consolatory, in spite of its realistic, disenchanted formulation: the history of capitalism is made of tragedies and human sufferings; why should the history of socialism be different? In the 1920s, the soviet economist Evgeny Preobrazhensky defended a similar idea when he theorized the process of "primitive socialist accumulation" by analogy to the horrors of the beginning of industrial capitalism.[36] Magri's reflection was neither naïve nor optimistic. He did not try to reduce the defeat of communism to simply a lost battle. In his book, he depicts such an event as an epochal turn that takes the features of tragedy. What remains of this assault on heaven? Almost nothing, he answers severely. The so-called bourgeois revolutions had durable consequences: the American Revolution created a still valuable constitution; the French Revolution produced the Declaration of the Rights of Man and Citizen. Today, their legacies form a shared whole of values and principles. After the Napoleonic Wars, the European Restoration did not erase all of the social and political conquests of 1789; in 1814, absolutism was over and the "persistence of the Old Regime" impeded neither the rise of industrial and financial capitalism nor the advent of its bourgeois elites.[37] The October Revolution had consequences not so deep and durable insofar as neither its property relations nor its political forms survived it. Whereas soviet democracy disappeared during the civil war of the 1920s, collectivist economy endured until the 1990s, but today nothing remains. Socialism passed over the twentieth century like a meteor without proving to be a historical tendency and nobody could seriously pretend it represented the future. "The 'old mole' continues to dig," Magri writes, "but he is blind and he does not know where he is coming from or going to; he digs in circles."[38] Just after the fall of the Berlin Wall, Perry Anderson formulated a complementary prognostic: he did not exclude a possible redemption of communism (like the triumph of neoliberalism after a long time in the wilderness) even under different forms, but lucidly imagined a possible oblivion, a destiny comparable to the disappearance of the indigenous communities created by the Jesuits in Paraguay between the seventeenth and the eighteenth centuries.[39] Communism had failed as both a political and an ethical project. It had proclaimed the emancipation of humankind but had created a new form of despotism: why should it survive such a gigantic heterogenesis of ends?

Positing oblivion as a possible destiny for communism means that its defeat at the end of the twentieth century could be more than a lost battle; it could be a lost war, a final defeat. In fact, Marxist thinkers disposed to admit such a possibility have always been very rare. Of course, the road to socialism was fraught with pitfalls, but in any case the final victory was assured. Of course, the history of revolutions is a history of defeats, because all of them have been followed by restorations, authoritarian turns, and Thermidorian reactions, but to learn the "upright walk" of human beings is a difficult task. We might easily extract from

Marx's (and Marxists') writings on revolution—as a kind of subtext—a theory of defeat that is an attempt at exorcism.

In *The Eighteenth Brumaire of Louis Bonaparte*, a work written in 1852, just after the putsch of Napoleon III in France, Marx emphasized a crucial difference between bourgeois and proletarian revolutions. Whereas the former ran "swiftly from success to success," he wrote, the latter (socialist) "constantly interrupted themselves in their own course, returned to the apparently accomplished, in order to begin anew."[40] They learned from their own defeats, which allowed them to better know their enemies, select their allies, choose their weapons, and define their projects. At the same time, they could not be overwhelmed by such defeats, because the future belonged to them: "the social revolution could not take its poetry from the past but only from the future."[41] Marx did not deny or trivialize the defeat of June 1848, which, in his words, paralyzed the workers of Paris and "rendered them incapable of fighting for years to come." The result was impotence and passivity—"the historical process would once again have to go on over their heads"[42]—but such a downfall could not be definitive.

In May 1871, just after the bloody repression of the Paris Commune, Marx wrote *The Civil War in France*, a report in which this dialectic of defeat was even more clearly and strongly reaffirmed:

> The soil out of which [socialism] grows is modern society itself. It cannot be stamped out by any amount of carnage. . . . Working men's Paris, with its Commune, will be forever celebrated as the glorious harbinger of a new society. Its martyrs are enshrined in the great heart of the working class. Its exterminators history has already nailed to that eternal pillory from which all the prayers of their priest will not avail to redeem them.[43]

The Paris Commune resulted in massacre. During the so-called bloody week, thirty-five thousand people were executed in the streets of the French capital through a systematic repression that took the form of a mass slaughter. Furthermore, ten thousand fighters were deported to New Caledonia. In short, one in every thirty Parisians had been killed or deported.[44] A campaign aimed to criminalize the insurgent workers followed the repression. In the wake of Zola and Lombroso, many

writers and scholars depicted the Commune as an eruption or an ata-
vistic resurgence of barbarism in the middle of a civilized society. The
dimension of such a defeat was overwhelming, but did not shake the
faith of Marx in the historical growth of socialism. Three decades later,
mass socialist parties existed in all European countries.

Marx's interpretation of the Commune did not differ, in its main
lines, from that of many of its actors. Jules Vallès, a representative of
Paris socialist Bohemia since the years of the Second Republic, had
actively participated in the Paris Commune as an elected member of
its Council and as the editor of its most popular newspaper, *Le Cri du
Peuple.* Exiled in London for almost ten years after having miraculously
escaped from the repression of the bloody week of May 1871, he wrote a
three-volume autobiographical novel, *Jacques Vingtras,* whose last part,
The Insurrectionist (1882), was devoted to the Commune. First published
as a feuilleton in *La Nouvelle Revue* just after his return to Paris in 1880,
when he benefited from the general amnesty proclaimed by the Third
Republic, this novel opened with a moving description of a historical,
tragic defeat, but finished with a promise of redemption. The exergue of
the book is a dedication to the Commune martyrs: "To the dead of 1871.
To all those who, victims of social injustice, took arms against a badly
made world and formed, under the flag of the Commune, the great federation of sorrows [*la grande federation des douleurs*]."[45] As melancholic
as the start is the end, which evokes the violence of counterrevolution
but includes, nonetheless, a message of hope. Having escaped from the
massacre, Vingtras crosses the border and, watching the French sky, be-
gins an exile conceived as an interlude between two moments of a life of
struggle: "I have just crossed a stream that marks the border. They won't
get me! And I will still be able to be with the people, if the people are
thrown back into the street and hounded down the battle. I look at the
sky over where I sense Paris to be. It's a harsh blue with red clouds. Like
a huge workers' smock, soaked in blood."[46]

The memoirs of Louise Michel, another charismatic figure of the
Commune, are replete with sadness and mourning. She wrote her autobiographical recollections in the first half of the 1880s, after she returned
from exile in New Caledonia and could participate anew in French political life. More than ten years after the tragic end of the Parisian revolution, she described its events by enveloping them in an atmosphere of
martyrdom, paying homage to the memory of her fallen comrades and

claiming the exemplarity of their sacrifice. She inscribed the Commune in a historical perspective, depicting it as a sort of announcement of a liberated future in which its anonymous heroes would be redeemed. "The Commune, surrounded from every direction," she wrote, "had only death on its horizon. It could only be brave; and it was. And in dying, it opened wide the door to the future. That was its destiny."[47] This vision of the Commune as a laboratory of socialism or "anarchic communism" to come shapes the writings of its actors in exile, as well as those of their interlocutors, from Elisée Reclus to Peter Kropotkin, from Karl Marx to William Morris. For all of them, remembering the bloody defeat of May 1871 was not an impotent or desperate mourning; it was the inescapable road through which the legacy of the Paris Commune—both its political imaginary and its practical experience of social transformation—could be assimilated and transmitted.[48]

In the wake of the Communards, Rosa Luxemburg sketched a similar statement in a famous article written in January 1919, at the end of the Spartacist uprising in Berlin, on the road to becoming herself a martyr and a symbol of that crushed revolution. Her last message—written shortly before being killed by the *Freikorps*, who threw her dead body in the water of *Landwehrkanal*—celebrated a defeat with words announcing a future victory. She was aware that the Berlin uprising was condemned to failure: the German capital was isolated and the social democracy had abandoned the insurgent workers (Gustav Noske became the symbol of their bloody repression). She was opposed to such a desperate insurrection, but assumed its leadership when she understood that it could not be stopped. In her article, she remembered the strong failures of all nineteenth-century revolutionary movements—from the weavers of Lyon in 1831 to the British Chartists, from the revolutions of 1848 to the Paris Commune—in order to stress that socialism always resurrected on stronger and wider bases. The Spartacist downfall belonged to this tradition of proletarian defeats and, like them, it promised an ineluctable rebirth. Her final sentence is paradigmatic of this socialist vision of defeat:

> The whole road of socialism—so far as revolutionary struggles are concerned—is paved with nothing but thunderous defeats. Yet, at the same time, history marches inexorably, step by step, toward final victory! Where would we be today *without* those "defeats," from which we draw

historical experience, understanding, power and idealism? Today, as we advance into the final battle of the proletarian class war, we stand on the foundation of those very defeats; and we cannot do without *any* of them, because each one contributes to our strength and understanding.[49]

Socialism, she concluded, "forged a link in the chain of historic defeats" and consequently "future victories will spring from this 'defeat.'" Differently from Marx, who observed the end of the Paris Commune from the outside, Luxemburg inspired the Berlin uprising and lived its repression, leading to her own death. More than consolatory, her vision is astonishingly optimistic. Defeats put into question neither the socialist goal nor the capacity of revolutionary forces to fulfill it. They only had to draw strategic and tactical lessons from their downfalls. There were no final defeats; defeats were only lost battles.

In other statements, nevertheless, Rosa Luxemburg had depicted a different landscape. In 1915, she had stressed without any optimistic accent the alternative that stood in front of Europe: socialism or barbarism. In her eyes, socialism was as possible as the fall of civilization into barbarism. It was a conscious rejection of the historical tendency toward barbarism. In "The Crisis of Social Democracy," an essay written from the jail where she expiated her opposition to the Great War, she did not exclude "the triumph of imperialism and the destruction of all culture, and, as in ancient Rome, depopulation, desolation, degeneration, a vast cemetery."[50] How are we to explain such a discrepancy in her writings? There is a simple answer: at the moment of defeat, she felt compelled to reaffirm her socialist faith.

She was not alone in adopting such a posture of willing resilience. In the fall of 1939, following the European events from his Mexican exile, Trotsky formulated the hypothesis of a victory of National Socialism in the Second World War, which would have meant "the grave of civilization." In this case, the Marxist vision of the proletariat as historical redeemer of the oppressed humanity had to be revised. At the beginning of a new world war, however, he reaffirmed the alternative of Rosa Luxemburg—socialism or barbarism—with the same irreducible anthropological hope: "the only way out for humanity is the world socialist revolution. The alternative to it is the relapse into barbarism."[51] In his eyes, the Fourth International, the new communist current that should have replaced Stalinism and whose building absorbed all his energies, was born "amid the roar of defeats," but would have led "the toilers to victory."[52]

On May 12, 1943, when only ruins remained of the insurgent Warsaw Ghetto, Shmuel Zygielbojm, the representative of the Jewish Labour Bund in London, committed suicide in protest against the silence of the world—first of all the Allied passivity—in front of the extermination of the Jews of Poland. His suicide was not an act of despair, but rather a testimony and a political warning: "My comrades in the Warsaw ghetto fell with arms in their hands in the last heroic battle. I was not permitted to fall like them, together with them, but I belong with them, to their mass grave. By my death, I wish to give expression to my most profound protest against the inaction in which the world watches and permits the destruction of the Jewish people."[53] Written in one of the most tragic moments of the history of the twentieth century, these words were followed by the usual reaffirmation of his faith in a socialist future. His death was meaningful insofar as it belonged to the struggle for socialism: "I wish that this remaining handful of the original several millions of Polish Jews could live to see the liberation of a new world of freedom, and the justice of true socialism. I believe that such a Poland will arise and that such a world will come."[54]

Zygielbojm's testament proves that even in the middle of a catastrophe, when all seemed lost, this dialectic of defeat displayed its therapeutic virtues. Walter Benjamin did not escape from this providential scheme. In "On the Concept of History" (1940), he evoked the possibility of a complete defeat in front of National Socialism: "even the dead will not be safe from the enemy if he wins, and this enemy has not ceased to be victorious."[55] But he also recalled the "weak messianic power" that his generation had inherited from the past and could use in order to blast out of the historical path toward this catastrophe. In his eyes, this "tiger's leap into the past"—a past made of defeats—was "the dialectical leap Marx understood as revolution."[56]

At the time of colonial revolutions, the darkest moments of the Second World War were replaced by a wave of political optimism. History ran toward socialism, not barbarism. In Bolivia, in October 1967, Che Guevara clearly understood that his guerrilla movement had failed, but the feeling that history was on his own side never abandoned him. In conversation with his guards, just before being killed, he admitted his failure but also added that revolution was "immortal."[57] Differently from the fighters of the Warsaw ghetto, he knew that his death would transform him into a martyr and his sacrifice would not occur in the middle of a silent, indifferent world.

It is in Latin America that this cycle of "glorious" defeats—celebrated as tragic, historical moments that, instead of putting into question the belief in socialism, strongly reinforce it—comes to end. On September 11, 1973, a military putsch destroyed the Popular Union government in Chile, establishing a brutal dictatorship that lasted twenty years and changed the political landscape of the continent. The last speech of President Salvador Allende, recorded that morning in the besieged Moneda Palace just before he committed suicide, perpetuated—and completed —this long tradition of socialist martyrdom. Pronounced without lyricism, his last words and images—the leader wearing a helmet and a shoulder-mounted machine gun, surrounded by his guards—immediately transferred him into the pantheon of socialism beside Che Guevara, giving to his sacrifice an almost mythical dimension. We do not know if he had previously written this text, foreseeing the catastrophe to come, but his message was clear. He was sure that his immolation would not be in vain: "sooner rather than later," he said without any emphasis in his voice, "the great avenues will open again where free men will walk to build a better society." The fascist military forces could prevail by violence, but the future belonged to the people: "History is ours, and people make history."[58] One year later, the Afro-Cuban singer Pablo Milanés offered to this image the lyricism it lacked with a famous air that explicitly referred to the words of Allende: "I will once again walk the streets / of what had been bloody Santiago / and in a beautiful liberated plaza / I will stop to cry for the absent."[59]

LEFT-WING MELANCHOLY

Melancholy was always a hidden dimension of the left, even if it came to the surface only at the end of the twentieth century, with the failure of communism. Pursuing a tradition that goes back to Tommaso Campanella, for whom melancholy and utopia hypnotically attracted and hated each other, left culture had occulted melancholy behind its messianic hopes. In *The City of the Sun* (1623), mourning was banned;

people could not wear black habits and during the fall should eat grapes, a god's gift against sadness.[60]

There are many definitions of melancholy, an ancient concept whose meaning has changed through the ages.[61] Its phenomenology spans from sorrow to lovesickness and resignation, but primarily focuses on loss and bereavement. The Ancients defined melancholy as a sickness engendered by an excess of "black bile" (μελαγχολία) in the human body. This would produce sadness and passivity, leading to serious diseases like epilepsy. An expression of a broken equilibrium of moods, melancholy was the opposite of isonomy (a system of perfectly balanced tempers). This state of mind corresponded to a season (the autumn, when cold is coming and nature changes) as well as to a specific age of the human body (maturity, the transition between youth and senility). In the Middle Ages, melancholy was no longer naturalized and became a sickness of the soul; it ceased to be considered an infirmity of the body and appeared as a disposition of mind. *Acedia* meant sadness, sorrow, despair, unhappiness, and desolation; in its most sharp forms it could correspond with impotence, passivity, torpor, laziness, and pusillanimity, up to disgust with life.

Mourning and resignation, however, remained the principal features of melancholy. In Vittorio Carpaccio's *Dead Christ* (1465–67) all seems lost: impotence overwhelmingly submerges the bereaved figures that inhabit this painting. The link between melancholy, death, and mourning is a topos in the history of painting, from the Renaissance to the Romantic Age.[62] It would not be difficult to find a secular equivalent of Andrea Mantegna's *The Lamentation Over the Dead Christ* (1480 [figure 1.1]) in many creations of modern left culture. Among them, the most significant is probably Käthe Kollwitz's woodcut *In Memoriam Karl Liebknecht* (1920 [figure 1.2]), created after the Berlin's Spartacist Uprising of 1919.[63] In more recent years, many biographers of Che Guevara stressed the affinities between the pictures of his dead body exhibited by his executioners in the Bolivian village of Vallegrande and the representation of Christian martyrdom in classical painting (figure 1.3).[64] Like Mantegna's canvas, from which it clearly draws its inspiration, Köllwitz's woodcut displays a scene of sorrow and gives it a choral, collective dimension. The proletarian bereavement around the dead body of the German socialist leader transcends the familial pietas of the Virgin, St. John, and

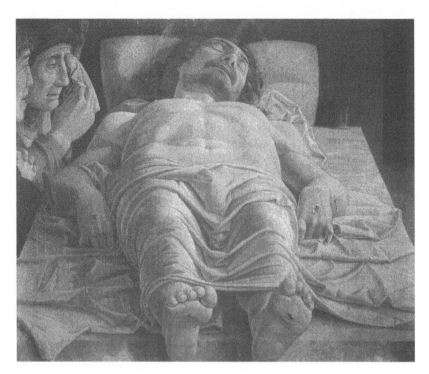

1.1. Andrea Mantegna, *The Lamentation over the Dead Christ* (1480), temper, Pinacoteca di Brera, Milano. © Art Resource, New York.

DIE LEBENDEN DEM TOTEN . ERINNERUNG AN DEN 15.JANUAR 1919

1.2. Käthe Kollwitz, *In Memoriam Karl Liebknecht; In Memory of January 15, 1919* (1920), woodcut, Private Collection © 2015 Artists Rights Society (ARS), New York / VG Bild-Kunst, Bonn.

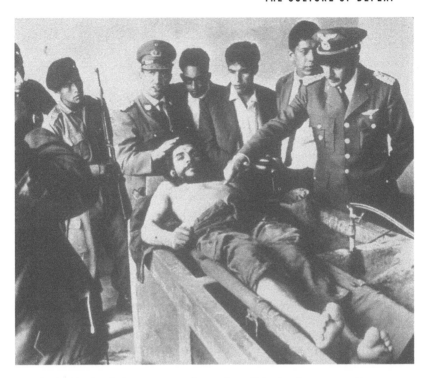

1.3. The dead body of Che Guevara, Vallegrande, Bolivia, October 10, 1967. From Richard Dindo, *Ernesto Che Guevara, le journal de Bolivie*, Arte France, Les Films d'ici (1994).

Mary Magdalene, but all of them mourn an iconic figure lying on a slab. The pictures of the corpse of Che Guevara belong to a different genre—military and police evidence—completely deprived of any religious aura or intent of consolation: a soldiers' war trophy rather than the invention of a myth. It is their immediate reception in a rebellious age that transformed them into iconic images of revolutionary mourning. As Régis Debray observed, "That Christ-like cadaver from which a legend emerged—eyes open, head supported by a plank, stretched out on a cement slab for display—was offered to the world by his enemies."[65]

Since the beginning of the sixteenth century, melancholy is identified with a copper engraving by Albrecht Dürer, *Melencolia I* (1514), a work that established an aesthetic canon and shaped a durable iconographical tradition in spite of its enigmatic, controversial meaning. According to Aby Warburg, Dürer's masterpiece is a positive, optimistic work in which the melancholic spirit triumphs against its enemies. The tools that surround the woman at the center of the image—the clepsydra, sphere, compass, sextant, ladder, and so on—symbolize her capacity to win against the elements, whereas, in the background, melancholy is depicted as a rising sun.[66] Saturn has been humanized, becoming a reflexive mood instead of a dark and frightening threat. According to Warburg, Dürer's engraving symbolized a fundamental step in the struggle of humanism against religious obscurantism.[67] In the Renaissance, this process just started and melancholia did not yet "feel free from the fear of the ancient demons," but this change could not be stopped. It is two disciples of Warburg, nonetheless, who have reversed this optimistic interpretation. For Erwin Panofsky and Fritz Saxl, Dürer represented the defeat of the human ambition to know the cosmos, unveiling its mysteries with the instruments of science. The melancholic spirit of the picture rises from the awareness of the limits of human knowledge that cannot subjugate nature. Dürer's meditating women expresses such a human impotence in front of God's creations (figure 1.4).[68] In the Renaissance, melancholy achieves a new fundamental feature: self-reflection. Beside contemplation appears introspection. Melancholy is no longer a simple feeling; it becomes a disposition of mind, a use of reason, and its symbol is Saturn. In some respects, Panofsky and Saxl's interpretation of Dürer corresponds with Lucien Goldmann's analysis of the tragic vision of the world that deeply shapes Pascal's philosophy and Racine's dramas.[69] They perceived the advent of rationalism as a threat to the holy order of the world and this awareness generated a vision of life as tragedy, as well as their retreat into faith. But Lucien Goldmann himself embodied a link between the classical tradition of melancholy and left culture. In fact, Dürer's engraving could allegorize both the crisis of Marxism and left melancholy, insofar as the defeat of the revolutions of the twentieth century refutes the old teleological vision positing socialism as the end of history. Pascal's and Racine's melancholy expressed the sufferings of a religious world's vision dismantled by reason, whereas left melancholy derives from the failure of a conception of socialism as science. In our secular age, however, escape into faith is no longer allowed (except for religious fundamentalism) and the culture of defeat takes the form of a melancholic retreat into meditation and introspection.

Most contemporary representations of melancholy express a feeling of emptiness, like the metaphysical paintings of Giorgio De Chirico

1.4. Albrecht Dürer, *Melancholia I* (1514), engraving. © Art Resource, New York.

where sad, meditating statues lie in the middle of deserted, geometrical squares darkened by powerful shadows. We cannot exclude the possibility that our descendants will remember the historical experience of twentieth-century socialism as an isolated monument in an empty square, a vestige of the past whose charm will lie in its "age value." The fascinating power of such remains, Alois Riegl emphasized in his famous essay "The Modern Cult of Monuments" (1903), derives from their temporal consumption. Differently from the "historical value," which singles out "one moment in the developmental continuum of the past and places it before our eyes as if it belonged to the present," the "age value" simply shows the traces of time, conferring on a monument the aura of a dead object.[70] In this case, as in Perry Anderson's hypothesis already mentioned, socialism would disappear from collective memory like the Christian collective communities of Paraguay. Except by a few romantic writers, they have been observed in the following centuries as "an artificial social construction, contradicting every known law of human nature, doomed to rapid extinction."[71] It is perhaps with the secret purpose of denying them even an inoffensive "age value" that, after 1989, all the monuments of real socialism have been systematically destroyed.

At the turn of the twentieth century, psychoanalysis enriched this melancholy constellation, rearticulating the elements inherited from the classical tradition. It is in 1915, when the First World War had begun to reveal its traumatic dimension, that Sigmund Freud published his famous essay "Mourning and Melancholy." His description of the symptoms of melancholy did not change the classical representation inherited from the Middle Ages, but he emphasized its pathological aspects: "The distinguished mental features of melancholia are a profoundly painful dejection, cessation of interest in the outside world, loss of the capacity to love, inhibition of all activity, and a lowering of the self-regarding feelings to a degree that finds utterance in self-reproaches and self-reviling, and culminates in a delusional expectation of punishment."[72] According to Freud, the symptoms of mourning are similar, except for self-despising, but mourning is a transitional state of mind whereas melancholy is a durable disposition. Melancholic people do not wish to abandon their status of sadness and suffering; they complain and, to a certain point, enjoy their pain.

Both mourning and melancholy derive from the loss (or the absence) of a beloved object that could be a person or even an abstract category (an ideal, the country, liberty, and the like) but their issues are different. Mourning is a process through which a person overcomes the suffering of such a loss and finally separates itself from this lost object. In this way, its libidinal energies can be transferred toward a different recipient (person, ideal, value, and so on) and the mourner recovers his equilibrium. Differently from the mourner who prevails over his sorrow, the melancholic remains narcissistically identified with his lost beloved object, transforming his suffering into an introspective isolation that cuts him off from the external world. In other words, melancholy is an unaccomplished, impossible, and "pathological mourning."[73] Today, notably thanks to the works of Robert Hertz, scholars tend to conceive mourning as a process of "transformation" of the relationship between the griever and the dead rather than as a simple "separation."[74] Death modifies and reshapes their relationship instead of breaking and exhausting it.

In Freud's terms, we could define "left melancholy" as the result of an impossible mourning: communism is both a finished experience and an irreplaceable loss, in an age in which the end of utopias obstructs the separation from the lost beloved ideal as well as a libidinal transfer toward a new object of love. This seems to be the interpretation suggested by Wendy Brown, according to whom left melancholy is a "conservative tendency" impeding subjects from finding a new "critical and visionary spirit."[75] However, one could observe that it is precisely the lack of a new spirit and vision that annihilates any attempt to distance oneself from the lost object and to overcome the loss. This "conservative tendency" could also be viewed as a form of resistance against demission and betrayal. Because of the end of utopias, a successful mourning could also mean identification with the enemy: lost socialism replaced by accepted capitalism. If a socialist alternative does not exist, the rejection of real socialism inevitably becomes a disenchanted acceptation of market capitalism, neoliberalism, and so on. In this case, melancholy would be the obstinate refusal of any compromise with domination. If we abandon the Freudian model and "depathologize" melancholy, we could see it as a necessary premise of a mourning process, a step that precedes and allows mourning instead of paralyzing it and thus helps the subject to become active again. In other words, melancholy could be seen as an enabling process in which, according to Judith Butler's lexicon, the subject experiences "a withdrawal or retraction from speech that makes speech possible" (a vision that Freud himself would have finally accepted in *The Ego and the Id*).[76]

THE ANTINOMIES OF WALTER BENJAMIN

In fact, there is a tradition of left melancholy. On several occasions, Benjamin had stigmatized the *acedia* of the historians who identified themselves through empathy (*Einfühlung*) with the dominant classes, as well as the "left-wing melancholy" of the writers belonging to the New Objectivity. In his eyes, *acedia* was both the methodology of historicism—embodied by a positivistic scholar like Numa Denis Fustel de Coulanges—and a political attitude epitomized by German social democracy: the former justified the results of history as objective, necessary accomplishments; the latter blindly believed in automatic progress, favoring passivity and a fatalistic acceptation of the order. Both revealed a similar "indolence of the heart."[77] Historicism postulated an apologetic vision of the past and erected a monument to the victors seen as its exclusive subjects, whereas social democracy rejected as a dangerous form of adventurism and extremism any attempt to change the course of history. It is precisely against them that Benjamin claimed a new conception of history and a revolutionary political action whose aim was both reactivating the past and transforming the present. In his eyes, this historiographical and political *acedia* had its aesthetic equivalent, during the Weimar years, in the New Objectivity. In 1931, he published an extremely violent attack against this aesthetic and literary current, pointing out one of its most successful representatives, the poet and novelist Erich Kästner. The radicalism of the New Objectivity was nothing else than an amusing, childish, and ludic façade behind which it was not difficult to recognize a shameful attitude of complacency toward the tastes of a new bourgeois elite fascinated by the aesthetical modernism of the avant-gardes. The main feature of brilliant writers like Erich Kästner and Kurt Tucholsky was their political impotence, which turned revolutionary ideas and goals "into objects of distraction, of amusement," with the result of reifying them as cultural commodities. Their works, Benjamin sentenced, were as vibrant and attractive as city coffeehouses after the closure of stock exchange. Echoing Siegfried Kracauer, who had pointed out the emptiness of the mass culture directed to the new bourgeois layers and the white-collar workers of Weimar society in his essay "Die Angestellten" (1930),[78] he stressed the "tortured stupidity" of the New Objectivity literary accomplishments. They unveiled the decomposition of bourgeois society and were the latest metamorphosis of a millennial melancholy: "The rumbling in [Kästner's] lines certainly has more to do with flatulence than with subversion. Constipation and melancholy have always gone together. But since the juices began to dry up in the body social, stuffiness meets us at very turn. Kästner's poems do not improve the atmosphere."[79]

Differently from Kracauer, who pointed out in Lukácsian terms the "spiritual homelessness" (*geistige Obdachlosigkeit*) of the intellectuals of the New Objectivity,[80] Benjamin depicted them as the embodiment of melancholia, a category borrowed from art history. His criticism reproduced the vision of *acedia* as sin, as a state of mind oriented toward acquiescence, laziness, and submission, which belonged to the culture of Renaissance, in which it began to be distinguished from melancholy, the illness produced by internal combustion of bodily tempers.[81] In *The Origin of German Tragic Drama*, Benjamin characterized Hamlet as "the paradigm of the melancholy man,"[82] giving to this definition a genuinely political connotation: melancholy meant first of all the political impotence of a king unable to command and decide. In other texts (or even passages of the same book), nevertheless, he suggested a different conception of melancholy. In a famous autobiographical, enigmatic fragment, he presented himself as "born under the sign of Saturn," the planet of melancholy, "the star of hesitation and delay."[83] And in another passage of his *Trauerspiel* book, he analyzed melancholy as an epistemological paradigm. The empathic and mournful exploration of the world reduced to a field of ruins, he suggested, engenders a new vision: "Melancholy betrays the world for the sake of knowledge. But in its tenacious self absorption it embraces dead objects in its contemplation, in order to redeem them."[84] In other words, he transformed the traditional vision of melancholy into a phenomenological approach to objects and images.[85] Of course, such a conception of melancholy moved him close to Kracauer. In his review of Kracauer's essay mentioned above, "Die Angestellten," Benjamin linked melancholy to the recollection of the past preceding its revolutionary redemption, a task he depicted through the metaphor of the "ragpicker" (*Lumpensammler*), the collector of abandoned, lost, and forgotten objects that could recall those scattered in Dürer's engraving already evoked:

> Thus, in the end this writer stands alone. A malcontent, not a leader. No pioneer, but a spoilsport. And if we wish to gain a clear picture of him in the isolation of his trade, what we will see is a ragpicker, at daybreak, picking up rags of speech and verbal scraps with his stick and tossing them, grumbling and growling, a little drunk, into his cart, not without letting one or another of those faded cotton remnants—"humanity," "inwardness" or "absorption"—flutter derisively in the wind. A ragpicker, early on, at the dawn of the day of the revolution.[86]

In short, Benjamin did not reject melancholia per se but only as a mood—epitomized by the aesthetic of the New Objectivity—voided of any political content and deprived of its critical potentialities. Against this fatalistic melancholia made of passivity and cynicism, he valorized a different melancholia consisting in a kind of epistemological posture: a historical and allegorical insight into both society and history that tries to grasp the origins of their sorrow and collects the objects and images of a past waiting for redemption. What emerges, Jonathan Flatley points out, "is the picture of a politicizing, splenetic melancholy, where clinging to things from the past enables interest and action in the present world and is indeed the very mechanism for that interest."[87] In the end, this is the core of historicity itself.

Benjamin's antinomies allow him to distinguish the peculiar features of communist melancholy, which always has been much more tragic than lighthearted. From the silent processions reaching the Communards' Wall in the Parisian cemetery of Pere Lachaise—I don't refer here to the solemn burials celebrated by the Stalinist regimes that embalmed their leaders like pharaohs in ancient Egypt—the workers movement has always practiced mourning as a secular liturgy of hope. The funeral of Palmiro Togliatti, the leader of the Italian Communist Party, which took place in Rome in 1964, was a moment of authentic popular emotion and inspired several works of art, from the movies of Pier Paolo Pasolini (*Uccellacci e Uccellini*, 1966, [figures 1.5–6]) and the Taviani brothers (*I sovversivi*, 1967) to a famous canvas of Renato Guttuso of 1972 (figure 1.7).[88] This painting is based on the contrast between the mourning faces of the characters—among whom many historical figures of the communist movement are clearly recognizable (Lenin, Gramsci, Sartre, Angela Davis, Enrico Berlinguer, among others)—and the red flags dominating the landscape. Symbolizing socialism and the future, these banners sublimate the loss of the dead leader: mourning is inseparable from hope.

THE MELANCHOLY WAGER

After 1989, nevertheless, this culture of mourning does not work anymore. The loss appears irreparable; it cannot be mourned and sublimated in the living flow of a political movement. The historical defeats

1.5–6. Pier Paolo Pasolini, *The Hawks and the Sparrows*, Water Bearer Films (1966).

1.7. Renato Guttuso, *Funerals of Togliatti* (1972), oil on canvas, Museo di Arte Moderna di Bologna. © Artists Rights Society (ARS), New York; SIAE/Rome.

evoked above—1848, the Paris Commune, the Spartacist Revolution, the Warsaw ghetto uprising, and the Bolivian guerrilla struggle of Che Guevara—possessed a great and glorious taste. They certainly deserved retrospective criticism but did not spread despair; they compelled admiration, inspired courage, and reinforced loyalty. They were not dark defeats that, according to Charles Péguy and Daniel Bensaïd, occurred "by deception and disenchantment," defeats from which "a generation cannot recover."[89] The end of communism sealed this kind of downfall.

Before being an epistemological posture or an allegorical vision of the past, melancholia, according to its classical definitions mentioned above, is a temper, a state of the mind, an atmosphere, and a mood. The melancholy of defeat described in this chapter did not result in defeatism or depression because it was supported by a world vision that had its core in revolutionary utopia. Life is made exclusively neither of moods and emotions nor of purely abstract values or ideologies. Between them, there is a relational continuity that the Marxist cultural historian Raymond Williams defined as "the structure of feeling": the way in which ideas and values are perceived, "lived and felt."[90] This is worth, especially for these ideas that, like socialism, have been embodied by collective movements and have innervated the "feeling" of many generations. The secret of this metabolism of defeat—melancholic but not demotivating or demobilizing, exhausting but not dark—lies precisely in the fusion between the suffering of a catastrophic experience (defeat, repression, humiliation, persecution, exile) and the persistence of a utopia lived as a horizon of expectation and a historical perspective. Perhaps it is because of their extreme character, "at the mind's limits," that Jean Améry's and Primo Levi's observations on the spiritual resources with which the communists deported to Auschwitz were able to endure violence and resist the process of dehumanization carried on by their persecutors depict quite well this dialectic of utopian melancholy, refractory to resignation. Both Améry and Levi, maybe too superficially, assimilate this utopia to a faith in an immediately religious sense, avoiding distinguishing between believers and political activists, but their testimony is valuable if we consider Marxist historical teleology as the secularized version of a messianic aspiration. Améry admitted his admiration for the militants who, in the most difficult conditions, found an "inestimable help" in their convictions:

> Whether they were militant Marxists, sectarian Jeovah's Witnesses, or practicing Catholics, whether they were highly educated national economists and theologians or less versed workers and peasants, their belief or their ideology gave them that firm foothold in the world from which they spiritually unhinged the SS state. Under conditions that defy the imagination they conducted Mass, and as Orthodox Jews they fasted on the Day of Atonement although they actually lived the entire year in a condition of raging hunger. They held Marxist discussions on the future of Europe or they simply persevered in saying: the Soviet Union will and must win. They survived better or died with more dignity than their irreligious or un-political intellectual comrades, who often were infinitely better educated and more practiced in exact thinking.[91]

Differently from the representatives of the tradition of humanistic skepticism, for whom Nazi violence was incomprehensible and overwhelming—not only materially but also spiritually irresistible—the "believers" could find unexpected and inexhaustible resources. According to

Améry, "they transcended themselves and projected themselves into the future. They were no windowless monads; they stood open, wide open onto a world that was not the world of Auschwitz."[92] Levi's remarks are very similar:

> Their universe was vaster than ours, more extended in space and time, above all more comprehensible: they had a key and a point of leverage, a millennial tomorrow so that there might be a sense to sacrificing themselves, a place in heaven or on earth where justice and compassion had won, or would win in a perhaps remote but certain future: Moscow, or the celestial or terrestrial Jerusalem.[93]

When communism fell apart, the utopia that for almost two centuries had supported it as a Promethean impetus or consolatory justification was no longer available; it had become an exhausted spiritual resource. The "structure of feelings" of the left disappeared and the melancholy born from defeat could not find anything to transcend it; it remained alone in front of a vacuum. The coming neoliberal wave—as individualistic as it was cynical—fulfilled it.

Left melancholy does not necessarily mean nostalgia for real socialism and other wrecked forms of Stalinism. Rather than a regime or an ideology, the lost object can be the struggle for emancipation as a historical experience that deserves recollection and attention in spite of its fragile, precarious, and ephemeral duration. In this perspective, melancholy means memory and awareness of the potentialities of the past: a fidelity to the emancipatory promises of revolution, not to its consequences. In this case—as Slavoj Žižek has pertinently observed—melancholy is identification with a *lack* rather than with a *loss*; identification with communism as it was dreamed and expected, not as it was realized (state socialism).[94] Such fidelity is the core of any possible attempt at working through the past.

In *Modern Tragedy* (1966), Raymond Williams observes that revolutions always tend to deny their tragic dimension. It is true that their actuality is eminently tragic, made of mass movements, violent confrontations between social forces and visions of the world that often become physical and murderous clashes between human beings. Revolutions, nevertheless, never conceive themselves as tragic events; their actors always emphasize their redemptive, liberating, emancipatory, not to say exciting or joyful, dimension. The tragic vision of the world derives from a feeling of despair. Tragedy arises when no issue is visible, when people feel definitively lost. That is why, according to Raymond Williams, tragedy and revolution reciprocally exclude themselves.[95] As a teleological vision of history, socialism did not admit tragedy. It historicized and "metabolized" defeats, removing or diminishing their painful, sometimes devastating character. The Marxist dialectic of defeat took the form of a secular theodicy: good could be extracted from evil; final victory resulted from an enchainment of defeats.

However, some Marxist thinkers tried to reintegrate tragedy into the struggle for socialism. In 1955, Lucien Goldmann published *The Hidden God*, a brilliant study devoted to the tragic world vision of Pascal and Racine, the representatives of French Jansenism. Facing the rise of rationalism (Descartes) and a new individualistic morality, Pascal affirmed the existence of God as an act of faith: a *wager* (*pari*). In the twentieth century, Goldmann analogously defended the hope of a communist future as a secular *wager*, neither mystical nor religious, but rather rooted in an idea of human community. Socialism, he thought, is not ineluctable; it is a hypothesis based on the emancipatory potentialities of human beings. In other words, he conceived of socialism as an anthropological act of faith. As he wrote in *The Hidden God*, "The Marxist faith is a faith in the historical future that men make themselves, or more exactly that we must make by our activity; it's a 'wager' staked on the success of our actions. The transcendence that constitutes the object of this faith is no longer either supernatural or trans-historical; it is trans-individual, no more but also no less."[96] This wager, he added, necessarily implies "the risk, the danger of failure and the hope of success."[97] The risk means that nothing is assured in advance; the danger of failure cannot be removed, because the defeat permanently threatens us; but the hope of success remains. In his *Prison Notebooks*, Antonio Gramsci defended the same idea when, parodying positivism, he wrote that the only "scientific" prediction was struggle.[98]

2 MARXISM AND MEMORY

ENTER MEMORY, EXIT MARX

A T first sight, Marxism and memory appear as two foreign continents. Since Marx, many scholars belonging to his intellectual tradition have elaborated philosophies of history or investigated historical temporalities—E. P. Thompson's studies on time and work discipline in early industrial capitalism are the most known—but have never conceptualized collective remembrance. Opened one century ago by Henri Bergson and Maurice Halbwachs, the scholarly debate on memory deeply shaped sociology, historiography, and philosophy without receiving any significant Marxist contribution. The rare assessments made by Marxist scholars on this topic simply reproduce a classical, positivistic dichotomy between history and memory: memory is the subjective and volatile recollection of a lived experience, whereas history rigorously reconstitutes the events of the past. In his preface to *History of the Russian Revolution* (1930), Leon Trotsky admits that his participation in this historical event as an outstanding actor "naturally makes easier his understanding, not only of the psychology of the forces in action, both individual and collective, but also of the inner connection of events." That being said, he immediately adds that such a position can become an epistemological advantage only if he does not write as a witness, that is, providing a "testimony of his own memory." Memory is unreliable, as he clearly explains in the following terms: "This work will not rely in any degree upon personal recollections. The circumstance that the author was a participant in the events does not free him from the obligation to base his exposition upon historically verified documents. The author speaks of himself, in so far as that is demanded by the course of events, in the third person."[1]

In presenting his autobiography a few years earlier, he had already stressed that, memory not being "an automatic reckoner," he preferred leaving it to "psychoanalytic criticism." In writing his book he had "persistently checked [his] memory by documentary evidence."[2] Historians use primary sources—notably archival materials—rather than unstable and unverifiable recollections; in spite of its title, My Life, his book was a work of historical investigation, not the report of a witness.

By a kind of symmetrical reaction, the scholars interested in memory almost completely ignored Marxism. In the last decades, their debate has been renewed by, among others, Pierre Nora, Henry Rousso, and Paul Ricoeur in France, Aleida Assmann in Germany, and Josef H. Yerushalmi in the United States, that is, historians who have never paid attention to Marxism, a current of ideas that remains outside of their intellectual horizon. The indexes of "memory readers" published in recent years do not include any reference to Marxism, except for a couple of pages drawn from Marx's Eighteenth Brumaire.[3]

A common view fixes in the middle of the 1980s the advent of a moment mémoriel shaping all Western societies. It significantly coincides with the publication of Zakhor (1982) in the United States and the first volume of Realms of Memory in France (1984). It corresponds also with the rise of the memory of the Holocaust in the public sphere, a process whose major steps were the Historikerstreit in Germany (1986) and the publication of Primo Levi's The Drowned and the Saved in Italy (1986), just after the international impact of Claude Lanzmann's Shoah (1985), a movie exclusively based on witnesses' recollections. Meaningfully, the emergence of memory in the public sphere has coincided with the intellectual turn known as "the crisis of Marxism."[4] Such a synchronism between the rise of memory and the decline of Marxism is highly emblematic. Marxism played a major role in the humanities when *society* was their dominant paradigm; its eclipse became almost complete in the 1980s, when scholarly research shifted toward the paradigm of *memory*.[5] This transition took place in a political context created by the "conservative revolution" in Britain and America, the Islamic revolution in Iran, and the Cambodian genocide: experiences that exhausted the postwar anti-imperialist wave. The fall of the Berlin Wall completed the process. Marxism left the stage, without applause or a curtain call, at the moment in which memory came out from the margins and installed in the foreground.

This chapter will explore the causes of such a missed encounter between Marxism and memory. Of course, this failure was not ineluctable, but it needs to be explained. On the one hand, I will consider Marxism as the dominant culture of the left throughout the twentieth century without reducing it to a doctrine codified in some canonical texts. On the other hand, I will approach memory in its double meaning: not only individual recollections but also collective representations of the past. I don't deny the distinction between memory and history, the latter being both the whole of the facts making the historical universe—*res gestae*, the literality of the events—and a discipline (history writing) that is a critical discourse on the past. Historical factuality is a magmatic kaleidoscope, whereas history writing is a work of reconstruction, contextualization, and interpretation of what has happened, a work that inevitably implies a textual re-creation of the past. I will also take into account the interaction between memory and history, precisely because the primary function of the latter consists in answering a demand of knowledge that rises from the society and is nourished by memory itself. Far from being immutable or frozen, memory changes permanently and transcends the recollections of a lived experience. Cultural practices, cultural industry, public policies, and even laws (sometimes penal laws) hugely shape and transform our representation of the past. Historiography cannot completely escape from the constraints of collective memory, because it is collective memory that suggests to historians their objects of investigation and molds their mental habitus. As a mirror of expectations, visions, and perceptions of the past, Marxist culture implies a certain conception of memory and, at the same time, gives interesting insights into the memory of the left itself.

The interaction between history and memory is grounded in a given *regime of historicity*: the experience and the perception of the past shaping a society at a particular moment. As we have seen in the previous chapters, the regime of historicity at the beginning of the twenty-first century discloses a deep crisis of utopic imagination. Often captured by the concept of "presentism," this experience of time shows a permanent acceleration within a "naturalized" and eternized social structure, that is, conceived and considered as immutable, without any possible alternative. The dialectical tension between past and future[6] is broken in a world withdrawn into the present. Once capitalism is naturalized, to think of a different future becomes impossible and the past appears as a warning against such a dangerous temptation. Pushed forward by the French and Russian Revolutions, the nineteenth and the twentieth centuries projected themselves into a future identified with "Progress" (industrial, technical, democratic, socialist). The twenty-first century, on the contrary, opens in a world without utopias, paralyzed by the historical defeats of communist revolutions. Abandoned by the "principle of hope," our age of post-totalitarian, neoliberal humanitarianism does not perceive the past as a time of revolutions, but rather as an era of violence. Its witnesses speak in the name of the victims[7] and the task of collective memory lies in an inexhaustible work of mourning: we have to impede their oblivion and learn the lessons of their suffering for the next generations. Young people are not summoned to change the world, but rather to not repeat the mistakes of those who, blinded by dangerous utopias, finally contributed to the building of a despotic order.

The turn of 1989 is the moment in which the changes accumulated over the previous decades suddenly condensed, leading to collapse. The end of communism introduced new tropes into our historical consciousness: the remembrance of the victims replaced that of the vanquished; only perpetrators and victims remained. Nowadays, the actors of the past need to achieve the status of victim in order to conquer a place in public memory. Burdened with its totalitarian past, Germany has become a privileged realm for this metamorphosis of historical consciousness. It is there that, since the 1980s, the memory of the Holocaust has symbolically replaced that of antifascism in the public space.[8] The official memory of the GDR has been erased. The monuments of the regime as well as the statues of the founders of communism have been destroyed. A solitary statue of Marx and Engels remains in Berlin, between the Museum Island and the Nikolaiviertel, exhibiting an ironic graffiti on its base: *Wir sind unschuldig* ("we are innocent"). At the same time, the recollection of the victims of National Socialism has redrawn the urban landscape until the creation, in 2005, of a gigantic Holocaust Memorial at the heart of the German capital.[9] This is the context of the crisis of Marxism, which is the mirror of a historical defeat.

MEMORY OF THE FUTURE

As the famous eleventh thesis on Feuerbach (1844) indicates, Marxism was born and developed as both an interpretation and a project for the revolutionary transformation of the world. The collapse of communism annihilated its utopic hopes and, consequently, erased its memory. In other words, it ceased to transmit the memory of the struggles for a better world. There is no need to reconsider old philosophical debates in order to recognize that utopia was the secret tropism of the Marxist conception of history. In *The Eighteenth Brumaire of Louis Bonaparte* (1852), memory is evoked as "the tradition of all dead generations," which "weighs like a nightmare on the brains of the living."[10] The modern revolutions directed against capitalism, Marx pursues, "cannot take their poetry from the past but only from the future."[11] They "must let the dead bury their dead" and throw off the "required recollections of past world history" (which blinded their ancestors) in order to project themselves into the future.[12]

Until the late twentieth century, teleology was a typical feature of Marxist historiography. Communism was postulated as a telos, as an end of history and, consequently, the cleavages of historical periodization were fixed by revolutions. A straight line linked 1789 to 1917, passing through the revolutions of 1848 and the Paris Commune.[13] In Lenin's *The State and Revolution*, a text written in 1917, the word "memory" does not appear, but several chapters are devoted to the revolutionary "experiences" of the nineteenth century, notably 1848 and the Paris Commune.[14] The Bolshevik leader considered this recapitulation as a necessary task in view of a revolutionary action. From October onward, the process became global and the ascending curve split in different lines crossing Europe (1968 in France, 1974 in Portugal), Latin America (1958 in Cuba), and Asia (1949 in China, 1975 in Vietnam). Adopting a similar compass, Albert Mathiez described the Bolsheviks as the inheritors of the French Jacobins[15] and the actors of May '68 were convinced of having experienced a "general repetition," like the uprising of July 1917 that preceded the October Revolution.[16] In short, revolutions seemed to sketch an ascending line. Eric Hobsbawm vividly summarized this vision of memory, quoting a British union activist who, in the 1930s, used to speak to the Tories in the following terms: "your class represents the past, my class represents the future."[17] History writing and memory were interwoven and reciprocally nourished themselves. In other words, memory was a memory for the future, insofar as it announced the battles to come. The remembrance of the past revolutions was not circumscribed to the exciting moment of emancipation experienced as a collective action; it could also bear the tragedies of their defeats. During the darkest days of the Russian Civil War, when the Soviet power was threatened and the revolution seemed in agony, the ghost of the Paris Commune haunted the Bolsheviks. A victory of the Russian White Guards would have led to a massacre such as the "bloody week" of May 1871, on an incomparably larger scale. As Victor Serge reminds in his memoirs, a White military dictatorship appeared as the most probable issue, with the consequence that the Bolshevik leaders would have been all executed. Far from spreading discouragement, nevertheless, this awareness encouraged them to resist: "Despite hunger, mistakes, and even crimes," he wrote in 1924, "We Reds are going toward the City of the Future."[18]

For a century, socialist-communist iconography has illustrated this teleological vision of history. Its images "etched" themselves in the memory of several generations of activists—from workers to intellectuals—and shaped their imagination. They played the role of "subliminal points of reference" or "unspoken points of address"—according to the beautiful formula of Raphael Samuel—whose interpretation can be as interesting as textual exegesis.[19] *The Fourth Estate* by Pellizza da Volpedo (1900 [figure 2.1]), one of the most famous paintings inspired by the socialist idea before the Great War, describes the advance of the laboring classes from a dark background toward the light: their march is a metaphor of history as a path from oppression to emancipation, from a somber past to an enlightened, resplendent future.[20] *The Fourth Estate* could be interpreted as a pictorial illustration of the socialist strategy described by Friedrich Engels, just before his death, in a famous and controversial preface to a new edition of Marx's *The Class Struggles in France* (1895).

2.1. Giuseppe Pellizza da Volpedo, *Il Quarto Stato/The Fourth Estate* (1901), oil on canvas, Pinacoteca di Brera, Milano. © Artists Rights Society (ARS), New York.

Observing a shift of the center of gravity of the European socialist movement from France (the locus of nineteenth-century revolutions) to Germany, the country where social democracy realized its most impressive electoral advances (from one hundred thousand votes in 1871 to almost two million votes in 1890), Engels registered a radical change of strategy. The time of street fights and the barricades was over. "Rebellion in the old style" appeared irremediably "obsolete" in comparison with the rise of the "great international army of socialists, marching irresistibly on and growing daily in number, organization, discipline, insight and certainty of victory."[21] Socialism was ineluctable and any attempt to accelerate its advent was useless, not to say dangerous: "If even this mighty army of the proletariat has still not reached its goal, if, a long way from winning victory with one mighty stroke, it has slowly to press forward from position to position in a hard, tenacious struggle, this only proves, once and for all, how impossible it was in 1848 to win social reconstruction by a simple surprise attack."[22]

Retrospectively, the revolutions of the nineteenth century had taken a "Blanquist" dimension, and this critique of the insurrectionary struggle was presented as the opposition between two historical temporalities: on the one hand, the speeding, sparking, disruptive time of revolution and, on the other hand, the slow but homogeneous and irresistible time of an evolutionary change. Then appeared the dialectics—later theoretically codified by Gramsci—between a "war of movement" and a "war of position." The future of socialism, Engels thought, belonged to the second one and, consequently, the memory of the barricades could be an obstacle for this gradual but tremendous growth. Suddenly, nineteenth-century revolutions had become, like populist terrorism in the eyes of the Russian social democrats, "an expression of political impatience," an ensemble of combats coming "ahead of their time," occurring "too early" and "too fast" to consolidate their conquests.[23]

The First World War rehabilitated revolutionary action with its sudden, disruptive time, but this acceleration was still inscribed into a utopian vision of socialism. After the October Revolution, utopia ceased to be the abstract representation of a liberated society projected into a far, unknown future; it became the unchained imagination of a world to be built in the present. In 1919, in the middle of the Russian Civil War and the revolutionary upheavals in many countries of Central Europe, Vladimir Tatlin elaborated the project of his *Monument to the Third International* (figure 2.2). Drawing inspiration from the myth of the Tower of Babel, he conceived this work of art in a constructivist style, as a building that had to be not only admired but also used, proving that art was a tool for constructing socialism. Much more than a symbol, its ambition was to give material evidence of the construction of a new world as a fusion between aesthetics and politics. "Radically anti-monumental," as Svetlana Boym has pointed out, this architectonic project deeply differed from all its forerunners.[24] It had nothing to do with the linear verticality of the Eiffel Tower, which simply celebrated industrial modernity, or with the Statue of Liberty, whose aesthetic was inspired by a conventional classicism, or even with Auguste Rodin's *La Tour du Travail*, a project—probably known to Tatlin—created for the Universal Exhibition of 1900 but never realized. In the spirit of the Third Republic, Rodin's tower glorified the redemptive virtues of work, depicted as a spiral ascending from manual labor to technique and science, vectors of a progress placed under the sign of Providence and

2.2. Vladimir Tatlin, *Monument to the Third International* (Model) (1919). © Art Resource, New York.

accomplished as sacrifice (figure 2.3).[25] Tatlin broke with this traditional conception of art and culture. Made of iron and glass, his "monument" integrated into a single structure three different rotating elements: a cube, a pyramid, and a cylinder. On the bottom, the cube would have hosted the Soviet government (Sovnarkom) and spun for one year; the pyramid provided accommodation for the Communist International

2.3. Auguste Rodin, *The Tower of Labour (Model for a Monument)* (1898–99), Musée Rodin, Paris. © Art Resource, New York.

(Komintern) and circled around itself once a month; the cylinder held the editorial board of its propaganda organ, published simultaneously in different languages, a conference room, a printing office, a telegraph office, a radio, and a projector of slogans onto the clouds on overcast days, and it would have spun daily.[26] The spiral evoked the evolutionary movement of science (the original idea of revolution as astronomical rotation) whereas the pyramid gave to the building a vertical character, like a wedge penetrating into the cosmos: revolution was a rupture and an attempt to storm heaven. The Babel of languages was a symbol no longer of confusion, but rather of a new international community conquering the future.

Other works of art were created in a similar spirit. In 1921, Lenin suggested that the Obelisk of Moscow, inaugurated by the Tsarist regime at the edge of the war in order to celebrate the Romanov dynasty, be transformed into a Memorial for the Great Socialist Thinkers, including utopian visionaries like Campanella, Thomas More, Saint-Simon, and Charles Fourier. In the same year, Kosntantin Yuon painted *The New Planet*, which depicted the October Revolution as the discovery or the birth of a new planet (figure 2.4). The advent of socialism was much

2.4. Konstantin Yuon, *The New Planet* (1921), oil on canvas, Tretyakov Gallery, Moscow. © Art Resource, New York.

more than a simple historical turn; it was a sort of Copernican Revolution that modified our vision of the world, or even a new big bang that changed the cosmos itself.[27]

During the 1920s, the Soviet propaganda showed Lenin with his arm stretched toward the future, like an assured guide in the middle of a world made of industries, chemistries, and machines where a multitude of workers feverishly acted to build a new society (figures 2.5–6). In 1933, the architect Boris Iofan won the competition for the Soviet Palace of Moscow (figure 2.7). His project will never be realized, but it was immediately publicized and shaped the Soviet imagination of the time. The skyscraper—the communist response to the Empire State Building inaugurated in New York two years before—culminates in a gigantic statue of Lenin, once again his arm stretched toward the future, surrounded by clouds and planes.[28] These posters and statues of Lenin are the secular version of an older biblical iconography showing Moses going down from the Mount Sinai, bringing the tables of the Law and stretching his finger toward the skies (figure 2.8).[29] This striking affinity between socialist and biblical iconographies reveals the permanence, in the communist tradition, of a religious impulsion that coexists—visually exhibited even if theoretically denied—with its dominant atheism. Marx inherited his anticlericalism from the radical Enlightenment and his disciples transformed it into Marxism's official doctrine, but insofar as this ideology became part of the culture of the left—that is, of social and political mass movements—it merged with hopes, dreams, and expectations that for centuries had taken a religious form. In other words, atheism and secularized religious trends intertwine in the famous definition of religion as "the opium of the people," which means both alienation and a wish of liberation: "Religious distress," Marx wrote in 1844, "is at the same time the expression of real distress and the protest against real distress. Religion is the sigh of the oppressed creature, the heart of a heartless world, just as it is the spirit of an unspiritual situation. It is the opiate of the people."[30] Communist iconography expressed this messianic tension toward a liberated world—a posthistorical realm according to Marx—reproducing its own version of Christian eschatology.

After the Second World War, the Soviet imagination remained projected into a future made of factories and space crafts, whose supersonic speed replaced the feverish, compressed time of revolutionary upheaval:

2.5. A. Strakhov, *Lenin* (1924), Soviet poster. © Art Resource, New York.

the march toward socialism was measured by the tons of steel, tractors, aircrafts, and missiles produced by the Soviet industry instead of the millions of votes won by the German social democracy at the elections, but history had not lost its telos. Like the avant-garde, Boris Groys pointed out, "Stalinist culture continues to be oriented toward the future,"[31] trying to shape everyday life and to magnify the material achievements

2.6. V. Shcherbakov, *A Specter Is Haunting Europe, the Specter of Communism* (1920), Soviet poster. © Art Resource, New York.

2.7. Boris Iofan, *Project for the Palace of the Soviets* (1933). Schusev Research Museum of Architecture, Moscow. © Art Resource, New York.

2.8. Gustave Doré, "Moses Coming Down from the Mount Sinai," *Bible's Illustrations* (1866). © Art Resource, New York.

of socialism. It is in the 1970s, during the time of Brezhnev's stagnation, that the march began to slow down and the future became uncertain. Then appeared in the USSR a "postutopian" art producing paintings such as Erik Bulatov's *The Horizon*, in which a group of Soviet people walk along the beach, toward the sea, but the horizon, in front of them, is invisible, cut by a huge, horizontal strip reminiscent of the Order of

Lenin. However, this sharp demystifying aesthetic was perceived as a critique of real socialism rather than a critique of socialism itself.

Even in Latin America, where socialist utopias very often merged with the cyclical time of the indigenous communities, visual representations of history could not avoid the mythology of an ascending path toward the future: the conquest of the sky (*el cielo por asalto*). In a diachronic, sumptuous perspective, the linear movement describing the advance of the laboring classes from a past of oppression toward a liberated future is shown by the murals of Diego Rivera decorating the Palace of Government's staircases in Mexico City (figure 2.9). The remembrance of both anticolonial struggles and peasant revolution naturally leads to the organization of the modern, multiracial, and multinational workers movement, which is put under the sight of the tutelary figure of Marx.[32]

Marxist teleology was not necessarily formulated in terms of deterministic causality; it could also take the form of Ernst Bloch's utopia,

2.9. Diego Rivera, "Karl Marx Pointing to Utopia," detail from *Mexico Today and Tomorrow* (1935), mural, Mexico City. © 2015 Banco de México Diego Rivera Frida Kahlo Museums Trust, Mexico, D.F./Artists Rights Society (ARS), New York.

that is, a philosophy and a politics of "anticipation" (*Vorschein*). Marxism built an "anticipatory consciousness," transforming the dream of emancipation that had haunted human societies since Antiquity into a philosophical vision of the future. That is why Bloch devoted to Marx the last chapter of his *Principle of Hope*, in a volume reviewing the "wishful images of the fulfilled moment."[33] Rather than a "cold utopia" depicting socialism as a future inscribed into the laws of history, Marxism was, in the eyes of Bloch, a social project routed into an anthropological optimism inherited from the Enlightenment: the long process through which humanity learns to rise up and walk upright. In a similar way, Herbert Marcuse explained the dialectical link between memory and the socialist utopia mobilizing the category of unconscious elaborated by Freud. The function of memory, he wrote in *Eros and Civilization* (1955), was "to preserve promises and potentialities which are betrayed and even outlawed by the mature, civilized individual." This unfulfilled but also unforgotten desire could be projected toward the future as a utopia of happiness. On this path, Proust joined Marx: "The *recherche du temps perdu* becomes the vehicle of future liberation."[34] This future-oriented memory needed to be educated and forged in opposition to the alienated memory of a class society: repressive civilization is made of discipline and submission and, consequently, it recollects duties rather than pleasures. It is a "memory linked with bad conscience, guilt and sin," in which images of freedom are "tabooed."[35] Marxist *countermemory* should focus on the engulfed happiness of humankind, joining utopia as a promise of freedom. This utopia, saved and carried on by memory, has a romantic dimension insofar as it reconnects a liberated future with an ancestral past. Similarly to fantasy's conservation of the structures and tendencies of the child's psyche in the adult individual, "imagination preserves the 'memory' of the sub-historical past," offering to the struggle for human emancipation "the image of the immediate unity between the universal and the particular under the rule of the pleasure principle."[36] In the wake of Bloch, Marcuse suggested a dialectical Marxism liberated from any form of historical determinism, admitting "the possibility that the path to socialism may proceed from science to utopia and not from utopia to science."[37] Science did not announce the advent of socialism but certainly could be mobilized by socialism in order to fulfill an ancestral dream of happiness. Even reinterpreted as utopia — or as a possible alternative to barbarism — socialism remained a historical *telos*, a goal orienting and building the recollection of an emancipatory movement. If we had to synthesize in a formula the Marxist conception of memory, we could adopt the intense definition suggested by Vincent Veoghegan: "remembering the future."[38]

These visual and textual documents prove that Marxist teleology implied remembrance as a key element of its utopian imagination. It was not a form of left futurism, that is, an avant-garde movement that, fascinated by velocity, technology, and modernity, pretended to conquer the future "abolishing history."[39] In the first years of Soviet power, Leon Trotsky criticized the mnemonic nihilism exhibited by the Russian Futurists and stressed the part of remembrance incorporated into revolutionary action. We can read the following assessment in *Literature and Revolution* (1924):

> A Bohemian nihilism exists in the exaggerated Futurist rejection of the past, but not in a proletarian revolutionism. We Marxists live in traditions, and we have not stopped being revolutionists on account of it. We elaborated and lived through the traditions of the Paris Commune, even before our first revolution. Then the traditions of 1905 were added to them, by which we nourished ourselves and by which we prepared the second revolution. Going farther back, we connected the Commune with the June days of 1848, and with the great French Revolution.[40]

What Marxism rejected in Futurism was not its subversive character and—in the case of Russian Futurism—its radical criticism of bourgeois society; it was rather its rejection of a revolutionary tradition. The trouble was not that Futurism rejected "the holy traditions of the intelligentsia," but rather in the fact that it did not feel itself "to be part of the revolutionary tradition. We stepped into the Revolution while Futurism fell into it."[41] According to Trotsky, revolution was not a tabula rasa; it had its own vision of the past, as a kind of countermemory opposed to the official interpretations of history. Revolution was the moment in which this vision "raised from the deeps of memory" and pushed its actors to "break a road into the future."[42]

Of course, that did not impede Trotsky from sharing the futurist faith in the machine as a tool for changing the world. Some passages from *Literature and Revolution* describe the socialist future in Promethean terms, merging Fourier's utopian vision of "universal harmony" with a typically nineteenth-century blind idealization of progress and technology. According to the Russian revolutionary, socialism should look like that:

> Man has already made changes in the map of nature that are not few nor insignificant. But they are mere pupils' practice in comparison with what is coming. Faith merely promises to move mountains; but technology, which takes nothing "on faith," is actually able to cut down mountains and move them. Up to now this was done for industrial purposes (mines) or for railways (tunnels); in the future this will be done on an immeasurably larger scale, according to a general industrial and artistic plan. Man will occupy himself with re-registering mountains and rivers, and will earnestly and repeatedly make improvements in nature. In the end, he will have rebuilt the earth, if not in his own image, at least according to his own taste. We have not the slightest fear that this taste will be bad. . . . Through the machine, man in Socialist society will command nature in its entirety, with its grouse and its sturgeons. He will point out places for mountains and for passes. He will change the course of the rivers, and he will lay down rules for the oceans. The idealist simpletons may say that this will be a bore, but that is why they are simpletons. Of course this does not mean that the entire globe will be marked off into boxes, that the forests will be turned into parks and gardens. Most likely, thickets and forests and grouse and tigers will remain, but only where man commands them to remain. And man will do it so well that the tiger won't even notice the machine, or feel the change, but will live as he lived in primeval times. The machine is not in opposition to the earth. The machine is the instrument of modern man in every field of life.[43]

In a rare Marxist excursion into science fiction, Alexander Bogdanov's novel *Red Star* (1908) had already prefigured socialism as a technological future whose accomplishment he located in the planet of Mars.[44] Unlike Bogdanov, however, the chief of the Red Army preserved a dialectical tension between memory and utopia. In a chapter titled "The Revolutionary as Historian" of his remarkable biography of Leon Trotsky, Isaac Deutscher describes the style of *History of the Russian Revolution*—narrative and analytical at the same time—as an emphatic reconstruction of the events in which October 1917 appears as a moment of proletarian self-emancipation burdened with memory. Painting the crowds' movements, Trotsky wished to share with the readers their happiness: "Of such men, even though they may be illiterate and crude, he is proud; and he wants us to be proud of them. The revolution is for him that brief but pregnant moment when the humble and downtrodden at last have their say. In his eyes this moment redeems ages of oppression. He harks back to it with a nostalgia which gives the re-enactment a vivid and high relief."[45]

MYTH AND REMEMBRANCE

Of course, this future-oriented memory nourished the Soviet myth of the "New Man," but the communist forerunner of emancipated humankind was very different from his fascist "homologous" heroes. The abyssal distance that separates communism from fascism does not concern only their vision of the future but also their description of the past. The past can inhabit the present as a myth or as a hot, blasting memory waking up and acting upon today's reality. Fascism is probably the most emblematic example of a modernity conceived and experienced as a timeless myth. The secret of the Conservative Revolution was precisely the fusion of technical and mechanical modernity with an ancestral, romantically idealized past made of traditional values and mythological heroes. It merged old and new, transforming the charismatic leaders into everlasting figures belonging to both the past and the future.[46] The "Thousand-Year Reich" celebrated its liturgies in the medieval city of Nuremberg and the fascist regime's ambition was to transform Rome into a *città eterna* where the Futurist cult of the machines incorporated the vestiges of Antiquity, creating a single, harmonic unity. In 1936, after the colonization of Ethiopia, Mussolini presented himself as a Roman emperor. The following year, the Mostra Augustea della Romanità was inaugurated in the Italian capital, celebrating the two-thousandth anniversary of the birth of Emperor Augustus. Rather than a historical reconstruction of the Roman Empire, this exhibition was conceived as a "rebirth" of the past in the present, according to the vision of *romanità* defended by Mussolini, for whom Rome was "a symbol and a myth."[47] Mussolini's profile dissolved into Augustus. The same year of the Roman exhibition, the Nazi painter Hubert Lanziger created a famous portrait of the Führer as a medieval knight in armor. According to Johann Chapoutot, the Nazis had replaced "the realm of history with the realm of myth"; they had abolished historical time, replacing it with the "eternity of the race, of its gesture and its combat."[48]

Just as the fascist historical imagination is a mythical construction, the revolutionary perception of time—its antipodal one—is shaped by memory, even if it is a "memory of the future," charged with eschatological expectations. Walter Benjamin grasped this feature when he wrote that revolutionary movements were "nourished by the image of enslaved ancestors rather than that of liberated grandchildren."[49] This might explain the relationship with the past established in the last decades by the revolutions in Latin America, waking up the shadows of Augusto César Sandino, Farabundo Martí, Emiliano Zapata, and, more recently, Simón Bolívar. In January 2006, at Tiwanaku, near Lake Titicaca, among the ruins of an old, pre-Inca town, Evo Morales was proclaimed president of Bolivia, a few days before his official investiture in La Paz. This Indian ceremony held in Aymara inscribed his victory into a cyclical time intertwined but distinct from the historical time of the state and of secular institutions (figure 2.10). The indigenous peoples desire to be actors of history but they will not submit their own past of "peoples without history," according to the classical Hegelian (and Engelsian) formula, to the codes of Western history (state, writing, archives, and so on). For them, the entrance into history means the beginning of a long cycle of oppression and resistance and, consequently, they define themselves against the state and history.[50] Evo Morales and Álvaro García Linera are not folkloric figures; they act politically in a secular world, but they know that their historical role is also intertwined with a temporality that does not belong to Western history.[51] In other words, they wish to build their future saving their past. As the Mexican Zapatistas say, they walk "putting one foot in the past and the other in the future" (*poniendo un pié en el pasado y otro en el futuro*).[52] This is an interesting attempt to preserve—through memory—a hope in the future without falling into the fatal illusions of teleology.

FUTURES' PAST

The monument of Tatlin to the Third International drew its inspiration from the biblical myth of the Tower of Babel (Genesis 11) that, as

2.10. Bolivia's President Evo Morales at Tiwanaku, December 2005.

we know, resulted in divine punishment for human beings guilty of a
demiurgic dream. The Tower of Babel could not be finished and fell into
ruin; its image was transmitted for centuries by a large iconographic tradition immortalized by the famous painting of Pieter Bruegel the Elder
(figure 2.11). After the fall of the Berlin Wall, the literary historian and
critic Hans Mayer chose this biblical myth in order to depict the end of
real socialism: it deserved to fail, but such a failure was not ineluctable,
and its beginning had not been as bad as its end.[53] The Tower of Babel,
to which he referred, is a lyric written in 1949 by the German expression-
ist poet Johannes R. Becher, who, ironically, became for several years
the minister of culture in the GDR. Reread in 1990, this lyric took on a
prophetic taste, especially in its conclusion, where the Tower of Babel,
which "speaks in all tongues" and "rises into the sky," ultimately "col-
lapses to nothing in its fall."[54]

Like Tatlin's tower, Babel had become the world revolution that
"speaks all tongues" but now it was a lie, Stalinism, which had transformed its universal message into an incomprehensible uproar and provoked its fall. The assault on heaven had turned into a pitiful collapse:
only ruins remain.

2.11. Pieter Bruegel I, *The Tower of Babel* (1563), oil on canvas, Kunsthistorisches Museum, Vienna. © Art Resource, New York.

Several vanguard creators anticipated the end of communism and depicted it as a memory break. In 1983, the exiled Russian artist Aleksandr Kosolapov painted a canvas presenting Lenin's head put on the soil, beside the base of its broken statue, in front of which there are three putti leaning over a journal titled *The Manifesto* and trying painfully to decipher its content (figure 2.12). The utopia has fallen and what had been announced as a radiant future lies as a field of ruins. Communism has become an incomprehensible text demanding to be rediscovered and reinterpreted. Lenin has fallen from his base, but his head is still entire and his sight somber; we do not know whether he directs his reproach against those who destroyed his statue or those who decided to build it, compelling him to play a role he had not chosen.[55]

The end of communism as the end of a utopia and an act of remembrance, as a ceremony of mourning both solemn and tragic, found its most poignant expression in Theo Angelopoulos's *Ulysses' Gaze* (1995), a movie devoted to the war in the former Yugoslavia. The erasing of the past, the rescue of its legacy, and the preservation of its memory are the film's connecting thread. The journey of its hero in the middle of

2.12. Aleksandr Kosolapov, *The Manifesto* (1983), oil on canvas. © 2015 Artists Rights Society (ARS), New York.

a country devastated by war, looking for a lost fragment of film—the first Greek movie, whose last copy is conserved at Sarajevo's film archive, in a besieged city—is the metaphor of a collapsed world whose fall has swept away its hopes and utopias. A famous tracking shot in this movie shows a broken statute of Lenin that traverses the Danube lying on a boat, his sight and his index finger directed toward the sky. Suddenly people appear, ranging in a crowded shore, in order to follow its

2.13–14. Theo Angelopoulos, *Ulysses' Gaze* (1995), Paradis Films, La Sept, Centre du Cinéma Grec.

2.15. Sergei Eisenstein, *October* (1927), Corinth Films.

passage. They are silent; many among them kneel down and cross themselves (figures 2.13–14). A sad melody accompanies this funeral of Lenin,
a broken and fallen statue leaving the stage of history. By an astonishing
reverse of Eisenstein's *October* (1927 [figure 2.15]), where the destruction
of the Tsar's statue symbolized the revolution, Angelopoulos depicts the
remembrance of communism as a work of mourning.

Like Danube in Angelopoulos's movie, in Marcelo Brodsky's exhibition *Buena Memoria* (2003), the realm of memory is another river: Rio
de la Plata. Marcelo Brodsky is an artist whose visual conceptualization
of memory corresponds to the representation of a former future—a
future past (*vergangene Zukunft*), according to Koselleck's definition—
which includes communism, not as a political regime but as a revolutionary utopia.[56] *Buena Memoria*, probably his best-known exhibition,
is a palimpsest that merges an identity quest, a family chronicle, a work
of mourning, the autobiography of a generation, and a piece of national
history, that of Argentina at the time of military dictatorship (1976–83).[57]
His pictures weave a plural memory in which the past reappears with its

horizon of expectation, its hopes and utopias. Three key images suggest an interpretation of the history of Argentina. In the first one, an old photo from a family album, a man is on the bridge of a ship (figure 2.16). He is uncle Salomon, the brother of his grandfather, coming to Buenos Aires at the beginning of the past century. He looks at the sea, the agitation of the waves before him, with a grave gaze that seems to search and scrutinize the future waiting him. Brodsky presents this picture with the following words: "The Rio de la Plata has been the arrival point and also the end point. My great-uncle Salomon, my grandfather's brother, came by the river at the beginning of the century. His image challenges the future, his posture expects everything."[58] The second picture shows two adolescents, the author and his brother, smiling for the camera, still on the bridge of a ship. They stand up, resting on the railing, next to a warning indicating that they are in a forbidden area ("proibido permanecer en este lugar") (figure 2.17). In the third picture, only the water remains, the waves of the Atlantic Ocean merging with those of the Rio de la Plata, the "boundless river" (*el río sin orillas*) in whose wake Juan José Saer narrated the history of Argentina (figure 2.18). By their juxtaposition, these three pictures build a narrative with multiple meanings and evocations, in which they tell at the same time individual destinies and the history of a nation.[59] The first one shows a European emigrant going to build his life in the New World, with his expectations and his hopes, like millions of immigrants who landed in Argentina in the nineteenth and twentieth centuries. The second one jumps two generations later. The inscription on the railing reveals a transgression and announces the revolt of the 1960s and 1970s. The third one is an image of horror: during the military dictatorship, the disappeared (*desaparecidos*) were often thrown in the river, sometimes still alive. They "have a grave in the water," we would say paraphrasing the words of Paul Celan's "Todesfuge."[60] The river became their cemetery. Fernando, the brother of Marcelo Brodsky, was one of them. *Buena Memoria* includes one of his last pictures, taken at the Naval Mechanical School (ESMA) of Buenos Aires, the biggest concentration camp of general Videla's regime (figure 2.19). The sequence of these three images tells the history of Argentina in the twentieth century, which is a broken history. The immigrant found a new home; his descendants grew up, became political militants, and suffered from fascist violence, one exiled and the other killed: the flowing

2.16–18. Marcelo Brodsky, "The River Plate" (triptych) © Marcelo Brodsky, *Buena Memoria* (1997).

2.16–18. (Continued)

2.16–18. (Continued)

water, a metaphor of the time, engulfed him. The waves no longer evoke continuity—the flowing water, the chain of generations—but rather an abyss. And also the past resurging in these pictures is futures' past, made of destroyed dreams. Alone, separated from the other images, the water recalls a natural temporality whose historical equivalent is a "homogeneous and empty" chronological time. This image takes on meaning when it is juxtaposed with the other pictures. It is their sequence that fulfills the time, transforming it into a historical time and allowing us to decode the past. In the wake of Walter Benjamin, we might see these pictures as "dialectical" or "thought-images" (*Denkbilder*) claiming a "redemption of the past."[61] In light of Koselleck's semantics of historical time, Brodsky's pictures build a negative dialectic: the former future is buried, or, better, swallowed up by the sea, without links to a "horizon of expectation" in the present. It appears as a trauma breaking the continuity of historical time.

A Marxism corresponding to our regime of historicity—a temporality withdrawn into the present, deprived of a prognostic structure—inevitably takes a melancholic tonality. Amputated from its principle of hope—at least in the concrete form it took in the twentieth century, when the utopia of a liberated society was embodied by communism—it internalizes a historical downfall. Its strategic dimension does not

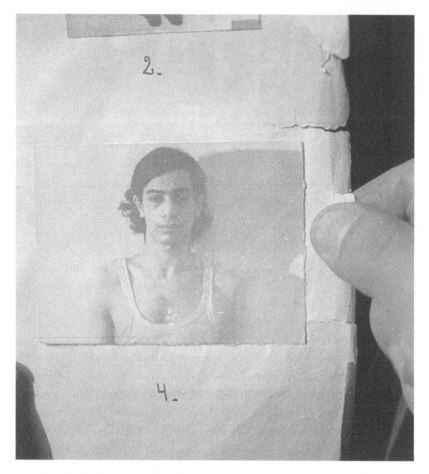

2.19. Marcelo Brodsky, "La camiseta" © Marcelo Brodsky, *Buena Memoria* (1997).

consist in organizing the suppression of capitalism, but rather in over-coming the trauma of a suffered collapse. Its art lies in organizing pessimism: to draw lessons from the past; to recognize a defeat without capitulating in front of the enemy, with the awareness that a new start will inescapably take new forms, unknown paths. The sight of the vanquished is always critical.2.19. Marcelo Brodsky, "La camiseta" © Marcelo Brodsky, *Buena Memoria* (1997).

③ MELANCHOLY IMAGES

FILM AND HISTORY

THE end of real socialism did not produce any significant film on the end of the communist hope. It inspired a wave of aesthetic creations that described the collapse of a world, ranging from tragedy to comedy, from the moral dilemmas and everyday lies to which a totalitarian power submitted individuals and human relations (Florian Henckel von Donnersmarck: *The Life of Others*, 2006) to the ironic nostalgia for a disappeared human environment (Wolfgand Becker: *Good Bye Lenin*, 2003). In Russia, Alexander Sokurov and Aleksei German depicted metaphorically the breakdown of the Soviet regime through the death agonies of Lenin and Stalin (respectively *Taurus*, 2001, and *Khrustalyov, My Car!*, 1998), whereas the former Yugoslavian filmmaker Emir Kusturica told the history of his broken country as a gigantic Balkan buffoonery in *Underground* (1995). In communism, Kusturica explained, "everything was a sham, a fiction, a hoax. Fundamentally, communism was a system that never evolved. And people bought into the fiction as if it were reality. In these cases, there is no choice; you are headed for disaster, for catastrophe. As George Orwell said, political language is designed to make lies sound truthful."[1] In most of these movies, communism appears as a strange, ungraspable, and often incomprehensible space of social disaggregation, a fathomless abyss. What remains is a vacuum. Pointing out Sokurov's predilection for "elegies"—this is the title of many of his documentaries—Giorgio Agamben recalls the etymology of this word, which in ancient Greek means both "funeral lament" and "political complaint": "the object of Sokurov's lamentation is power or, more precisely, the central vacuum of power."[2]

Perhaps, this vacuum was deeper and transcended power. The end of real socialism did not engender but simply revealed the eclipse of the socialist hope. In 1989, Nanni Moretti realized *Red Wood Pigeon* (*Palombella rossa*), a movie in which this vacuum becomes amnesia. His hero is an Italian communist who, after a car accident, has lost his memory. Pieces of the past—his own as well as the collective past of the Italian left—fragmentarily return during a water polo match, a sport that gives him a feeling of community in a universe of individualism, leaving him angry and astonished in front of an almost unrecognizable country. One year later, Moretti filmed the rank-and-file debates leading up to the congress in which the Communist Party changed its name (becoming the Left Democratic Party). The abandonment of any reference to communism—and consequently the separation from cultures, ideas, experiences, and identities forged over many decades—made way for something unknown and uncanny, a mysterious object: *The Thing* (*La cosa*, 1990).[3] Nevertheless, the movies of Nanni Moretti—"the egocentric Cassandra of the left"[4]—do not excavate this left-wing amnesia and usually simply mirror it, with an ironic gaze. One should look elsewhere for a visual language able to scrutinize the eclipse of the socialist hope and the legacy of the defeated revolutions of the past century.

This chapter deals with what Antoine De Baecque called *camera historica*, that is, "the cinematographic form of history," and Hayden White *historiophoty*, that is, the "representation of history and our thought on it through images and filmic discourse."[5] Differently from the historiography that is a critical discourse on the past—an attempt to reconstruct and interpret occurred events—historical films are often inaccurate and approximate in depicting a bygone time, with which they can take liberties that any serious scholar working with verifiable sources never could imagine. Historical films as well as historical novels, nonetheless, can excavate or overcome events in order to reach a "subjective" dimension of the past, telling the way in which events had been experienced by human beings and the meaning they took from them. Historical films, Natalie Zemon Davis suggests, can be "a thought experiment about the past"[6] that, without pretending to describe the facts "as they occurred" (*wie es eigentlich gewesen* in Rankean terms), deliver us one of its truths. This chapter will scrutinize films as barometers of left consciousness, as revealers of its dilemmas and changes. Without pretending to completeness, it will analyze several movies that, explicitly or allegorically, depict revolutionary and left defeats. This necessarily implies a selection of sources, whatever their subject or celebrity: films shot by politically committed artists as contributions to the left culture; films that politicize culture and stimulate a critical thought; films, in short, that, beyond their aesthetic value, unveil the mental and emotional landscape of the left.

THE EARTH TREMBLES

The most impressive filmic representation of a left defeat is probably Luchino Visconti's *La terra trema* (*The Earth Trembles*), where it takes an allegorical form. It is not a movie about socialism—with the exception of a couple of hammers and sickles that fugitively appear on the screen—but it was conceived (and perceived) as a parable of the class struggle. Presented at the Venice International Film Festival in September 1948, it mirrored the end of the expectations of the postwar years, when Italy seemed to be at the edge of revolution. In 1945, the Communist Party was in government and armed workers controlled almost all the factories of the industrialized northern regions of the Peninsula. In the Mezzogiorno, the southern regions, a massive movement of land occupations had conquered a law of agrarian reform and put into question the ancestral rule of feudal latifundia owners. Three years later, with the beginning of the Cold War, the Communist Party remained a powerful force but had been completely isolated and social movements had been defeated everywhere. On April 1948, Christian Democracy, the new dominant force of conservatism, won the political elections and three months later a murder attempt perpetrated in Rome against Palmiro Togliatti provoked an insurrectional wave across the country that—promptly controlled by the Communist Party—symbolically closed the political effervescence of the postwar years. Meanwhile, a coalition of Christian Democracy, the mafia, and the large landowners had prevailed in the South. An emblematic moment of this social and political restoration was, on the first of May 1947, the massacre of Portella della Ginestra, where a gang of bandits instigated by landowners killed eleven and wounded twenty-seven peasants, seven of whom died in the following days. The struggles to destroy feudalism and establish egalitarian social relations in rural Italy had been smashed. According to Paul Ginsborg, this defeat took "historic proportions, for it determined the values of contemporary southern life."[7]

It is in the middle of this dramatic social and political restoration that Visconti realized *La terra trema*: the shooting began in November 1947 and finished at the end of April of 1948; the editing took place in Rome during the following months. It was the second film of Luchino Visconti, one of many intellectuals who had joined the Communist Party in the war years and participated in the Resistance. In 1944 he had been arrested and miraculously avoided deportation to a German camp; one year later he filmed the execution of Pietro Koch, the Italian chief of the torture centers in Rome and Milan under German occupation.[8] At the end of the war, he was, with Roberto Rossellini, Cesare Zavattini, and Vittorio De Sica, one of the founders of neorealism, the new tendency of Italian cinema, created by intellectuals and artists who wished to describe the real life of "people," made of suffering, oppression, and struggle. Like the Russian Populists one century earlier, they idealized the "people" and decided to transform it into the "hero" of their movies, where it played a central role, far beyond a simple aesthetic representation. Their films were shot in the streets, often played by nonprofessional actors.

Originally, *La terra trema* was conceived as a documentary. Visconti accepted the job of shooting it as a propaganda film for the elections of April 1948, financed by the Sicilian federation of the Communist Party. It was intended to be the first part of a trilogy devoted to the struggles of the laboring classes on the island: the fishers, the miners, and the peasants. The initial project described the fight of the fishers against the wholesalers, the workers' strikes against the closure of sulfur mines, and the victorious peasant occupation of the lands as a single, lyric fresco, merging into a dialectical unity of aesthetic creation, representation of social reality, and political commitment. In fact, this project was quickly abandoned: the documentary became a fictional movie and Visconti was compelled to find many additional financial sources, including his own properties. The political purposes of the aborted documentary were transferred to the movie, where, because of the mutilation of the redemptive second and third parts, only an allegorical representation of defeat remained.[9] Another communist filmmaker, Giuseppe De Santis, realized in those years similar projects with *Caccia tragica* (1947) and *Non c'è pace tra gli ulivi* (1950). These neorealist movies delivered an optimistic, emancipatory message, whereas *La terra trema* finished with defeat.

Free from any documentary constraint, Visconti could finally realize an old idea: the filmic transposition of Giovanni Verga's *The House by the Medlar-Tree* (1881),[10] one of the masterpieces of Italian nineteenth-century literature. This naturalist novel tells the story of the Malavoglia, a family of poor fishermen in Aci Trezza, a village of the Sicilian coast, near Catania. In Visconti's movie, the family is named Valastro and its story happens in the twentieth century, but the plot is quite faithful to the novel. Ntoni, the Valastro son, wishes to overcome his ancestral condition of submission and exploitation by selling the family house and buying a small fishing boat with which he can directly sell the catch at the market of Catania, without giving it to the rapacious wholesalers of the village. Unfortunately, a storm destroys the boat (called Providence in the novel), leaving the entire family in despair. The father is sick, the daughters abandon Aci Trezza, and their respectability is deeply affected. Ntoni is compelled to return to fishing for the wholesalers but he does not lose his dignity. He understands that his individual rebellion was inevitably condemned to failure: most fishermen of the village share his condition and they have to organize themselves for collective struggle.

La terra trema was shot in Aci Trezza and real fishermen acted in the film, speaking their Sicilian dialect ("Italian is not the language of poor people," we learn at the beginning of the movie). The dialogues are almost incomprehensible but the voice-over explains the sequences and suggests some keys for interpreting this tragedy. Faithful to the codes of neorealism, Visconti showed society and human beings as they were, without any artificial embellishment, but his neoclassical sensibility often pushed him to frame natural landscapes as Renaissance paintings, to sculpt bodies as Greek statues, and to depict fishermen as mythological heroes. These features, however, did not hide the political dimension of his film, which was pointed out by many critics in the dramatic context of 1948.

Visconti surely shared with Verga a similar populist attraction to the vanquished and a certain aristocratic touch, but differently from the Sicilian novelist, a conservative romantic who idealized poverty in a world made of immutable hierarchies, he inscribed this fishermen's saga into a historically determined social structure. In Verga's novel, poverty is a fatal destiny for the Malavoglia and their attempt to escape such a condition is pitilessly punished with a tragic failure. Oppression is an ancestral, compelling, almost ontological malediction. In Visconti's movie, on the contrary, oppression does not mean fatality but injustice and does not deserve pity but rebellion. The topic of this film, he wrote just before shooting it, was "the life of these people, their difficulties, their fight that almost always results in catastrophe, their resignation."[11] Nevertheless, *La terra trema* transmits a political message enounced by the voice-over in the last sequence: "Ntoni resumed his job. He is vanquished and isolated, but now experience has taught him that he lost because he was isolated."[12]

Posteriorly, Visconti indicated that Gramsci's writings on the "southern question" were a crucial matrix for his film. Verga's novel had offered him a literary source, whereas the Marxist thinker from Sardinia had inspired his vision of the social and economic framework in which the fishermen lived. Reading Gramsci he understood that southern Italy was an enormous space of "social disaggregation, a market of colonial-like exploitation by northern ruling classes." His movie, he added in Gramscian terms, was a plea for "the alliance between the north workers and the south peasants."[13] *La terra trema* was released in 1948, the same year as the first edition of Gramsci's *Prison Notebooks*, whereas the essay on the "southern question"—written in 1926—was published by the communist journal *Rinascita* in 1945.[14] The Italian discovery of Gramsci followed Visconti's movie and consequently his testimony should be received with some reservations. Nevertheless, the idea of an Italian socialist revolution accomplished by a "historical bloc" comprising the working class of the industrial North and the peasants (and fishermen) of the

South was crucial for Italian Marxism, and was spread by communist propaganda before the systematic publication of Gramsci's writings.[15] Visconti could not illustrate this idea in his movie; it was deprived of its second and third parts—whose hero should have been the mass in action—and remained a sumptuous celebration of defeat. In 1948, the tragedy of Ntoni Valastro allegorized the defeat of Resistance and the communist movement.

A similar fusion between a positive, confident message—Visconti claimed Gramsci's "optimism of the will"—and a lucid recognition of defeat shapes several paintings by Renato Guttuso, the communist artist who devoted many works, at the end of the war, to the land occupations in Sicily. Canvases like *Marsigliese Contadina* (1947) and *Occupazione delle terre incolte* (1949) represent the peasant struggles through multiple references to both old and recent pictorial models, from Delacroix's *Liberty Leading the People* (1830) to Picasso's *Guernica* (1937), passing through Pellizza da Volpedo's *The Fourth Estate* (1901): popular struggle faces a violent reaction, arouses passions, and endures pains. In his last canvas on this topic—*Portella della Ginestra* (1953)—only death and suffering still remain.[16]

This combination of catastrophe and hope so typical of *La terra trema* and Guttuso's paintings reflected the spirit of those years. The social and political downfalls of 1948 were only lost battles; the socialist project did not change. Everywhere across the peninsula, the popular classes had been put on the defensive, but they continued to exist as a strong, organized proletarian army aware of its strength and confident in the future. In the 1950s, the Italian Communist Party reached its historical peak of two million members as well as a dominant position within the national culture. Of course, there were conflicts between the defenders of communist orthodoxy and free spirits, but communism confidently pretended to embody progress and indicate the direction of history: the years of Zhdanovism also corresponded with its largest influence among the intellectuals.[17]

Other postwar movies represented defeated revolutions and crushed struggles or explored the existential dimension of political downfalls. They scrutinized history, detecting its prosaic and ugly sides hidden behind a misleading façade. Treason, mistakes, resignation, and denials were not ignored, but history transcended them. Its "horizon of expectation" had not disappeared. In 1972, the Taviani brothers shot *Saint*

Michael Had a Rooster, a film on the tragedy of a nineteenth-century Italian anarchist freely inspired by "The Divine and the Human" (1906), a short story by Leo Tolstoy devoted to Russian populism.[18] The hero of *Saint Michael Had a Rooster* is Giulio Manieri, a bourgeois intellectual who, like the *narodniki*, becomes a passionate revolutionist and decides to "go to the people." During the 1870s, he crisscrosses the country, organizing insurrections and subversive actions until being sentenced to death. At the last moment, his punishment is commuted to life imprisonment under the most severe conditions. Completely isolated for ten years, he does not change his beliefs, sustained by a messianic desire for vindication. He displays an incredible vital energy—in a remarkable performance by Giulio Brogi—and survives by re-creating an imaginary world around him, with his comrades, his books, and passionate discussions. Transferred to another prison, he travels enchained through the Venetian lagoon when his small boat crosses that of another group of younger, socialist prisoners. For the first time after a decade, he can converse with them, discovering that since his imprisonment society and politics changed. They speak a different language and defend a new idea of socialism in which a mass movement has replaced the old method of the "propaganda of the deed." The world of Giulio falls apart. Suddenly conscious of belonging to a dead past, of his useless and meaningless life, he commits suicide by plunging into the cold water of the lagoon.

Representing the conflict between anarchism and Marxism, this film stressed the tragic dimension of the history of socialism, made of sacrifices and illusions, but it never put into question the socialist hope itself. This post-Risorgimento drama was a contemporary story, as Vittorio Taviani explained in an interview: "all our movies tell the past in order to speak of the present."[19] Seventy years after Tolstoy, Paolo and Vittorio Taviani could reinvent and update "The Divine and the Human"; today, nevertheless, *Saint Michael Had a Rooster* describes only the past. Both Giulio Manieri and the young socialist he meets on the Venetian lagoon belong to a closed chapter of history.

AGAINST COLONIALISM

The filmmaker of glorious defeats—one almost could say, oxymoronically, "victorious" defeats—is Gillo Pontecorvo, another Italian communist intellectual who, like Visconti, had been involved in the Resistance and began to make films in the atmosphere of neorealism (his vocation resulted from seeing Roberto Rossellini's *Paisà*). He devoted his first films—both documentaries and fictions—to the Italian postwar workers' condition, showing their poverty, their struggles, and their hopes (*Giovanna* and *Pane e Zolfo*).[20] In 1956 he broke with the Communist Party after the Soviet intervention in Hungary, but far from abandoning any political commitment, he radicalized his anticolonialist and revolutionary spirit. This evolution is tangible in the change of focus of his movies from the victims—*Kapò* (1959), telling the story of a Jewish girl deported to the Nazi camps—to the rebels, who are the heroes of *The Battle of Algiers* (1966) and *Burn!* (1969). Reviewing *Burn!*, the American critic Pauline Kael depicted him as "the most dangerous kind of Marxist, a Marxist poet," a definition he certainly would not have rejected (nor would his scriptwriter, Franco Solinas, have).[21] Edward Said, for whom *Burn!* was "a masterful work, extraordinarily prescient and analytical," shared this appraisal.[22]

Released when the rebellious wave of the 1960s was reaching its peak, *Burn!* appears retrospectively as a seismograph of that turbulent decade. It was shot in Colombia, ten years after the Cuban Revolution and two years after the death of Che Guevara in Bolivia. Pontecorvo had already achieved international fame thanks to *The Battle of Algiers* (awarded the golden lion at the Venice Film Festival in 1966) and this new film clearly echoed the Vietnam War, which had just experienced the victorious Tet Offensive of the guerrilla forces and the mass protest of the American antiwar movement. In Europe, France had been shaken by the revolt of May '68, Northern Ireland seemed to be exploding, and Italy was going to experience its most powerful wave of strikes after the Second World War. In such a context, the representation of a revolutionary defeat could not but appear as a reminder of the long, epic, and difficult road toward an impending victory. From its first images, accompanied by the music of Ennio Moricone, *Burn!* runs as an incitation to fight.

Sometimes criticized for its didacticism, this film illustrates the history of colonialism and depicts the process that transforms an oppressed people into a historical subject.[23] This tale of the fictional Caribbean island of Queimada, whose autochthonous population has been smashed by the colonizers and mostly replaced by African slaves, condenses many past and contemporary events. The two heroes of the movie, William Walker (Marlon Brando) and José Dolores (Evaristo Márquez), epitomize the relationship between the West and the Third World. They also evoke two real historical figures: William Walker was an American filibuster who tried to colonize Nicaragua by his own means, shortly controlling the country in 1856, and José Dolores—today a Nicaraguan national hero—was the military commander of the indigenous army who drove him out of the country. In *Burn!*, Walker is a British agent with some features of the adventurer, embodying all the ambiguities of Enlightenment and the hypocrisy of classical liberalism. Dolores is a kind of modern Spartacus, an allegorical representation of both Toussaint L'Ouverture and Che Guevara. At first, Walker instigates slaves to rebel against Portugal and achieve independence—a change supported by the British Empire—but ten years later he comes back to the island in order to defend the interests of the Royal Sugar Company. An expert in antiguerrilla warfare, he is charged with crushing a new rebellion led by Dolores from the mountains, where he has established his guerrilla bases. Captured in a military operation that destroys his bases, burning the mountains (a sequence reminiscent of both Vietnam napalm bombings and the Bolivian downfall of Che Guevara), Dolores is sentenced of death. Walker is deeply torn between his cynical job—violent repression—and his affection conflated with admiration for Dolores, who incarnates moral purity and collective commitment. He could shield him from execution, even save him with a visa for expatriation, but Dolores does not accept this privilege and goes to death, knowing that his sacrifice would help his emancipatory cause.

Burn! depicts two parallel trajectories: on the one hand, the moral abyss into which neocolonialism pushes its agents and, on the other, the progressive development of a political consciousness among the ruled people.[24] When Walker meets Dolores, he believes in civilization and progress, with the illusion that anticolonialism and British trade merge into a common cause. Ten years later—a period condensing the contradictions of a century, as he points out in a dialogue with the corrupted and parasitic elite of Queimada—he has lost his illusions and his Western culture is reduced to pure instrumental reason: he likes to do his work well and is interested exclusively in "how," not in "why," to do it. Dolores, on the contrary, knows he fights for liberation even if he

3.1. Gillo Pontecorvo, *Burn!* (1969), Produzioni Europee Associate.

still does not know "how" to realize his goal. Illustrating Frantz Fanon's vision of colonialism as a process of destruction of autochthonous cultures (*déculturation*), he understands that if civilization is "civilization of white man, then we are better uncivilized."[25] At the end of the film, when he is going to be executed, he ends his silence and speaks to Walker with premonitory words: "Inglés. Remember what you said? Civilization belongs to Whites! But what civilization, and till when?" (figure 3.1).

In many interviews, Pontecorvo stressed the influence of Fanon's *The Wretched of the Earth* (1961) on his vision of violence.[26] In 1972, he said he considered anticolonial struggle as "one of the most difficult moments of the human condition," adding that the entire Western civilization was built "within this matrix: on the shoulders of colonial people, we draw all our strengths, and our manner of thinking and our culture depend always to a greater or smaller degree on this fact."[27] In both *The Battle of Algiers* and *Burn!*, violence is depicted as a fundamental step in the liberation struggle. Of course, it results from the violence of colonialism, which is destructive and genocidal (Queimada means "burnt" in Portuguese), but it transcends a purely reactive dimension and becomes a moment of political education: it is through such a "Manichean" violence, symmetrical to the enemy's violence, that the oppressed achieve the awareness of their own strength. According to Fanon, armed struggle brings a colonized people to the consciousness of embodying "a collective history."[28] In *The Battle of Algiers*, Ali La Pointe becomes a leader of the FLN by learning how to organize sabotage and terrorist attacks, and the Algerian women committed to the liberation war affirm their dignity and independence by transporting pistols and depositing bombs. In *Burn!*, violence is openly claimed by the rebels: "we must cut heads instead of cane."

Shot like a newsreel in order to reinforce its realism, *The Battle of Algiers* was the chronicle of a defeat that became a crucial step in the Algerian struggle, which would achieve independence three years later. *Burn!* adopted a different style, midway between an adventure movie and a revolutionary saga—it merged Hollywood and neorealism, juxtaposing a world star like Marlon Brando with a nonprofessional actor like Evaristo Márquez—but transmitted a similar message, presenting the death of Dolores as an announcement of victory. Walker himself, explaining the methods of antiguerrilla warfare to Queimada authorities, foresaw the destiny of Dolores as a kind of nineteenth-century Che Guevara: repression transforms the leader of a mass movement into a hero; once killed, he becomes a martyr and his aura turns him into a myth.

According to these films, victory could be impeded neither by the defeats of the Algiers's insurrection, nor by the execution of the leader of Queimada's guerrilla. As Pontecorvo himself explained in several interviews, *The Battle of Algiers* had been possible because of Algerian independence, and *Burn!* had been shot with the feeling of representing through images a liberation process that once begun could not be stopped. The vision of history subjacent to both films is a kind of revolutionary historicism that posits guerrilla conflict and revolution as ineluctable. Perhaps this is the reason, as Edward Said suggested twenty years later, for the persistent silence of Pontecorvo after his masterpieces. From the end of the 1970s until his death in 2006, he retired into a position of waiting and passivity, only broken by marginal participation in collective documentaries (about the funerals of the communist leader

Enrico Berlinguer in 1984 or the demonstration against the international summit of Genoa in 2001). It was a blockage, Said writes, as if he could not "actually go anywhere, do anything, say anything. It was as if his own feeling of impotence were writ large on the political scene everywhere."[29] He was a filmmaker of battle, not of mourning.

REALMS OF MEMORY

After 1989, neither Visconti's nor Guttuso's, not to speak of Pontecorvo's, visions were defendable. Defeat had turned communism into a *realm of memory*. According to Pierre Nora, the French historian who conceptualized them, the "realms of memory" appear precisely at the moment in which the traditional "milieus of memory" have been dissolved. The recognition of the places, sites, objects, and symbols crystallizing or embodying the past is possible when we feel that it does not live longer, has abandoned our present, and is threatened by forgetting. The "realms of memory" express a lost past, supplying a memory that is no longer transmissible. It can only be conserved, in a reliquary form, as a testimony of an experience related to history by an emotional link. History writing is a "cold," rational, and critical exercise. Memory captures the meaning of the past as a lived experience. Referring to the French national memory, Nora evokes a "sacred" link that takes a secular dimension as the civil religion of the French Republic. His book is a gigantic, sumptuous historiographical monument to the national past, from the Old Regime to the Fifth Republic, built in a time in which its continuity seems put into question, broken, and threatened by the advent of global modernity. We do not need to share the conservative purposes of his approach—inventorying a national patrimony—in order to apply his concept to the closed experience of twentieth-century communism. As Nora writes:

> Our interest in *lieux de mémoire* where memory crystallizes and secretes itself, has occurred at a particular historical moment, a turning point where consciousness of a break with the past is bound up with the sense that memory has been torn—but torn in such a way as to pose the problem of the embodiment of memory in certain sites where a sense

of historical continuity persists. There are *lieux de mémoire*, sites of memory, because there are no longer *milieux de mémoire*, real environments of memory.[30]

This definition is useful in order to investigate the colorful and heterogeneous accumulation of communist vestiges constituted by objects, sites, symbols, and images. The realms of memory are an archived past. Rigorous and almost normative, Nora's canonical opposition between history and memory is certainly debatable, insofar as it posits their mutual exclusion and does not recognize any symbiotic relationship between them.[31] Reduced to its basic elements, it results in a rigid dichotomy in which memory is systematically opposed to history like life to death, presence to remoteness, subjective involvement to objective reconstruction, affection to reason, hot to cold, sacred to secular. The memorial moment of our societies, Nora points out, results precisely from their forgetfulness, from a past that does not palpitate any more in their present. Realms of memory fulfill the need of preserving an affective relation with an exhausted past threatened with oblivion. Going away from Nora's patrimonial nationalism, we could observe, quoting Walter Benjamin, that realms of memory are *relics*, dead objects captured by a contemplative, melancholic gaze, "in order to redeem them."[32] Many movies shot in the postcommunist era accomplish these kind of memory duties, gathering a mosaic of moments and objects that condense both the meaning and the flavor of a finished experience.

As we already observed in a previous chapter, there is a striking contrast between the vision of the past suggested by the movies of the beginning of the twentieth century and those of its end. Eisenstein's conception of film is emblematic of a strategic vision of the past as a reservoir of experiences whose selection allows the construction of both an aesthetic form of history and a political message. His movies of the 1920s, from *Strike* and *Battleship Potemkin* (1925) to *October* (1927), illustrate Russian history as an unfolding path toward revolution. The symbol of this break with the past and utopian projection into the future is *October*'s scene of the fall of the Tsarist statue in the middle of an insurgent crowd, already analyzed in the previous chapter. In Theo Angelopoulos's *Ulysses' Gaze* (1995), as we have seen, it is a broken statue of Lenin that epitomizes communism itself. Its procession along the Danube symbolizes its displacement out of the stage of history, its transformation into a realm of memory. It is also a return to the origins: communism needs to be rethought and rebuilt. Angelopoulos's movie tells a journey through the Balkans—Greece, Albania, the former Yugoslavia, Bulgaria, and Rumania—until Sarajevo, where a modern Ulysses (Harvey Keitel) finds, in the film archives of a besieged city, in the middle of a civil war, the first films shot in Greece almost a century before. Ulysses comes back to Ithaca, like this melancholic broken statue of Lenin that, running through the Danube, goes to Germany, where communism was born in the nineteenth century. Their trips are charged with an epiphanic taste insofar as they simultaneously describe an end and a return to the sources. Lenin's traveling across the Danube followed by a praying crowd, accompanied by the mournful orchestral music of Eleni Karaindrou, is both a funeral and a revelation. This secular funeral is an announcement in the Christian tradition: Angelopoulos enveloped this scene "in a burial tone,"[33] but its final meaning is contained in a formula he borrowed from T. S. Eliot and attributed to one of his film heroes: "In my end is my beginning."[34] According to Arthur J. Pomeray, this scene possesses also a mythological dimension—so typical of Angelopoulos's filmography—suggesting an analogy with the journey of Dionysus depicted in a famous Exekias's vase conserved in the Bavarian Museum of Antiquities of Munich. Like Dionysus in Greek mythology, Lenin could reborn.[35] This is not an announcement of victory; it is a socialist wager, based on the recognition that all has to be rebuilt.

RED SHADOWS

Eisenstein reappears in Chris Marker's *Le fond de l'air est rouge*, a film shot in 1977 but shortened and revised in a new version in 1993, at the moment of its second release, and in 2003, when it became available to the English-speaking audience as *A Grin Without a Cat*. The French original title of this movie—something like "the bottom of the air is red"—catches the atmosphere of the 1960s and the 1970s, whose struggles it depicts through a vortex of images showing a world in which revolutionary utopia was taken to the streets. Marker conceived this movie after discovering, in the back of the leftist bookshop La Joie de Lire, many abandoned documentary films, mostly excerpts of unfinished shots, on two decades of revolutionary struggles. As he explained in his introduction to the movie's script, he was fascinated by "these images that remain in the bottom drawers when a film is finished, these sequences that finally disappear from montage, these film trims." Realized as a montage of fragmented sequences and images enveloped in Luciano Berio's *Night Music in the Streets of Madrid*, his movie is not a chronology of these combats, but rather an attempt to catch their spirit. He defined his movie as "our image-unconscious" (*notre refoulé en images*).[36] The red thread crossing the entire movie is the Vietnam War, described as a second Spanish Civil War that could be won, as the core of a vertiginous spiral of struggle and rebellion in which other continents, from Europe (the Prague Spring and May '68) to Latin America (Cuba and other guerrillas) and the United States (the march on the Pentagon of 1967), are growingly involved.

We don't know whether Marker was familiar with "microhistory," the historiographical current created in the 1970s by a group of Italian scholars such as Carlo Ginzburg and Giovanni Levi. His procedure, nevertheless, clearly reveals a similar "evidential paradigm."[37] *A Grin Without a Cat*, he explains, was conceived as a "detective story," even if he tried to find the "authors of the innocence" rather than those of a crime. His method consists in "going back patiently the other way, looking for evidence, and finding clues, butts, and footprints."[38] Like in microhistory, *A Grin Without a Cat* focuses on some features, going back from a detail to the entire picture, from the particular to the general. But the general, in this movie, is less a long shot than a magisterial montage of close-ups.

Marker's gaze is neither naïve nor idyllic. Sometimes, his observations are extremely critical and severe. He distinguishes between different experiences and his empathies are variable, in spite of his choice to not defend an ideological position. He does not criticize Fidel Castro, but recognizes his own astonishment in front of Fidel's approval of the Soviet invasion of Czechoslovakia in 1968, which appeared so contradictory with the road followed by Cuban socialism until that moment. His description of the underground congress of the Czech Communist Party during the Prague Spring, as well as his interviews with Latin-American communist leaders concerning the catastrophic Bolivian experience of Che Guevara, indicates that he does not wish to oppose the New Left to the traditional communist currents, but rather to describe the choral character of the revolutionary movements, with their contradictions and internal conflicts. The 1960s had engendered the "lyrical illusion" that allowed these multiple voices to meet; in his movie, montage becomes a language mirroring the "polyphony of history."[39] In his eyes, 1967 saw the birth of a new generation, a "new race of adolescents" who "resembled each other" and shared a "silent knowledge." Montage expresses this feeling of a new generation of political rebels beyond the borders—today one would say a "global" revolt—showing a succession of interwoven images of hands belonging to young people of different races. As the voice-over explains: "Their hands were incredibly skillful in hanging posters, exchanging paving stones, writing on the walls short and mysterious sentences that remained engraved in memories, while they were looking for other hands to which to transmit a message they were aware of having received without being able to completely decipher it."[40] Marker reminds us of the expectations and enthusiasm generated by May '68, when people floated in a "zero-gravity" atmosphere and all seemed possible, evoking his meeting with the philosopher Louis Althusser: "For him, as for others, revolution was in the air, and had to be, like the grin of the Cheshire Cat. He would always see that grin. And would not (nor would anyone) ever see the cat."[41] On the other hand, he points out that, compared to other insurgent experiences—from Vietnam to Latin America's guerrillas—the Parisian barricades were a joyful masquerade: "We lived with the fantasy to storm the Winter Palace, [but] nobody ever thought of marching on the Elysée."[42] Conflating Eisenstein's Odessa steps and the assault on the Pentagon in October 1967 with a magisterial montage composition, Marker suggests that such an uprising was purely symbolic and finally inoffensive. Differently from Mexico, where, a few months later, three hundred students were killed in the Square of the Three Cultures, the Washington police did not seek a massacre; the demonstrators could enter the building but they didn't; their goal was a spectacular protest, not a military insurrection. In Latin America, revolution was bloodily defeated; in the West, it never took place. It remained "the unending rehearsal of a play which never premiered."[43]

Thus, Eisenstein reappears, evoked not by the broken statue of the Tsar that opens *October*, but rather through the famous steps of Odessa in *Battleship Potemkin* (1925). Marker recalls that the massacre depicted in this film never took place; it was a genial invention of Eisenstein suggested by the architectural site itself. He did not know, Marker adds, that such aesthetic artifice would have created "the imagination of a generation."[44] Quoting *Battleship Potemkin*, the opening sequence of *A Grin Without a Cat* juxtaposes the images of Eisenstein's movie with excerpts from a documentary video of a Washington march in 1967, creating a spiral of correspondences—the crowd, the marching soldiers, the attack, the bloody face of a wounded woman and that of a demonstrator, and so on—which, far beyond a purely aesthetic resonance, inscribes the movements of the 1960s into history, the history of revolutions (figures 3.2–5). The extraordinary intensity of both sequences lies in the same principle of "camera-life" that—according to Siegfried Kracauer—consists in building and revealing reality instead of representing it. This does not mean an illusory "impersonal" reproduction of the world of life, but that films can interpret reality only by exploring, "embodying" real life rather than "illustrating" it.[45] From this point of view, the demonstrations and funerals of Chris Marker's movie belong to the "long procession of unforgettable objects [that] has passed across the screen" as legitimately as the cruiser Potemkin.[46] In both Marker's and Eisenstein's movies, the hero is the mass, not the anonymous, monolithic, passive, and purely ornamental mass of totalitarian propaganda but a living body made of human beings whom action transforms into a historical subject and whose emotions are captured by the camera. In their movies—like in microhistory—close-ups become "pars pro toto,"[47] fragments of experience that, charged with an enormous evocative power, transmit the meaning of a historical time.

In Marker's movie, Eisenstein's Odessa steps play a double function. In the first part ("Fragile Hands"), they join similar images selected from pictures and videos of the demonstrations of the 1960s and 1970s, stressing the continuity of the revolutionary tradition and describing a certain lyric dimension of revolt. *A Grin Without a Cat* opens with the voice of Simone Signoret remembering her emotion watching this classical movie, followed by an interview with a young guide of Odessa (shot in the 1970s), who introduces the visitors to this famous site. The steps of Odessa are an aesthetic invention of Eisenstein, but the posterior images that punctuate Marker's film (the demonstrations of Washington, Berlin, Prague, Tokyo, Mexico, Washington, and Paris)

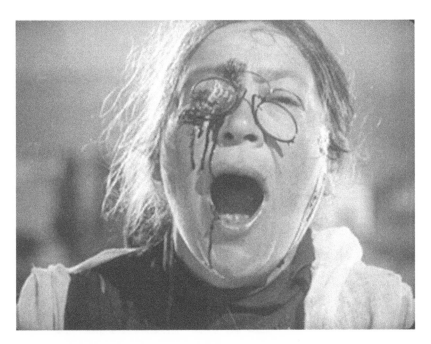

3.2. Sergei Eisenstein, *Potemkin* (1925), Mosfilm.

3.3. Chris Marker, *A Grin Without a Cat* (1977, 1996), First Run/Icarus Films.

3.4. Sergei Eisenstein, *Potemkin* (1925), Mosfilm.

3.5–6. Chris Marker, *A Grin Without a Cat* (1977, 1996), First Run/Icarus Films.

3.5–6. Continued.

had transformed them into a real collective experience. In the second part ("Severed Hands"), they become the symbol of a "futures past," of the struggles of a finished age. In short, they become a visual realm of memory. The parenthesis is closed: the attempt to transfer Eisenstein's images of revolt into the reality of the 1960s and the 1970s failed. The second part reshapes the entire movie, giving it a new character, transforming it into a sort of epitaph of the last revolutionary hopes of the twentieth century. The strange, fascinating strength of this film lies in this double dimension: on the one hand, it transmits the freshness of the engagement of the 1960s and 1970s and, on the other hand, it is a posthumous homage to a closed time.

Significantly, the commentaries added in 1993 do not appear as a separated part, annexed or foreign to the first version. This means that the awareness of the end of a cycle was already implicit in the original movie, at least as the intuition of an ineluctable turn. The melancholic dimension of *A Grin Without a Cat* is not the result of a retrospective perception or a posterior revision; it is its proper character. As Marker points out, when he decided to realize this movie, he had in mind "the crushing of guerrillas, the occupation of Czechoslovakia, the Chilean tragedy, the Chinese myth" (the Cultural Revolution), all events that had turned the years after May '68 into "a long sequence of defeats."[48] The film is punctuated with images of burials—Che Guevara, Roque Dalton, Carlos Marighela, Victor Jara, Miguel Enriquez, George Jackson, Pierre Overney, Ulrike Meinhof—which suggest a symbiotic relationship between revolution and death. But far from symbolizing the end of a communist hope, such mass funerals are experienced as one of its expressions. Already in its first version, this movie was dedicated "to the activists who fought against a power that would erase their memory."[49] The final sequence of the film is a meaningful counterpoint to its beginning, where an archival video of the Vietnam War shows a B52 pilot who describes his excitement in bombing villages in the jungle with napalm. At the end, we see a pack of wolves that are being shot from a helicopter. One of them raises its head and looks toward the aerial camera (figure 3.6). In a commentary added in the version from 1993, Chris Marker's voice-over observes that fifteen years later some wolves still survive. Like them, revolution is won but it is not dead.[50]

Death haunts also *The Last Bolshevik* (1993), the film Chris Marker devoted to his friend Alexander Medvedkin (1900–89), a filmmaker whose life corresponded with the trajectory of the USSR and whose work completely identified with communism, from the enthusiasm of the 1920s to the censorship and oppression he suffered under Stalinism. The film ends with the image of a herd of galloping horses—reminiscent of Isaac Babel's *Red Cavalry*—superimposed on the grave of Medvedkin: "that lyricism," Marker's voice-over explains, "was dead."[51]

SPANISH GHOSTS

Ken Loach's *Land and Freedom* was released simultaneously with *Ulysses' Gaze* and both of them were awarded by the Cannes Film Festival. In this movie, it is revolution itself that becomes a realm of memory, evoked and "revived" with empathy and a poignant nostalgia. But Loach's melancholic gaze is quite the reverse of resignation. Beyond homage to the Spanish revolution, his movie wished to shake the conformist Zeitgeist of the 1990s, as well as to contest the conventional representation of the Spanish Civil War as a kind of humanitarian catastrophe. From this point of view, *Land and Freedom* appears almost antipodal to *Soldiers of Salamis* (2001), the acclaimed novel by Javier Cercas in which the tragic dimension of the Spanish Civil War does not leave any place for hope or for the reasons of a political commitment.[52] Ken Loach's movie, nevertheless, does not come back to the old canonical representations that for decades shaped the filmography of such an event, from the movies shot during or immediately after the war—Luis Buñuel's *España 1936* (1936), Joris Ivens's *Spanish Earth* (1937), Sam Wood's *For Whom the Bell Tolls* (1943), and André Malraux's *Days of Hope* (1945)—to those of the Francoist decades—first of all Frédéric Rossif's *Mourir à Madrid* (1963)—that were propaganda works celebrating a still unfinished struggle.[53] Differently from all of them, *Land and Freedom* comes back to a closed historical experience that, epitomizing the defeat of twentieth-century socialist revolutions, clearly transcends the Spanish borders. Loach and Jim Allen, his scriptwriter, wished also to break the cliché of the Spanish Civil War observed by foreign intellectuals accomplishing their ritual trip to Barcelona, Madrid, and Valencia in defense of the Republic. The hero of his movie is a young proletarian from Liverpool, David Carr (Ian Hurt), who does not travel to Spain to attend an international conference in defense of culture, but rather to fight as a member of the International Brigades. There he completes his political and sentimental education, developing values and convictions he will not abandon for the rest of his life.

Ken Loach's movie starts with the death of David Carr, struck by a heart attack in his modest working-class apartment in Liverpool, in the middle of the 1990s. Kim, his granddaughter, discovers, among the objects he conserved at home in an old bag, many pieces belonging to his militant past, from the magazines of the 1930s—*The Socialist*—to the leaflets produced during the miners' strikes in 1984 against Margaret Thatcher's government. In an old box, she finds a red neckerchief with a handful of Spanish earth, a remembrance of the collectivization of 1936 (figures 3.7–8). The movie displays a touching flashback of the crucial moments of a revolutionary struggle. This handful of earth plays the role of a relic—or a "sensible" archive[54]—as the inherited vestige of a meaningful, necessary, and inspiring but lost battle. The last scene of the film depicts the burial of its hero: his granddaughter reads a poem of William Morris, "The Day is Coming," which reaffirms the socialist vision

3.7–9. Ken Loach, *Land and Freedom* (1995), PolyGram.

of memory: "Come / join in the only battle wherein no man can fail / Where whoso fadeth and dieth / yet his deed shall still prevail."[55] Then, she undoes the neckerchief knot and throws the earth of Spain into the grave (figure 3.9). They have been defeated, but others will pursue their combat and will win. This conventional conclusion closes a film that is a monument to twentieth-century revolutions.

Mourning surely does not constitute the exclusive dimension of this movie, which is built as an epic fresco and a moment of socialist pedagogy. Loach depicts the passionate debates on land collectivization, the violent clash of May 1937 inside the Republican camp, the radical difference separating an insurgent militia (the Partido Obrero de Unificación Marxista [POUM], and the anarchists) from a regular army led by Soviet military advisors, the tension between liberation and submission experienced by the combatant women, as well as other crucial issues. His vision is neither dogmatic nor idyllic, in spite of the lyricism of many scenes. He deliberately avoids propaganda and tries to show how such historical drama was experienced by its actors rather than delivering a prefabricated message. The land collectivization in a village in Aragon is not announced with an eloquent speech; it is depicted as the result of an animated and controversial discussion involving both peasants and militiamen (including militia-women). Loach does not impose his point of view; he avoids close-ups and lighting that would emphasize this radical choice. He shows a collective deliberation in which many points of view are taken into account. The character that embodies the anticollectivization tendency—Gene Lawrence (Tom Gilroy), the young American member of the communist Lincoln Brigade—does not appear as a negative hero. Arguing that war and revolution cannot be realized simultaneously and that, consequently, collectivization has to be postponed, he defends an option that was debated all along the civil war. When he comes back as a member of a regular army for disarming the revolutionist militia of the POUM, Loach does not depict him as a traitor, but rather as a tragic figure confronted with the extreme, inevitable logic of his political choice.[56] Still open among historians, this dilemma of opposing war and revolution is represented in this movie as a dramatic confrontation experienced by living human beings. The choice of postponing revolution—which meant the liquidation of the POUM and the anarchist forces—did not save the Spanish Republic, but Ken Loach does not say that a different option would have surely been successful. He shows that, far from being purely ideological, such a conflict broke hopes and friendships, and became a human tragedy.

The beauty of *Land and Freedom*, nevertheless, lies in the romantic goal it admirably fulfills: engraving the Spanish Civil War in the heart of left memory, particularly in the heart of a generation for whom this historical experience was no longer an inherited legacy. Finally, the message of this movie is the same delivered by George Orwell in *Homage to Catalonia* (1938), a testimony that certainly remains one of its main sources of inspiration. The Spanish Civil War resulted in a double, historical defeat: on the one hand, the collapse of the Republic in the face of fascism and, on the other, the burial of revolution by a Stalinist government.[57] The legacy of this experience was the discovery of socialism as a possible form of human life organization. In a sequence at the beginning of *Land and Freedom*, its hero says: "Now I am a soldier of the people's army. . . . We elect our officers. . . . It's socialism in action." In *Homage to Catalonia*, we can read the following passage that perfectly captures the spirit of Ken Loach's movie:

> The thing that attracts ordinary men to Socialism and makes them willing to risk their skins for it, the "mystique" of Socialism, is the idea of equality; to the vast majority of people Socialism means a classless society, or it means nothing at all. And it was here that those few months in the militia were valuable to me. For the Spanish militias, while they lasted, were a sort of microcosm of a classless society. In that community where no one was on the make, where there was a shortage of everything but no privilege and no boot licking, one got, perhaps, a crude forecast of what the opening stages of Socialism might be like. And, after all, instead of disillusioning me it deeply attracted me. The effect was to make my desire to see Socialism established much more actual than it had been before.[58]

This socialism—a form of society in which human beings feel equal— was not an idyllic *image d'Epinal* because it was organically connected with the tragic dimension of war, of civil war, which is the most terrible and atrocious of all conflicts. It was an ephemeral, fragile, and circumscribed experience—in *Homage to Catalonia*, Orwell pointed out that in 1937 Barcelona already had lost the communitarian enthusiasm it had one year earlier—that engendered a socialist memory able to survive defeat. Like Orwell's autobiographical account, Ken Loach's movie avoids and questions stereotypes. It is not conceived as the filmic version of Robert Capa's *The Death of the Loyalist Soldier,* the iconic picture that fixed—or fabricated—the traditional vision of the Spanish Civil War as a glorious defeat.[59] Ken Loach's hero is not a martyr; he is an anonymous activist accustomed to lost battles, from the Spanish revolution in the 1930s to the miners' strike in the 1980s. In *Land and Freedom,* he does not wish to tell the story of a hero, but rather to depict the pride of a vanquished combatant whose life corresponds with the trajectory of twentieth-century socialism.

SANTIAGO REMEMBRANCE

Carmen Castillo's *Santa Fe Street* (2007) is another epitaph, devoted to the Latin-American revolutions of the 1970s.[60] In this movie, it is a house of a peripheral street in Santiago that materializes a realm of memory (figure 3.10). There, the soldiers of Pinochet's dictatorship killed her husband, the leader of MIR (Movimiento de Izquierda Revolucionaria), Miguel Enriquez, on October 6, 1974. Miguel Enriquez was thirty years old when he died; Carmen had worked as an employee at the Moneda Palace, beside President Allende, between his election and the putsch of September 1973. After that date, they lived together in this house, which was one of the underground bases of the MIR leadership. At that moment, Carmen was pregnant and, seriously wounded, miraculously survived this police attack thanks to the neighbors who called an ambulance.[61] Her movie tells a story of exile, the rediscovery of her country after the end of the military dictatorship and also—this is perhaps the most moving dimension—of the living legacy of the MIR among a new generation of Chilean activists. The opening sequences merge documentary scenes from the years of Unidad Popular—journals, leaflets, and demonstrations—with objects that evoke this house as a place of domestic intimacy in the middle of military repression. They were young and wished to change the world, she says with her hoarse voice-over, and they wished to live. An old photograph shows her beside Miguel,

111

3.10–13. Carmen Castillo, *Rue Santa Fé* (2007), Les Films d'ici.

as lovers (figure 3.11). In a recent autobiographical text, she recalls the months of underground life, after the putsch, stressing the cleavage between a fearful outside—her dangerous movements in Santiago, where she accomplished political tasks—and a warm, protective inside, when she returned to Santa Fe Street. Laughing, playing with her daughters, cocking, reading, and making love: all of that gave her the illusionary feeling of living a normal life.

> I try to remind where and how fear reappeared. I was torn. A part of myself acted with coldness, going through the streets of Santiago from

3.10–13. (Continued)

a meeting point to another. The other part of myself only appeared within the light blue house of Santa Fe. Charm. I closed the door, took off bags and caps, needed an instant, after copiously kissing Miguel and the children, and recovered the everyday life gestures of an ordinary family mother. I breathed and acted. Nothing more. There were intense days and nights and many laughs, voluble hours I could no longer describe, which always occupy a place in my mind without leaving me quiet: go, woman—tell me these moments of life, don't leave, be serious! I lived swinging, with ups and downs, like everybody. And this was true life.[62]

On the sixth of October 1974, this precarious harmony was definitely broken. After that day, she felt herself "a survivor."

In the second part of the film, this realm of memory crystallizes a moment of critical self-consciousness. Carmen desires to buy the house on Santa Fe Street and transform it into a museum, but finally she abandons this project when, talking with young Chilean left activists, she understands that for them the MIR is a living legacy, not a dead object. Miguel Enriquez is an example, not an icon for cult and veneration. As she explained in a conversation with Daniel Bensaïd when her movie was released, she gradually changed her mind. Her first trips to Santiago, after the end of the dictatorship, had thrown her into "a deep melancholy": she felt "the arrogance of the victors and the sadness of the vanquished" in a country that had been hugely transformed and that she could no longer recognize. Then, after she met some young activists, this superficial screen broke up and she discovered a different landscape of human relations, generosity, and unprejudiced commitment: "I understood that these young people were us. I found Miguel again, the same vivacity, the same insolence, the same eagerness to learn without any pretention. These groups of present activists take over the tradition and the memory of the vanquished because they find there a source of dignity, leaving any rhetoric of heroism."[63]

Carmen Castillo was not a political leader and her purpose is not a critical reassessment of the MIR history, which remains in the background. She recalls some crucial moments—the choice of continuing the struggle with arms and the rejection of exile in 1973, the catastrophic decision of returning to Chile five years later, the "mysterious" dissolution of the movement in 1989—without questioning them, as simple, necessary landmarks. She questions the subjective dimension of a political experience, exploring which way such choices affected individual trajectories and what remains of this universe of revolutionary ideas, consumed energies, tragic dilemmas, destroyed hopes, and broken lives (at least eight hundred MIR activists were killed and disappeared).[64] Her movie transmits a message of hope without celebrating martyrdom, defending a thesis, or suggesting an apologetic interpretation. In a previous work—*La Flaja Alejandra* (1994)—she interrogated the trajectory of a traitor, a MIR leading member who had been captured and agreed to collaborate with the DINA, the secret police of the dictatorship. The activists interviewed in *Santa Fe Street* are not idealized: they vigorously defended a project of liberation and paid a very high tribute; of course, they made mistakes but, finally, they did what they were able to do. A former MIR leader tells her, in response to a question, that most of those who were responsible for the organization were less than thirty years old in 1973; the MIR had been created in 1965 and they had not had experience enough for facing a military putsch and a fascist dictatorship.

The most poignant moment, among many others included in this movie, is the interview with Luisa and Manuel Vergara, the fathers of three young MIR activists killed by the police in 1985 (figure 3.12). They belonged to the second MIR generation, formed under the military dictatorship. Luisa tells their story, her suffering, and her capacity to survive such a terrible loss. She was afraid when they told her their decision to go underground and she did not believe she would be able to survive after their assassination. Then, she understood that she had retreated into a prison of fear and suffering whereas her sons had chosen the struggle: "they looked for life, and their reasons were stronger than mines." They did not look for sacrifice or martyrdom and their political choice was rooted in a vital desire of freedom (figure 3.13). "What survives is desire; they cannot kill this desire. We reached the mystery of happiness and they could not accept that," Carmen affirms in her conversation: "My film does not transmit only a wounded remembrance; it transmits also a recollection of happiness."[65]

This movie convincingly exemplifies Jacques Rancière's observation that, in the last decades, the aesthetic realm has become "the privileged site where the tradition of critical thinking has metamorphosed into deliberation of mourning."[66] We could go further, recognizing in such a movie a shift from the *political* to the *emotional*: differently from *Land and Freedom*, which explains the conflict between revolution and Stalinism during the Spanish Civil War, *Santa Fe Street* does not investigate the reasons of past defeats, but rather explores the emotions such failures aroused and left behind them. Nonetheless, its critical self-reflexivity puts into question the dominant tendency to transform the realms of memory into neutral, aseptic, and dead objects belonging to an archival patrimony. This film shows a tension between subjective and collective memory, between individual lived experience and collective recollection of the past that is fruitful. Its object, beyond the trajectory of Miguel

Enriquez and her own exile, is a historical defeat—Pinochet's putsch of 1973—and the film is an attempt to work through such an experience, without denying or suppressing it. Recalling some illuminating pages of Primo Levi on the genesis of his testimonies on Auschwitz, one could add that Carmen Castillo's movie accomplishes a cathartic therapy, as a kind of interior liberation, becoming the "equivalent of Freud's divan."[67] But *Santa Fe Street* does not simply stage a trauma; it also shows the steps of a rebirth that joins the historical consciousness of the Chilean left.

Carmen Castillo is certainly not alone in creating a visual memory of the Chilean left. In 1973, Chris Marker helped the Latin-American film-maker Patricio Guzman to start *La Batalla de Chile*, a movie devoted to the experience of Allende's Unidad Popular that was finally completed in exile. The following year, when the military putsch compelled Guzman to leave his country, Marker waited for him at the Orly airport in Paris. They did not see each other frequently, but their friendship lasted until Marker's death.[68] In Patricio Guzman's *Nostalgia for the Light* (2010), memory does not float in the air; it runs through the skies and lies in the earth. This documentary tells different but intertwined stories in the Chilean desert of Atacama, on the top of the Cordillera. There both astronomers and archeologists work: the former because this desert hosts one of the most powerful telescopes in the world, which benefits from the extreme purity of the air and crystalline clarity of the sky; the latter because this exceptionally dry land preserves the oldest remains of animal and human life. Astronomers explore the skies, capturing images of the cosmos that belong to the life of planets as if it were thousands and thousands of years ago; archeologists scrutinize the vestiges of our prehistorical ancestors. But astronomers and archeologists are not the only presences in such a lunar landscape. There are also some relatives of the victims of the military dictatorship, which established concentration camps in this lost Chilean land. In the desert of Atacama, Pinochet's army secretly killed and buried many of its enemies. For years, many people came here to search the remains of their children, brothers, and sisters. Today, only a small group of women still persists; this search is the purpose of their life. The bones of some victims have been identified thanks to DNA analysis. Coexistence is sometimes difficult for the inhabitants of Atacama, but they learned to respect one another; all of them are searching for a truth in the past.[69] After decades of work on Chilean memory, depicted as an arm of the struggle for democracy,

3.14. Patricio Guzmán, *Nostalgia for the Light* (2011), Atacama Productions.

socialism, and the human rights —*La Batalla de Chile* (1975–79), *La Memoria obstinada* (1997), *Le Cas Pinochet* (2001) and *Salvador Allende* (2004)—Guzman realized his most beautiful movie through depicting memory as an impossible work of mourning (figure 3.14).

U-TOPIA

From Eisenstein to Pontecorvo, from *Battleship Potemkin* to *Burn!*, left movies described struggles and announced victories; since the 1990s, they have also begun to work through the past, assuming defeat as the starting point of their retrospective inquiry. Until the end of the 1970s, left movies described self-confident mass movements and announced ineluctable victories, even when they celebrated the downfalls of the past; since the 1990s, they have mourned defeats, even when they depict revolutions. Realized in 1977 and recomposed in 1993, *A Grin Without a Cat* marks emblematically the shift from the first to the second age of left filmmakers.

Angelopoulos's, Castillo's, Guzman's, Loach's, and Marker's movies draw a portrait of the twentieth century as a tragic age of wrecked revolutions and defeated utopias, remembering the vanquished of its lost battles. Death floats over all of them as their fatal destiny. This is the aesthetic dimension of a work of mourning that affects the culture of the left at the beginning of the twenty-first century, as the collective sorrow of a generation of activists, far beyond a political and intellectual elite. The heroes of the movies considered above are ordinary people.[70] Angelopoulos depicts an anonymous crowd that attends the apparition of Lenin's statue traveling down the Danube. Loach does not illustrate the autobiography of George Orwell; he tells the story of David Carr, a young, unemployed man from a working-class district of Liverpool. The relationship with the "History" of his movies' heroes can also take an ironic, ludic form, such as with the Latino immigrant workers of *Bread and Roses* (2000), who, arrested during a strike, answer the policeman who asks them their names by adopting the identity of Latin-American revolutionary heroes: Ernesto Guevara, Emiliano Zapata, Simon Bolivar, Augusto César Sandino, and so on. Chris Marker interviews intellectuals and political leaders, but the true subject of his movie is the mass movement that shook the world for more than a decade, emerging synchronically in different countries and continents. Carmen Castillo was the wife of a leader, but her remembrance of Miguel Enriquez changed when she shared her recollections with a multitude of young activists. After two decades of exile, she understood that her mourning had not been isolated. Patricio Guzman describes the abnegation of unknown people, relatives of the vanquished like Violeta, whose silent, crazy search unveils an enormous potential for love and dignity. Differently from Pierre Nora, all these portraits and characters do not build the gallery of a museum, rather a Pantheon of ordinary people with shared values and hopes whose virtues have been forged by collective action. The realms of memory depicted in these "thought-images" cannot become museums or official sites of mourning insofar as they belong to a private, intimate, affective and "sensible" sphere—a house, a neckerchief, a family picture—in which collective experiences intersect individual destinies. Not sealed with an official stamp, they are hidden, secret, Marrano memories with which everybody can identify in spite of their irreducible uniqueness. This concerns even the symbols of the former regimes of bureaucratic socialism—for example, the Lenin statue—that need to be broken and "desacralized" in order to become the melancholy guards of a defeated utopia.

In his speech upon reception of the Georg Büchner Prize, published under the title "The Meridian" (1960), Paul Celan distinguished between *u-topia* and *utopia*. *U-topia*, literally "no-place," is a nonexisting locus, whereas utopia means a hope, an expectation, a vision of the future, something not existing yet. According to Ernst Bloch, utopia is a prefiguration, the realm of "not yet" (*noch nicht*). This is also the meaning of Celan's utopia, "something open and free" to which poetry could give a form.[71] Today, after the collapse of twentieth-century revolutions, utopia does not appear as a "not yet," but rather as *u-topia*, a no-longer-existing place, a destroyed utopia that is the object of melancholy art. Realms of memory are places (*topoi*) created in order to remember hopes turned into no-places, something that no longer exists. The utopias of the twenty-first century still have to be invented.

4 BOHEMIA

BETWEEN MELANCHOLY AND REVOLUTION

SOCIOLOGY

POPULARIZED by a novel by Henri Murger in 1846,[1] then consecrated by Puccini in his famous opera, the idea of Bohemia, in its current use, implies a lifestyle and a particular attitude toward aesthetics. Rejection of bourgeois conventions, lack (or voluntary renunciation) of a fixed abode and regular work, frequent visits to cafés, cabarets, and popular taverns, a taste for nocturnal life, ostentatious sexual freedom, a keen penchant for alcohol and drugs, the fair communal share of meager available resources, and even, at times, a certain "sectarianism" colored by the use of secret codes shared only by a select brotherhood of initiates: these are the classical features of Bohemian life. Bohemia is visually expressed in long hair, strange clothes, and an untidy appearance, and usually goes hand in hand with an artistic ideal pursued as a marginal vocation. This is developed, in spite of the norms, outside such dominating, legitimate establishments as the Academy, and is inspired by a transgressive tendency: freedom against what is forbidden, conformist, and powerful; debauchery against repressive morality. In 1849, Théophile Gautier in his review of Murger's novel described Bohemia as "love of art and hatred of the bourgeois."[2]

The term appears in France in its political sense first during the July Monarchy, and then it spread out across the continent. The Bohemian, it can be seen, needs those forms of the modern world no longer governed by the moral norms and aesthetic canons of the aristocracy, or at least it needs to break away from their grip. His existence implies the independence of the artist and the man of letters (the woman of letters somewhat more rarely) in relation to court and patronage. He builds his home in the interstices of bourgeois society and his public no longer comprises nobles, but his equals: other outsiders or, sometimes, "renegades" who stem from the dominant classes, those members of the bourgeoisie disowning their origins.

In the mid-nineteenth century, the industrial bourgeoisie dominated the economy in England and Germany, but its style and mentality remained shaped by the landed gentry and the *Junkertum*. Capitalism had firmly entrenched its *Zivilisation*, but had not yet absorbed or replaced the old *Kultur*. Industrial modernity was developing, wrapped in old cultural forms and linked to archaic social relations. In France, it is the revolution that fertilized the soil for the rise of the bourgeoisie as a dominant class, not only in terms of production, but also in terms of social ethos. From 1830, under the July Monarchy, the bourgeoisie emerged for the first time in Europe as a truly dominant class. Bohemia then appears where the "persistence of the Old Regime" is at its weakest.[3] Its main historian, Jerrold Seigel, juxtaposed the *Bohemian* and the *bourgeois* as positive and negative poles in the same magnetic field, excluding each other at the same time as getting involved, needing, and attracting each other.[4] In relation to the bourgeoisie, incarnating a social and political order firmly installed and on the ascent, the Bohemian represents the tramp of modernity, a figure of instability, displacement, disorder; in brief, the "gypsy of the mind,"[5] according to the etymology of the word, a metaphor for the condition of authentic Gypsies originating from Central Europe, mainly from Bohemia.

It is not the Bohemian who appears in nineteenth-century England but the *dandy*, the George Brummel type of beau who distances himself from the triumphant bourgeois world by ostentatiously parading a luxury and style belonging to a past age, the age of nobility, whose privileges and means he does not enjoy any more, and even less its political awareness. But he definitely shares its style and taste.[6] Instead of expressing a civilization in its completeness in an organic and polished way, the dandy retains from the past only the external appearances of an aristocratic splendor. He pushes them to an extreme, by almost turning them into a caricature, in a context in which, from that moment, they are out of place. He is reduced to eccentric poses. Unlike the type of dandy who displays a haughty and perfectly aristocratic scorn for the masses and the various crowded meeting places, and who would not dream of soiling his impeccable outfit in a popular café, the Bohemian finds therein his natural environment, his nurturing cocoon. He needs the city with its kaleidoscope of images, sensations, and stimulations. He has to immerse himself in urban crowds, "as into a reservoir of electric energy,"[7] writes Walter Benjamin. He could not live without the protection offered by cities, the only places where, instead of appearing as a lonely rebel, he can build his own "countersociety," admittedly marginal, but decidedly real, consisting of cafés, inns, studios, concert halls, clubs, and magazines. However, his love of crowds does not lead him to negate his own personality. His cult of the self prevents him from disappearing into the anonymous, fragmented crowd. If the Bohemian looks for the crowd, it is not in order to be absorbed by it, but to hide in it, to inhabit it as a protective cover, to be inspired by it, to "use" it as a source of aesthetic experiences (the *Erlebnis* of the *flâneur*), or else to model it, orientate it, and make it a conscious subject (Blanqui's conspirators). For the conservatives, this Bohemian, who is in tune with the crowd, will remain subversive vis-à-vis the social and moral order, a dangerous adventurer, keen on alcohol and violence, as portrayed by Tocqueville in his *Memoirs*, from 1848.[8]

Engendered by the mass society that is born in the industrial age, Bohemia could not have existed in the eighteenth century, except as the malaise of intellectuals toward a nobility whose tutelage was becoming increasingly stifling (D'Alembert's essay on "men of letters" in his *Encyclopedia* is proof of this). Philosophers did not want to hide from society in an elitist ghetto, but wanted to establish their values such as humanity and reason as society's norms; they did not pretend to fight the dominant social and political régime, but wanted to transform it and improve it. At the time, as Norbert Elias has brilliantly shown in his analysis of Mozart's situation, artists did not consider the market as a source of social injustice or alienation of their talents, but as a way of freeing themselves from the claustrophobic grip of the court.[9]

With its antibourgeois attitude, Bohemianism displays a typically romantic aspect. It expresses the attempt to revive, in an age of modernity, a *community* (formed by artistic, intellectual, or political affinities) that escapes from the constraints of money, market, and utilitarian and calculating bourgeois rationale. It opposes its qualitative values to the quantitative universe ruled by the laws of market production. The anarchist poet Erich Mühsam found this in the Bohemian way of life, which he described in his memoirs for future generations and which he thought displayed the "possibility of being free in fraternity." It was a question of creating, on the fringes of capitalist society, a microcosmic community, able to foreshadow the universal human community of the future.[10]

A strong utopian spirit always accompanies this romantic dimension. Foreshadowing an authentic human community, Bohemia is experienced by its followers as a space of freedom wrenched from the much more prosaic surrounding reality and as an anticipation of the liberation to come. It is a place haunted by hope, where plans for the future are being constantly worked out (literarily, artistically, and politically). Its members display an irreducible dissatisfaction toward the present, totally lacking possibilities of compromise. They are, to use the title of a novel by Jules Vallès, *réfractaires.*[11]

Individualism is also a part of Bohemia where, indeed, egotistical temperaments are to be found in great numbers, but it is an artist's and an intellectual's individualism, careful to preserve the unique personality. It is different from the individualism postulated by classical liberal philosophies, focusing on the property owner or the consumer. It is not the individualism of the citizen either, unless it takes the form of a cosmopolitan citizenship. The freedom of the Bohemian consists in denouncing oppression and in claiming rights for those who are denied them; it is not concerned with adopting a juridical form.

All the fundamental features of the capitalist ethos described by Max Weber—the work discipline, worldly asceticism, virtuous and moderate behavior, productive rationality, the search for stable and continuous profit—are the reverse of the Bohemian ethos.[12] It scorns money, and has antiproductive and antiutilitarian morals, a precarious existence, a penchant for adventure, a taste for excess, and a derision of decorous and bourgeois respectability. It makes a cult of freedom, lives a disordered existence, and rejects all external constraints. If one wants to describe Bohemia in one formula, one could see in it the synthesis between an anticapitalist and romantic ethos and an anticonformist and transgressive lifestyle, a synthesis represented by two archetypal figures, distinct but not incompatible: the accursed artist and the political plotter.

In his major work, *Bohemian Paris*, Jerrold Seigel quotes a Parisian, a man of the theater of the Orleanist period, whose identity remains unknown, but thanks to whom we have an extremely precise portrait of Bohemians:

> That class of individuals whose existence is a problem, condition a myth, fortune an enigma; who have no stable residence, no recognized retreat, who are located nowhere and whom one encounters everywhere! Who have no single occupation and who exercise fifty professions; of whom most get up in the morning without knowing where they will dine in the evening; rich today, famished tomorrow, ready to live honestly if they can and some other way if they can't.[13]

One found among them, adds Seigel, as many unknown geniuses as scoundrels, all stuck in the same swamps, halfway between resourcefulness and criminality.

The economic precariousness of this group of people, who cannot live outside the bourgeois society in which they occupy no stable position and who are excluded from production, places them between the intelligentsia and the lowest depths. In the beginning of the 1920s, the sociologist Paul Honigsheim saw Bohemia as a marginal group, a class of "pariahs" (*Pariaklasse*), which he compared to the Jews, members of a banished and "disqualified race."[14] In his eyes, one typical aspect of Bohemia resides in its rejection of the monetary economy, not necessarily as a social or philosophical criticism of private property, or as an explicit form of political communism. More importantly, they reject the monetary economy in aspects of their practical behavior and lifestyle; and they base this not on a theory, but on "the power of emotions [*gefühlsmäßig*]." Bohemia's normal proclivity, far removed from the law of the market, is for the sharing of property (*Konsumptionskommunismus*) and this determines the anticonformism and the anticapitalist feelings of its members.[15]

These characteristics make Bohemia a haven for all kinds of fringe artists and marginal writers who are misunderstood because they are innovators, or condemned because they are subversive. It is a natural haven for intellectuals and revolutionaries in exile. Because it banishes such values as the family and the nation, Bohemia attracts rebellious women, foreigners, half-castes, uprooted people, all those who belong to excluded and persecuted minorities. Being an openly spiritual community, as well as a caste of social pariahs, it thrives in a cosmopolitan atmosphere. It recruits a great number of its members among Russian, Polish, German, and Italian exiles who came to settle in France in the course of the nineteenth century. Having reached the rest of Europe at the turn of the century, it will become the refuge, according to Robert Michels, of a huge intellectual proletariat that has been marginalized for political reasons and as a result of national, ethnic, religious, or racial prejudices. A new type of emigrant who lives in rented rooms and move from one city to another, like "modern nomads," will come to represent the idea of Bohemia.[16] In his work on Jacques Offenbach, conceived as a "social biography" of Paris during the Second Empire, Siegfried Kracauer analyzed Parisian Bohemia as a meeting place for political exiles and "internal emigrants." They were in search of an "extraterritorial" space that would provide refuge from political oppression and from generally accepted behavior and moral conventions.[17] In the same way, Honigsheim underlines the affinity uniting the Jewish intellectual of the big cities, excluded from the universities and often deprived of a fixed income, and the "littérateur" and, therefore, in an indirect way, the "Bohemian."[18] The socioeconomic precariousness of this artistic and intellectual proletariat makes Bohemia a difficult, transitory, and rarely endless state; its most usual prospects tend to be, adds Michels (paraphrasing Murger), the academy or the hospital, sometimes the morgue.[19]

The economic instability and the extreme social fragility of Bohemia also determine its changeable political character. On the one hand, its antibourgeois nature makes it a center for revolt where many groups of conspirators find shelter, foreshadowing the "professional revolutionaries" of the twentieth century. On the other hand, the poverty of its members exposes them to temptations of corruption, denunciation, and betrayal. Its unclear dividing line favors police infiltration. At its lowest level, Bohemia is close to petty criminals and informers, often getting mixed up with the subproletariat, which is at the mercy of demagogues, constituting the social basis of any nationalist and populist political movement. Erich Mühsam does not seem to worry about this fact, which he even tries to emphasize: "Criminals, tramps, whores, and artists: this is Bohemia, which leads the way to a new culture."[20]

Crime as revolt: it has been claimed that this aspect of Bohemia— stigmatized by its enemies in order to confuse it with delinquency—has even been proudly idealized by its supporters, first by Jean Genet in *Thief's Journal*.[21] Its most frequent political drift is terrorism: the terrorist attack as a symbolic gesture or more simply as an aesthetic one. This has often been a temptation for the anarchist Bohemia and sometimes for the socialist movement, particularly in Latin countries (a non-Latin example would be the assassination of Count Sturgh by Friedrich Adler in 1914). This proximity to the *Lumpenproletariat* and its forms of violence explains the tendency of Bohemia to break up, as, for example, in the course of the social and political crisis of 1848. Torn between contradictory forces, it is spontaneously attracted by barricades, and then, once the revolution has failed, becomes the object of seduction by the most reactionary circles.

The active participation of the Parisian Bohemia in the events of February and June 1848 is recorded in Baudelaire's poems but also in the memoirs of two spies, Adolphe Chenu and Lucien de la Hodde, both police infiltrators in republican circles.[22] Its conservative drift inspired many literary figures. Hussonet, one of the heroes Gustave Flaubert placed at the core of his *Sentimental Education*, is part of this literary Parisian Bohemia during the July Monarchy, after which he joins the Party of Order, later to become a man of power during the Second Empire.[23] In other words, Bohemia is a divided, heterogeneous social and cultural microcosm. Helmut Kreuzer distinguishes its three principal currents: the *green* (freedom, art, youth, hope), the *black* (distress, poverty, despair), and the *red* (rebellion).[24] They are not incompatible and can merge, depending on the times, with a predominance of one color or another. But a closer look shows that black Bohemia is only the material background shared by the other two: the artistic tendency as described by Murger, whose archetype is a poet like Rimbaud, a musician like Offenbach, and a painter like Modigliani, and the political tendency represented by figures such as Auguste Blanqui and Jules Vallès in France, Gustav Landauer and Erich Mühsam in Germany, Oscar Wilde, George Orwell, and John Reed in England and the United States.

MARX

Marx's writings on the 1848 revolution in France contain many references to the Parisian Bohemia. He underlines its politically ambiguous character, as well as its status as a floating layer of society, constantly polarized between the fundamental classes of society. The author of *The Communist Manifesto* describes Bohemia sometimes as a source of insurrection, sometimes as one of the bastions of Bonapartist counterrevolution. These two visions cross in texts often written only a few months apart. This leads one to believe that their author was never aware of such a contradiction. In any case, he never attempted to offer an explanation for this dichotomy.

In 1850, Marx and Engels published in the *Neue Rheinische Zeitung* a long review of the books written by the two informers mentioned above, Lucien de la Hodde and Adolphe Chenu: *The Birth of the Republic in February 1848* and *The Conspirators*. Using these sources, Marx and Engels distinguish two different kinds of agitators in the center of secret societies feeding the revolutionary movement: on the one hand, there are the occasional conspirators, who take part in group action at the same time as they carry on other activities; on the other hand, the professional conspirators, "who dedicated all their activity to conspiring and lived from it" (what Lenin, half a century later, would call "professional revolutionaries"). The editor of the Cologne paper emphasizes the extreme precariousness of these specialized plotters, whose existence depended "more on chance than on their activity." Indeed, their existence was characterized by "a dissolute life" whose only regularity was frequenting "the taverns of the *marchands de vin*, the places of rendezvous of the conspirators."[25] This refers implicitly to Marc Caussidière, prefect of police in the first provisional government in February 1848, persecuted and forced to go into exile after the June repression. This highly colorful character, who had taken part in Lyon's *canuts* insurrection in 1831 and collaborated with the activities of republican circles during the July Monarchy, was a wine and spirits representative. This job meant that he traveled all over the place, so it allowed him to maintain contacts between provincial and Parisian conspirators. It is Caussidière who denounced Chenu and de la Hodde as spies. They, in turn, devote a large part of their writings to him, where he appears as the incarnation of revolutionary Bohemia. Following this, Marx and Engels mention the acquaintance that this type of conspirator had with "all kinds of dubious people" mixing with "that social category which in Paris is known as *la Bohème.*"[26] In most cases, they were "democratic bohemians of proletarian origin," but as they also attracted part of the *Lumpenproletariat,* they were controlled and persecuted by the police like thieves and prostitutes.[27]

This picture of "professional conspirators" constitutes the first formulation of the Marxist criticism of "Blanquism." The conspirators had one single goal: the insurrection, the overthrow of the government, which they tried to achieve by their own methods, without caring about being understood or supported by the mass of the workers. Here is a description of the members of a Blanquist club:

> The leap at inventions which are supposed to work revolutionary miracles: incendiary bombs, destructive devices of magic effect, revolts which are expected to be all the more miraculous and astonishing in effect as their basis is less rational. Occupied with such scheming, they have no other purpose than the immediate one of overthrowing the existing government and have the profoundest contempt for the more theoretical enlightenment of the proletariat about their class interests.[28]

Hence it is "plebeian" and not "proletarian" anger that they display toward the "*habits noirs,*" the intellectuals who lead the workers movement and refuse to engage in a separate war against power.[29] In short, if the ultimate aim of Bohemia was on an aesthetic level *art for art's sake,* on a political level its equivalent was *insurrection for insurrection's sake.* Their illusion, through naïveté, lack of consciousness, or a sort of utopian impatience consisted, according to Marx and Engels, "to anticipate the process of revolutionary development, to bring it artificially to crisis-point, to launch a revolution on the spur of the moment, without the conditions for a revolution." They agitate truly like "alchemists of the revolution."[30] Such a severe judgment, where Bohemia on the barricades seems to be represented by adventurers, not to say authentic *putschists*, contrasts remarkably with a very famous passage of *The Eighteenth Brumaire* where Marx pays homage to Blanqui and his followers by presenting them as "the real leaders of the proletarian party."[31]

In this work, written a few weeks after Louis Bonaparte's coup d'état and therefore about a year after the account given by Chenu and de la Hodde in the books cited above, the image of Bohemia, as described by Marx, goes through another metamorphosis. The conspirators now appear in it as the leaders of the revolution, and Blanqui as their head. On the other hand, Bohemia suddenly departs from the revolutionary circles to identify itself totally with the urban mob, the basis of Bonapartist reaction. The Society of the 10th of December, which became instrumental in the Napoleon III coup is described thus by Marx:

> Alongside decayed *roués* with dubious means of subsistence and of dubious origin, alongside ruined and adventurous offshoots of the bourgeoisie, were vagabonds, discharged soldiers, discharged jailbirds, escaped galley slaves, rogues, mountebanks, *lazzaroni*, pickpockets, tricksters, gamblers, *maquereaux*, brothel keepers, porters, *literati*, organ-grinders, rag-pickers, knife grinders, tinkers, beggars—in short, the whole indefinite, disintegrated mass, thrown hither and thither, which the French term *la Bohème*.[32]

For Marx, Louis Bonaparte was the natural leader of "this scum, offal, refuse of all classes," therefore a fully fledged Bohemian, a representation in all its most disgusting and sinister aspects.[33] It was thanks to the mobilization of Parisian Bohemia that he could install his power.

Such a diagnosis was not just what Marx thought at the time, in the heat of the moment, straight after the coup d'état. In *The Civil War in France*, written twenty years later about the Commune, one finds a very similar definition: proletarian Paris against Versailles, where the Bonapartist reaction had taken refuge, surrounded by his own Bohemia. Marx here refers to its "high Bonapartist and capitalist Bohemia," which had fled the capital in the hands of the Communards: "a phantom Paris, the Paris of the *francs-fileurs*, the Paris of the Boulevards, male and female—the rich, the capitalist, the gilded, the idle Paris, now thronging with its lackeys, its blacklegs, its literary *bohème*, and its *cocottes* at Versailles, Saint-Denis, Rueil, and Saint-Germain."[34] However, one knows that the identification of the Commune with Bohemia will become received knowledge in the Third Republic, thanks to the propaganda of the conservative press as well as the testimonies of those involved. As early as in 1871, Elme-Marie Caro, future member of the French Academy, indicated in the *Revue des Deux Mondes* that the main leaders of the insurrection came from Bohemia, for example, Raoul Rigault, the prefect of police, and Jules Vallès, the education minister.[35] The latter celebrated the union between Bohemia and the Commune in his novel *L'insurgé*, the third part of his autobiographical trilogy on Jacques Vingtras. In *Les Hommes de la Commune*, one of the first works devoted to the event, published toward the end of 1871, Jules Clère described Jean Longuet, the editor-in-chief of the *Journal Officiel* of the revolutionary government, as "the most perfect example of a Bohemian one could meet."[36] But the Commune did not have, as in the 1848 revolution, a paper called *Le Bohémien de Paris*. The Commune supporters and gravediggers in turn used the term that had by then acquired a rather negative and scornful taste, each to describe its enemies. Toward the end of the nineteenth century, the term belonged to the conservatives and the antirepublicans, who used it as a synonym for the "decadence" of civilization, or, as in the case of Max Nordau, as a typical symptom of the "degeneration" of the modern world.[37] Édouard Drumont, the author of *La France juive* (1886), took over the task of reconciling conservative hatred for Bohemia with antirepublicanism and anti-Semitism.[38]

In his essay on Eduard Fuchs, written in exile in 1937, Walter Benjamin sums up the image of nineteenth-century France in Marx's writings. The German critic suggests that Paris appears there as the origin of three important revolutions, as a haven for exiles, as the fatherland for utopian socialism, and as the place of the Communards' martyrdom.[39] Thus, Marx's vision is based on more than just literary reminiscence. As he was sketching the portrait of Paris secret societies in 1850, Marx was certainly using Chenu and de la Hodde's testimonies, but he was also using the memories of his own experience. After his exile in Paris from October 1843 to February 1845, the French police, following pressure from the Prussian authorities, expelled him. He was then forced to settle in Brussels. In Paris, the young Karl Marx had been in contact with young German exiles (thousands of them taking part in a fairly large number of clubs and journals), including the poet Heinrich Heine. It is in Paris that, in 1844, he completed his passage from left-wing Hegelianism to communism, being under the influence of German immigrant circles and French political organizations originating from Babeuf. It is in Paris, where he was in close contact with French socialism, that he discovered revolutionary action, becoming aware of the necessity of "transforming" rather than merely interpreting the world. It is again in Paris, where he lived as a young exile and outsider, that he devoted an important part of his *Manuscripts* of 1844 to the concept of alienation (*Verfremdung*).[40]

The Communist League, whose program Marx and Engels composed in 1847, was originally the League of the Just (*Bund der Gerechten*), which was, in its turn, the outcome of a rift in 1836 from the League of the Proscribed (*Bund der Geachteten*). Made up of exiled German craftsmen, most of them self-taught intellectuals, all these movements contributed to enlivening what one could describe as the cosmopolitan, political, and revolutionary component of the Parisian Bohemia of the Orleanist period (red *Bohemia*, according to Kreuzer).[41] The interest Marx took in the life of French socialist circles during his stay in Paris is well illustrated in a passage from the *Economic and Philosophical Manuscripts* (1844). In this text, he described them as a kind of a countersociety in which workers could establish communal, brotherly connections of solidarity, the opposite of the dominant social relationships in the world outside. The purpose of their meetings was propaganda and the organization of possible revolutionary action, but the means they had chosen—their meetings would often develop as very convivial dinners—tended to become a goal in itself (the *community*). The description Marx gave of these meetings had a strong Bohemian flavor: "smoking, drinking, eating." All these actions, which were propitious for "good company, association, conversation," were for them ends in themselves. "Human brotherhood," he concluded, "is not a phrase but a truth and the nobility of humanity radiates from their features hardened by hard work."[42] Passages from *The Eighteenth Brumaire* and *The Civil War in France* quoted above seem therefore to show signs of repression with regard to the prehistory of the Communist League and even in relation to his own intellectual and political trajectory. According to Marx, the revolutionary and conspiratorial phase of Bohemia seems to stop in 1848, after which date it would only act in a deeply reactionary way.

GUSTAVE COURBET

From the July Revolution of 1830 to the Paris Commune, Bohemia was a privileged realm for conflating art and politics. It was a free space in which nonconformist and antibourgeois painters could fraternize outside of and against the academy and respectable institutions. Before 1870 many impressionist artists like Manet, Degas, and Fantin-Latour, later joined by younger painters such as Renoir, Pissarro, and Monet, usually gathered at Café Guerbois, 11 rue de Batignolles. Later, their preferred place became Le Chat Noir, in the heart of Montmartre.[43] Among them, a colorful Bohemian was Gustave Courbet, whose attraction for brasseries and cafés extirpated him from his workshop, as his friends Charles Baudelaire and Champfleury sometimes complainingly observed.[44]

Courbet was a socialist and an admirer of Fourier. In several texts and letters, he presented himself as a socialist, a democrat and a republican, "a supporter of the whole revolution."[45] In fact, he was a kind of individualistic anarchist inspired by the philosopher Joseph Proudhon. His political commitment was not lineal: he did not participate directly in the revolution of 1848, in spite of his sympathies for the insurgent workers of June. In solidarity with his friends involved in the barricades (first of all Baudelaire), he affirmed his socialist views in the 1850s. In 1868, when his reputation was solidly established, he rejected the Legion d'Honneur offered by Napoleon III in name of a radical opposition to academy and the Second Empire, artistic conformism and political reaction. In those years, Courbet became a close friend of Proudhon and Jules Vallès, one of the representatives of the political and literary Bohemia. In 1871, he actively participated in the Paris Commune, in which he was an elected member of its Council as well as delegate for the fine arts. It is as one of the main inspirers of the cultural politics of the Commune that, on April 27, he requested the demolition of the Vendome column, a symbol of French militarism and imperialism, which he suggested to replace with a new monument celebrating the insurrection of March 18. After the defeat of the Commune, he paid with prison for his political involvement and, once liberated, retired in exile to Switzerland.[46]

According to the art historian T. J. Clark, Courbet's Bohemianism did not express a condition of social marginality; it was rather a conscious choice of self-exclusion from the bourgeois world. Antibourgeois as well was his predilection for rural subjects against the celebration of bourgeois institutions and power symbols. In the second half of the nineteenth century, Clark explains,

> Bohemia was a life-style and a social situation. It meant a dogged refusal to abandon the aims of Romanticism, a manic and self-destructive individualism, a "cult of multiple sensations": "wine and hashish compared as means for multiplying individuality," as Baudelaire puts it in 1851. It meant a place between the *classes dangereuses* of proletarian Paris and the intelligentsia; between two classes that were themselves strange, intricate misfits in any class system, and remained unsure on whose side they were on.[47]

In a letter of 1850 to his friend Francis Way, Courbet described his Bohemian taste in very clear terms: "In our civilized society, I need to live like a savage; I need to go far away from the governments. My sympathies are with the people; I must speak to it directly, draw my knowledge from it, live by it. This is the reason for which I choose to embrace the great, independent, and vagabond life of Bohemians."[48]

In 1848, the people—the laboring classes—irrupted into politics through the June insurrection and two years later entered into art through the canvases of Courbet exhibited at the Salon of Paris: *The Stone Breakers*, *Peasants of Flagey*, and *Burial at Ornans*. Courbet claimed to realistically represent the "people" as it was, not as a symbol, a metaphor, or an idealized social entity.[49] From this point of view, the difference that separates him from most of his contemporary painters is impressive. In his artwork, Jean-François Millet depicted peaceful, submitted peasants who accept their oppression as a natural condition. In *The Angelus* (1859), he celebrated Catholicism and the traditionalism of rural culture. Highly appreciated by the bourgeois and aristocratic classes, Millet was a very successful artist, whose conservatism perfectly corresponded to the taste of the bourgeois elites of the Second Empire.[50] With *Burial at Ornans* (1850), Courbet astonished the audience, depicting a grandiose scene in which ordinary people occupied a central position usually reserved for the ruling classes, for the kings and the emperors (figure 4.1). Courbet's "realism" was the opposite of Jacques-Louis David's *The Coronation of*

4.1. Gustave Courbet, *Burial at Ornans* (1849), oil on canvas, Musée d'Orsay. © RMN-Grand Palais, Art Resource, New York.

Napoleon (1806). Reviewing the Salon of 1851, some art critics defined Courbet "the Proudhon of painting" and qualified his canvas as "an engine of revolution" in which "art makes itself part of the people."[51]

Of course, Courbet's people were not Marx's proletariat and his enthusiasm for the popular uprisings of nineteenth-century France was combined with a Fourierist vision of "universal harmony" that shaped many of his canvas. *The Meeting* (1854) reinvents the traditional iconography of the wandering Jew (popularized by a feuilleton of Eugene Sue ten years earlier), transforming a symbol of oppression and persecution—the Jew—into a messenger of utopian socialism. Courbet depicts himself as a wandering Jew—the bearer of Fourierist utopia— who finally comes face to face with the art collector Alfred Bruyas, his friend and patron, accompanied by his servant. This canvas suggests a vision of universal harmony as cooperation between art, people, and the industrialists, which is also a meeting between the enlightened bourgeoisie, the laboring classes, and the Bohemian artists.[52] The same characters can be distinguished in *The Painter's Studio* (1855), where they are opposed to the representatives of power and authority located on the other side of the canvas (a heteroclite vision of authority embodied, according to Proudhon's conceptions, by Napoleon III, Kosciuszko, Kossuth, and Garibaldi).[53]

Apart from his conception of socialism and his realist representation of the people, Courbet was probably the most significant and penetrating aesthetic interpreter of the revolutionary defeats of the nineteenth century. His pictorial work builds a culture of defeat that reveals the melancholy dimension of Bohemian and pre-Marxist French socialism. Of course, he was neither alone nor the first artist to depict the end of the barricades, but nobody had previously done it with such a degree of empathy and emotional involvement. In both the Second Empire and the early Third Republic, official art aimed to erase the traces of a rebellious past—the urban landscape changed to exhibit the symbols and the monuments of a new order—while the Bohemian artists created mournful visions of the lost battles. In a beautiful book devoted to the legacy of 1848 in European literature, Dolf Oehler sharply indicates the extent to which the poetry of Baudelaire and Heine and the novels of Flaubert and Herzen—four writers who had experienced the revolution in Paris—were haunted by the remembrance of the massacres of June, a time when, according to the words of Proudhon, "the vanquishing bourgeois [became] ferocious like tigers."[54] Under the Second Empire, Haussmann sagaciously redesigned the Parisian landscape: eliminating the squares and the streets that evoked the barricades, demolishing entire neighborhoods that embodied and preserved a revolutionary memory. Over the fountain in the Square Saint Michel appeared the statue of an archangel whose sword threatens a submitted Satan. It is, as Oehler highlights in quoting Baudelaire, an allegorical representation of the imperial order that had smashed the revolution, of the political and moral victory of the bourgeoisie against the "evil" of the popular uprising (figure 4.2).[55] In 1851, Delacroix's painting of the ceiling of the Apollo galleries at the Louvre fulfilled a similar celebration: the image of Apollo killing a demon clearly evoked the triumph of the order against the forces of anarchism and popular insurrection. Far from this neo-classical, pompous, and self-satisfied cult of the bourgeois order, the revolutionary artists accomplished a parallel work of mourning, creating a melancholy culture that represented and transmitted the memory of the vanquished. In the same year as the inauguration of the Apollo

4.2. Francisque-Joseph Duret and Gabriel Davioud, *Fontaine Saint-Michel* (1858–60).
© Archive Timothy McCarthy/Art Resource, New York.

4.3. Gustave Courbet, *The Killed Hart* (1867), oil on canvas, Musée d'Orsay.
© RMN-Grand Palais/Art Resource, New York.

galleries at the Louvre museum, Courbet painted *A Burial at Ornans*, the first realistic representation of the people in modern art, which was pertinently interpreted as the funeral of the revolution of 1848.[56] In the 1860s, he devoted a cycle of canvases to hunting whose recurring theme is the death of hounded animals. The most famous of them, *The Killed Hart* (1867), shows a dying deer, lying on the ground and exhausted, being whipped by a hunter while dogs are impatient to dismember it. This painting is an extraordinarily intense and uncanny allegory of the defeat of the revolution of 1848 (figure 4.3).[57] A similar symmetry can be seen in many works Courbet painted after the Paris Commune. In 1871, the Basilica of the Sacred Heart was built to celebrate another "moral order," that of the Third Republic born from the massacre of the Communards. At that moment, Courbet represented the fallen through a cycle of allegorical canvases that, in the style of still life, simply depicted trout. Rarely has the suffering of human beings found an expression as poignant as in these images of agonizing fishes (figure 4.4).

4.4. Gustave Courbet, *The Trout* (1873), oil on canvas, Musée d'Orsay. © Erich Lessing/ Art Resource, New York.

WALTER BENJAMIN

Walter Benjamin, one of the few critics who studied the Marxist interpretation of Bohemia, found in Baudelaire the embodiment of its political antinomies.[58] He stresses the fact that the poet gives a voice to the rebellious spirit of Bohemia, a rebellious spirit undeniably antibourgeois, but whose aim is never clear in advance and whose goal can change or be diverted, confiscated, or even distorted. He remembers how the author of *Les Fleurs du Mal* took part in the events of February 1848, as he was marching down Paris streets shouting: "Down with General Aupick!" (his own stepfather), and then quotes another passage where this time the poet seems to spell out the nature of his rebellion: "I say 'Long live the revolution!' as I would say 'Long live destruction! Long live penances! Long live chastisements! Long live death!' I would be happy not only as a victim; it would not displease me to play the hangman as well—so as to feel the revolution from both sides! All of us have the republican spirit in our blood as we have syphilis in our bones. We have a democratic and syphilitic infection."[59]

According to Benjamin, this shows the typical signs of the "metaphysics of the provocateur" that will culminate in the twentieth century with Sorel and Céline. Both nihilism and radical anti-Semitism in *Bagatelles pour un massacre* are not devoid of links with a note from Baudelaire's diary: "A fine conspiracy could be organized for the purpose of exterminating the Jewish race."[60] An aphorism, writes Benjamin, quoting the Blanquist Rigault, with many equivalents to be found in the writings of nineteenth-century French socialists and conspirators.[61] In other words, the rebellious spirit of Bohemia can find an outlet in an active participation in the revolution of 1848, as well as feed reactionary subversion, leading to Bonapartism and fascism in the twentieth century.

It is, therefore, in Bohemia that the "first burgeoning" appears of what the historian Zeev Sternhell called the "revolutionary Right."[62] This was born in France at the end of the nineteenth century out of the synthesis between an antibourgeois and antidemocratic populist left and an antirepublican nationalism, which is no longer nostalgic for the Old Regime, but has turned instead toward a new order.[63] Following this, Céline, Barrès, Drieu la Rochelle, and Brasillach in France, as well as Marinetti in Italy and Moeller van den Bruck and Gottfried Benn in Germany, could be considered as representatives of a fascist culture colored by Bohemian roots. There is a path leading Bohemia to fascism, as certain avant-garde currents illustrate. In futurism, the myth of youth becomes a cult of virility, the aesthetic idealization of speed and modern technology stimulates a celebration of war, and, finally, national strength and the subversive mind are channeled and neutralized in the "revolutionary" liturgies of the regime. A few months before Mussolini came to power in Italy, Gramsci mentioned, in an article in *L'Ordine Nuovo*, the "subversive past" of this "new reactionary" former leader of the radical socialist party. He felt that Mussolini was not totally wrong to advertise his "Blanquism," but he pointed out that it was a type of Blanquism that had lost its revolutionary and utopian dimension and was reduced to a mere technique for making a coup d'état. The forces of reaction could indeed exploit such a heritage. A similar itinerary, although much more provincial and entirely alien to any type of avant-garde, was the case of Hitler, whose biographers emphasize his "Bohemian" side during his youth in Vienna and in Munich before the First World War.[64] Economic precariousness as well as the lamentable failure of his artistic aspirations marked this period of his life.

Benjamin underlines, in the wake of Marx, the possibility of a reactionary drift in rebellious Bohemia. But he also shows, in relation to surrealism, the road leading to socialism and revolution. All the typical aspects of Bohemia—its exclusion from production, its social marginality, its penchant for eroticism and drugs, as well as its anticonformism—attracted the surrealists. Nadja, the heroine of André Breton's eponymous novel, is a complete repertory of every aspect of Bohemia: woman, prostitute, artist, drug dealer, visionary, tramp with no fixed abode, indifferent to money, pillar of café life, indulging in ephemeral and fleeting relationships.[65] Thus, at the source of Benjamin's project of writing a book on Parisian life was the impact of Surrealism, particularly the influence of a text by Louis Aragon, *Le Paysan de Paris* (1926). It is this meeting with Surrealism that directs him toward a new interpretation of the nineteenth century through the prism of Paris, its "capital," and toward a rereading of Baudelaire, which brings him to discover Bohemia with its characters, from the conspirator to the poet, from the *flâneur* to the rag-picker. But his interest in Surrealism has also something to do with a preoccupation of a political nature: the necessity of politicizing art and culture in the face of the aestheticization of fascist politics.[66] Surrealism appears to him as an example of artistic and literary creation, able to activate the revolutionary potentialities of dreams, eroticism, and utopia and therefore an example of a revolutionary use of a social imagination that has found its first modern historical expression in Bohemia. To conclude, Surrealism is seen as surpassing, in a revolutionary sense, the political ambiguities of the nineteenth-century Bohemian revolt, whose symptoms he had clearly detected in Baudelaire, and as an alternative to the drift into fascism in the twentieth century as represented by Céline.

A certain affinity with the Marxist analysis of Bohemia also seems to appear just beneath the surface, in his critique of Surrealism. In an essay from 1929, Benjamin singled out this movement as the first and only one that had been capable of giving expression to a radical idea of freedom that had disappeared in Europe after Bakunin.[67] At the same time, he grasped the limits of this anarchistic rebellion in its indifference to the methodical and conscious preparation of the revolution, a task that he described as necessary and urgent at the same time.[68] The danger awaiting Surrealism was to find itself isolated, in a deadlock, like the *flâneur*, who leads his own guerrilla warfare against the market and the capitalist organization of time: his ascetic elation in front of the phantasmagoria of the mercantile society (he looks without buying) and his individual challenge to the productive organization of time (he walks around aimlessly and without consulting his watch) certainly have something to do with the rejection of bourgeois values without nevertheless challenging the order or its foundations.[69] Thus, Surrealists were antipodal to the Blanquist conspirators. The latter organized insurrections while forgetting the real proletarian movement; the former expected the fulfillment of an emancipatory action, without bothering to connect their creative effort to the political practices of the workers movement, and so renounced their roles as revolutionary intellectuals. In both cases, rebellion against the dominant order was likely to exhaust itself in solitary and impotent action.

LEON TROTSKY

Trotsky looked mainly at Russian and German Bohemia in *Literature and Revolution*, published in Moscow in 1923. He devoted a chapter of this book to Mayakovsky and to Russian Futurism, adding in the second part several texts from 1908 concerning the journal *Simplicissimus* and Frank Wedekind's work. According to Trotsky, artistic, urban, and cosmopolitan Bohemia comprised various elements stemming from all social classes, ranging from the public dormitory regulars to the guests of aristocratic salons who thought they had formed a new community, which was in reality made up of "déclassés." What united them was a shared feeling of aesthetic rebellion, but this "chaotic radicalism" masked a lack of social focus and the absence of a clear political orientation.[70] The critical and mocking style of the Bavarian *Simplicissimus*, displaying no pity for morality and bourgeois conventions, was considered with some complacency by the government that had nothing to fear from its excesses. In contrast, the exiled Russian intellectuals, a kind of "messianic order" founded on poverty and the deprivation of rights and roots, exhausted with their "aesthetic nihilism": "first hour decadentism, the cult of the tramp, and perfectly powerless Nietzscheanism."[71] The first historical turn would have inevitably done away with these heterogeneous and confused elements. During the Great War, Trotsky observed, *Simplicissimus* did not resist the wave of German and Austrian chauvinism and tried "to reconcile the shades of Bebel and Bismarck in

Heaven."[72] Similarly, shortly after the War, Italian Futurism would join fascism, attracted by its "revolutionary methods." On the other hand, Russian Futurism would "plunge" into revolution, bringing in its Bohemian spirit. It had joined forces with the Soviets, encouraged by the rejection of old art forms, by the dynamic élan, and by the promise of building a completely new culture. From this perspective, it provided "a necessary step" in the process of transforming art and literature in the core of the workers' state. However, Trotsky could not hide his irritation toward a movement whose rejection of the past reflected "the nihilism of Bohemia" rather than "the revolutionary proletarian point of view."[73] He felt that the latter was more interested in assimilating a "bourgeois" culture that had always excluded it rather than "destroying" it. Therefore, he deplored Mayakovski's showy agitation: his subjectivism was the mirror of "individualistic and Bohemian arrogance"; his naïve criticism of the bourgeoisie, illustrated by the old-fashioned cliché of the fat-bellied American capitalist, only demonstrated "Bohemian silliness";[74] all his poems bore "the much too obvious mark of the artistic cabaret, of café life and everything else associated with it."[75] In short, for the head of the Red Army, the genuine revolutionary was not a Bohemian.

BOHEMIA AND REVOLUTION

In the works of Marx, Courbet, Benjamin, and Trotsky, Bohemia appears as a place of revolt that tends to split into two antipodal camps: a revolutionary one, going from the July Monarchy to Surrealism, from Blanqui to Mayakovski and Breton; and a reactionary one, going from the Bonapartist circles in 1848 to the Italian Futurists, Céline, and fascism. Baudelaire, in between both, is witness to a revolt that has not yet found its way, and is likely to go in either direction. In this deadlock, the Bohemian threatens to metamorphose himself into a *dandy*, his dialectical counterpart. Indeed, Baudelaire celebrated the dandy as a representation of a "haughty caste," of a "new type of aristocracy" that had withdrawn into the cult of the self, scared by the marks of bourgeois society such as work and money, but, in fact, perfectly incapable of opposing it. Dandyism, concludes Baudelaire, "is the last heroic feat in decadent times," an aristocratic heroism "without warmth and full of melancholy," which does not rebel against oppression and the injustices of capitalism but against "the mounting tide of democracy."[76] In his essay on Baudelaire, Sartre noted the "useless" character of dandyism that, in contrast to the politically engaged literature of Hugo, Sand, and Pierre Leroux, has never threatened dominant regimes, content to contemplate only a perfectly innocent "child's game."[77] In his *Treatise on Elegant Life*, Balzac defines the dandy as a man who becomes "a piece of furniture for a boudoir, an extremely clever mannequin which can sit on a horse or a couch, who bites or cleverly sucks the end of a cane," but who has definitely renounced being a "thinking person."[78] Reduced to a purely aesthetic rebellion, which has been isolated and pushed to the extreme, Bohemianism is in danger of turning into dandyism. The Bohemian then finds himself confronting his own caricature: George Brummell's clothes, a kind of Blanqui reduced to his passion for black gloves. The dandy's coldness, with his blasé attitude and his indifference, stands poles apart from Bohemian passion and carelessness, where one can find human warmth and the pariah's love for the world, implacable resistance to the rational, social, and even national codes of the bourgeois world.[79]

Far away from dandyism, the theoretical and political movement that is most closely connected to the Bohemian ideal is certainly anarchism. Its political romanticism, its decentralized organization, its utopian spirit striving toward a human community, possible through the abolition of the state, its rejection of all authority ("neither god nor master!"), and its cult of revolt have a deep affinity with the Bohemian ethos. This affinity—as underlies much libertarian literature—is in some cases openly acknowledged by such representatives as Gustav Landauer and Erich Mühsam. In 1904, these two Munich anarchist intellectuals vehemently expressed their disagreements with the distinction established by Julius Bab between the revolutionary who struggles for a new society and the Bohemian, "asocial" nihilist who is opposed to any form of organized society.[80] For Mühsam, anarchists were "the most consciously minded Bohemians."[81] As for Landauer, he distinguished Bohemia from anarchy, the former not being based on a clear political project, but he emphasized that "the anarchist must often lead a Bohemian life."[82]

It would therefore not be wrong to identify an anti-Bohemian aspect in the Marxist critique of anarchism, in spite of some significant convergences, political (from Germany in 1919 to Spain in 1936) as well as theoretical (the shared goal of a stateless society). In Bohemia, communism found many traveling soul mates, not a model for life or organization. However, examined carefully, the intellectual and political trajectories of Marx, Courbet, Benjamin, and Trotsky reveal many features that make them Bohemians according to criteria defined by Michels and Honigsheim. They were undoubtedly sui generis Bohemians, but they were nevertheless Bohemians. We have already mentioned Marx exiled in Paris, at the beginning of the 1840s, when he took part in the activities of democratic and protocommunist circles of German emigrants. But Marx lived most of his life as an exile in London, where he pursued his research and his political battles outside any academic institution, without any public acknowledgment, in extremely precarious conditions of existence, verging on poverty. Debts, a chronic shortage of money, and a pressing necessity of economic aid in order to secure the most immediate needs for his family monopolize a great part of his correspondence with Engels, his friend and patron, and with various members of his family. In the British capital, Marx's house was constantly open to visitors coming from all over the world, particularly the representatives from the international socialist movement, intellectuals, and exiles from Central Europe. In short, Marx lived his life, devoted for a great part to the study of the capitalist economy, as a permanent war against the constraints of a relentlessly hostile *Geldwirtschaft*. Because of his position as a foreigner and as a Jew, his poverty, his intellectual anticonformism, and his political engagement, he was always marginal. His biography is inscribed in a sociological and cultural context shaped by the striking features of his socially precarious exile, cosmopolitanism, and revolutionary engagement, all sharing a typically Bohemian *Stimmung*. As for his lifestyle, the report of a Prussian spy who visited his flat in Dean Street, in Soho, gives us a vivid idea:

> He lives in one of the worst and cheapest of the London districts. He occupies two rooms. Neither of them is clean nor furnished with any equipment in good state, everything is broken, torn to shreds, each object covered with a thick layer of dust. Manuscripts, books and newspapers, his wife's sewing, handless cups, dirty towels, knives, forks, lamps, an inkwell, mugs, pipes, tobacco ash lie, next to children's toys, on the same table. When you enter the room the smell of tobacco and smoke overpowers you to the point that you feel you are groping in a cave, until you get used to it and take care to move some objects in the haze. Here

is a three-legged chair, there another one, on which children are playing with cooking utensils, looks safe. It is offered to the visitor, but the
children's food has not been removed and you risk staining your trou-
sers. But this does not embarrass Marx or his wife. You are welcomed
in a most friendly way and are cordially offered a pipe, tobacco and the
rest. Then an interesting conversation starts which makes up for all the
domestic shortcomings and makes the discomfort bearable.[83]

It is true that, with a wife and children, Marx does not correspond to the
stereotype of the young student and lonely Bohemian, but the material
environment, a radical antithesis of a Victorian or Prussian bourgeois
décor, recalls the atmosphere of Henri Murger's novel. Isaiah Berlin,
who quotes this passage in his biography of the author of *Capital*, adds
that Marx was not a Bohemian, and that his difficulties affected him in
a tragic way. One could say that if Marx were a Bohemian, it was not by
choice, but, according to Landauer's diagnosis, by necessity. His mem-
bership in a Bohemia of exiles and revolutionaries did not derive from
an aesthetic impulse; it was, rather, the price to pay for an intellectual
and political choice. Several biographical details, such as, for example,
his pride in having married someone from the Prussian aristocracy (a
von Westphalen), the suppression of his Jewish origins, or even his relatively conformist behavior with his daughters' suitors (Paul Lafargue
particularly), indicate quite clearly that he did not consider himself and
he would not have liked being considered a Bohemian. On the other
hand, he must have been rather flattered by the way the British press, for
example, referred to him as the famous "red terror doctor."[84]

Born to a bourgeois family—his father was a landowner of Ornans,
in Eastern France—Courbet was not a pariah and his Bohemianism certainly did not come from his social condition. Differently from Marx
(and Benjamin and Trotsky), nevertheless, he claimed his belonging to
the Bohemia in which he saw a realm of freedom opposed to the bourgeois order. In his eyes, true artistic creation was directed, by definition,
against bourgeois conformism and authoritarian order. Courbet's Bohemianism was a calling; it was an exhibited style of life rather than a
necessity. In spite of this comfortable Bohemianism—or perhaps thanks
to the dispassionate criticism allowed by his relative prosperity—he was
able to illustrate the melancholy dimension of defeat. Rooted in a deeply
emphatic relationship with the popular classes, his allegorical realism

did not express a condition of personal despair but described the sorrow of the vanquished.

Walter Benjamin's case, as a refugee in Paris after 1933, is somewhat different. A literary critic reduced to surviving in exile thanks to meager support from an exiled German institute (the Frankfurt Institute for Social Research transferred to the United States), he lived alone in small hotels or rented rooms and mixed in circles of German émigrés, sometimes marginal circles of French intellectuals outside official institutions such as the Collège de Sociologie. His Bohemian features derive not only from the sociological elements cited above—cosmopolitanism, exile, social precariousness, cultural anticonformism—but from a more profound intellectual vocation, as demonstrated by his interest for Surrealism, drugs, eroticism, and dreams as literary experiments, as well as his interest in Baudelaire and his period. There is a striking homology between Benjamin and the object of his research: it is as an exile that he found nineteenth-century Parisian Bohemia with its émigrés, conspirators, *flâneurs*, ragmen, in short, all marginal men.

Finally, the case of Trotsky is particularly emblematic, as he is the only commentator on Bohemia among those who have been examined so far to have actually led a revolution. His intransigent criticism of artistic Bohemia seems to fit in well with the image we have of the leader of the Red Army, of the theoretician of the militarization of labor and the dictatorship of the Bolshevik Party. But this would only be a unilateral and misleading image. The years he spent as the leader of the Soviet state were a rather brief parenthesis in a long revolutionary career spent essentially in exile, in almost always precarious material conditions, surrounded by intellectuals and isolated militants, often persecuted, constantly putting up with the juridical constraints of statelessness, hence often deported. As a journalist and a Russian conspirator who emigrated to London, Geneva, Paris, Munich, Vienna, and New York before 1917, and as the former leader of the Soviet state, exiled and stateless in Prinkipo, Paris, Oslo, and Mexico after his expulsion from the USSR in 1929, until his death in Mexico, Trotsky himself in his existential itinerary spread the Russian Bohemia of the beginning of the century. The quarrels of Russian social democracy before 1917 with its clandestine congresses infiltrated by Okhrana, watched by all the police forces of Western Europe, had nothing to envy in the meetings of the Blanquist conspirators of the July Monarchy and the Second Empire. The Coyoacan house, protected like a bunker, where he settled in 1937, certainly did not have the atmosphere of the Paris and Vienna cafés before the First World War, but the little groups of regular visitors—from German and Russian exiles to American Trotskyists, from Mexican painters to French Surrealist writers, not forgetting the menacing and fatal presence of an infiltrated Stalinist agent—certainly bring back the revolutionary Bohemian flavor, a conspiratorial, utopian haven in a world on the brink of the abyss.

Exactly like Marx, Trotsky was for several years a déclassé intellectual, perfectly integrated into a picturesque Bohemia, which he assessed, on the basis of a severe and implacable diagnosis, in all its limitations, but which he described with a wealth of detail betraying an intimate familiarity with his subject. In an article written in 1908 for the Russian daily *Kievskaya Mysl,* he gave the following description of the atmosphere of a Latin Quarter café:

> A mixed flavor of coffee, tobacco, and concentration of human bodies hangs in the air. It was now past one a.m. The Café d'Harcourt, the most lively in Saint-Michel, was crammed full. People were piling up around the tables, knocking each other's knees and elbows. The free spaces were half filled with added chairs. God knows where all the students, clerks, journalists, local prostitutes came from, from theatres, cabarets, and streets: the heterogeneous Latin Quarter Bohemia. They smoked, drank, came in and out, bumped into each other without apologizing. This scramble created an absurd physical intimacy. Feet trod on piles of sawdust waiting to clean the floor on the following day. The prostitutes were walking between the tables, looking very much the part. Waiters, in their white aprons stained with wine and coffee, impeccable in their automatic gestures in spite of exhaustion, sailed through the crowd with the blasé expression of those who attend daily to the same spectacle.[85]

The regular visits Trotsky paid to Viennese Bohemian circles are recorded, outside his writings, by a rather amusing anecdote. In 1916, in the course of a conversation with his friend Rudolf Hilferding, a brilliant economist and future minister of the Weimar Republic, the Austrian social democrat Emil Lederer was expressing his fears about the imminent revolution in Russia. Hilferding looked at him skeptically, then added: "And who is supposed to make this revolution? Herr Trotsky at the Café Central?"[86] In his memoirs, the Belgian socialist Hendrik de Man, who had known Trotsky during his first exile, described him as an intellectual who spent his nights talking in literary cafés, looking like a "virtuous Bohemian pianist" and demonstrating "the uncontrolled nervousness which is typical of artists." When he heard of the appointment of Trotsky to the head of the Red Army, de Man first imagined it as a "propaganda bluff," only to realize that leaders of revolutions should not be judged on the image one had of them in exile.[87]

Trotsky's Bohemian lifestyle in exile—both before and after 1917—reveals an intellectual antiauthoritarian and libertarian sensibility that strikingly differs from his conduct in power. Many articles he wrote as a journalist and a political émigré show how attracted he was by this artistic and literary trend. A certain libertarian spirit undoubtedly inspired his debate in 1904 against the Bolsheviks' centralism and Jacobinism, in which he sensed the symptoms of an authoritarian conception of Marxism and the dangers of a bureaucratic stifling of the revolutionary spontaneity of the masses.[88]

A similar striking contrast exists between his defense of "aesthetic nihilism" in the texts of his last Mexican exile and the essentially pedagogical vision of art he defended in 1923 in *Literature and Revolution*, going as far as to make a discreet apology for "revolutionary" censorship. In his famous manifesto "For a Revolutionary and Independent Art," written in 1938 with the collaboration of André Breton (and to which Diego Rivera added his signature), Trotsky launched the slogan "absolute freedom in art," and advocated among all the revolutionary tasks in the field of intellectual creation to "establish and secure from the start an anarchist régime of individual freedom. No authority, no constraint, not the slightest hint of command!"[89] This text was preceded by a lesser-known article, published in New York in the pages of the *Partisan Review*, where Trotsky denounced socialist realism as a symptom of Stalinist perversion in the USSR and expressed his own conception of the relationship between art and revolution. Revolution should help to revive the subversive spirit of "artistic Bohemia" he wrote, whence came all the avant-gardes, from Cubism to Futurism, from Dadaism to Surrealism, which bourgeois society had attempted to discipline and assimilate by making them climb the steps of the Academy.[90]

MOVEMENTS AND FIGURES

The examples of Marx, Courbet, Benjamin, and Trotsky could be multiplied. Many avant-garde artists, heretical Marxists, "professional revolutionaries," socialist intellectuals, and exiled antifascists experienced conditions of life similar to the Bohemian. All knew poverty, precarious juridical status, no fixed abode, all met and frequented different cultural and political circles, all discovered the marginality of the exiles, the cosmopolitan ghetto of the excluded and the stateless, the underground existence of conspirators, the total exclusion from official institutions, the occasional feeling of living in disconnection from the real world, but also the aesthetic, psychological, and intellectual freedom permitted by the lack of ties. Such a condition has not often been, as we have seen, the result of a conscious choice.

The characteristics of the Bohemian—with his love for adventure, but also with his tragic dimension—undoubtedly color the life of such a libertarian communist writer as Victor Serge, who had chosen his existence between the "Bonnot Gang" and Spanish anarchism, between Russian Bolshevism and the French literary salons, between the Komintern and the Siberian camps, and ended his life in exile in Mexico. His memoirs contain one of the most striking descriptions of Parisian anarchist Bohemia, at the beginning of the century, the picturesque multitude of people on the fringe who lived between Belleville and Montmartre, who were often also on the fringes of the law, who aspired to freedom and dignity and were constantly on the brink of going to prison.[91]

At the turn of the century, the American press often used the word "Bohemia" for Greenwich Village, in New York, where an artistic and literary avant-garde of "outsiders" had congregated, strongly attracted by anarchism and socialism. Their political radicalism was expressed in papers such as *The Masses* or *The Liberator*, which led a campaign of support for the struggles of seasonal workers organized by the Industrial Workers of the World (IWW). The Village Bohemians sometimes introduced themselves as the urban equivalents and the intellectuals of the "hobos," the homeless tramps who lived a permanent wandering life between the two American coasts. The most gripping testimony of this cosmopolitan literary avant-garde can be found in John Reed's reports. He had taken part in the Villa and Zapata Revolution, then in the Russian Revolution. If he owes his fame to *Insurgent Mexico* and *Ten Days Which Shook the World*, his articles on New York, collected on the eve of war in *The Day in Bohemia, or the Life Among the Artists*, should not be forgotten.[92]

To think of the relationship between Bohemia and revolution as a simple playful adventure, superficial and ephemeral, would be extremely restrictive: one might run the risk of not understanding its nature. Revolutions have often been the time (resulting from a transitory, ephemeral historical constellation) when Bohemia (or at least some of its components) has come out of its marginality, has abandoned its ghetto and embraced the forces in movement in society. It has found in revolution its natural accomplishment, as it has been one of the places for its spiritual preparation, its aesthetic anticipation, its utopian prefiguration, sometimes its intellectual elaboration and its political organization. Those who have been exiled and banished and have lost their fatherland stop swimming against the current and take their place in the center of the movement that strives to overthrow the dominant order. The installation of a new order will be able to do without them, will want them to settle, or will exclude them once more: postrevolutionary Russia will not have any Bohemians. It is in ephemeral significant moments, when it completes its *pars destruens*, where the task at hand is not the organization of society on new foundations, but the uncontrollable and irrepressible expression of all liberating drives, which has accumulated gradually through the years, that Bohemia meets revolution. But Bohemia can also become the melancholy realm where, behind the façade of the restored order, the vanquished retire and meditate on their defeat.

5 MARXISM AND THE WEST

ZEITGEIST

LIKE all classics, Marx both "transcends" his own time and remains a thinker of the nineteenth century. With an incredibly imaginative strength, he was able to grasp tendencies that, still embryonic in his epoch, developed spectacularly during the following century. This astonishing modernity has led many scholars to interpret his works in naïvely anachronistic terms, as if they had been written in our age. Marx contributed to the forging of our lexicon, but many concepts through which we today apprehend the nineteenth century—for instance, imperialism—simply did not exist during his lifetime, or did not have the same meaning we give them nowadays. This concerns particularly the concept of the "West," which in his era meant essentially Europe, with the exception of the Russian Empire; West and East were not yet geopolitical categories, as they would become in the years after 1945.[1]

Europe dominated the world, viewing itself as its economic and cultural core. In his lifetime, Marx observed the rise of the great European empires, which were conquering Asia and Africa, and passed away long before the advent of the American world hegemony, which took place only at the end of the First World War. The rule of Europe was historically transitional, but its economic, political, and military elites were not aware of that, nor were its intellectuals. To blame Marx for his "Eurocentric" views means, in some way, to blame him for having lived in the nineteenth century and for having inscribed his thought in the intellectual and epistemic horizon of his time. There are two symmetrical misunderstandings that consist either in denying the Eurocentric dimension of his work, as many devotees obstinately do, or in stigmatizing it with a retrospective, completely anachronistic wisdom.

Belonging to the zeitgeist of the nineteenth century, Marx's Eurocentrism shapes his theoretical works as well as his articles devoted to contemporary events. In a well-known passage of *The Communist Manifesto* (1848), Marx and Engels depicted capitalism as both a system of exploitation of man by man and a historical progress driving civilization forward through an extraordinary growth of the forces of production. Thanks to its development, capitalism destroyed feudal societies, created a world market, and unified the planet, submitting it to the law of profit. Highly cosmopolitan, it generated a world after its own image and crushed prejudices, narrow cultures, and different forms of obscurantism inherited from the past. The world market resulted in the "universal inter-dependence of nations" and created a "world literature." But capitalism also engendered its own gravediggers because its economic cosmopolitanism was the material basis of proletarian internationalism, the project of an emancipated society, made of free and equal human beings on a global scale. In other words, socialism carried on the "revolutionary" role played by the bourgeoisie when it appeared on the stage of history. Capitalism, Marx wrote, "draws all, even the most barbarian, nations into civilization," compelling them to "introduce what it calls civilization." A crucial passage of *The Communist Manifesto* presented the bourgeoisie as a vector of progress: "Just as it has made the country dependent on the towns, so it has made barbarian and semi-barbarian countries dependent on the civilized ones, nations of peasants on nations of bourgeois, the East on the West."[2] In another equally famous passage in his preface to *A Contribution to the Critique of Political Economy* (1859), Marx depicted universal history in teleological terms as an enchainment of evolutionary stages: "In broad outline, the Asiatic, ancient, feudal and modern bourgeois modes of production may be designated as epochs marking progress in the economic development of society."[3] Similarly, in his preface to *Capital* (1867), he sketched an evolutionary scheme of historical development in which "the country that is more developed industrially only shows, to the less developed, the image of its own future."[4]

It is known that, in his writings on Russia of the second half of the 1870s, Marx nuanced his assessments. Responding to one of his Russian critics, he warned against the transformation of his "historical sketch of the genesis of capitalism in Western Europe into an historico-philosophic theory of the general development, imposed by fate on all peoples, whatever the historical circumstances in which they are placed." In other words, his historical description of capitalist accumulation was not a compelling narrative "whose supreme virtue consists in being supra-historical."[5] Rejecting such fatalism, he envisaged the possibility of a social revolution that, by transplanting modern socialism into the rural communities (*obshchiny*) of the traditional Slavic world, would avoid in Russia the misfortunes experienced by Western Europe during the period of primitive capital accumulation. This hypothesis, nevertheless, was quite exceptional. On the one hand, it depended on the peculiar conditions of Russia, where ancient communitarian forms still survived. On the other hand, it supposed a social revolution in the West, as he clearly indicated at the end of his life: once in the grasp of "the bosom of the capitalist regime," Russia could no longer escape from capital's "pitiless laws [*unerbittlichen Gesetze*]."[6] A few years later Engels recognized that Russia had lost such a "great historical chance"[7] and the Russian Marxists, according to the compelling definition suggested by Sheila Fitzpatrick, "had fallen in love with Western-style industrialization."[8]

It is true that Marx nuanced his theory at the end of his life, rejecting the idea of a linear development of capitalism with its related teleological interpretations of history. His observations, nevertheless, were formulated mostly in letters or occasional articles published by newspapers and marginal journals. This was not enough to impede, in the following years, the emergence of a positivistic Marxist philosophy of history whose doctrinal codification was to be assured by Karl Kautsky, the "pope" of the Second International. A subtle and rigorous scholar like Kevin Anderson is certainly right in observing that, especially in his late writings, Marx developed a "dialectical theory of social change that was neither unilinear nor exclusively class-based," putting into question the evolutionism and the "traces of ethnocentrism" of *The Communist Manifesto.*[9] The problem is that whereas Anderson very carefully reads many minor texts, he tends to neglect the most important ones mentioned above, which his disciples, at the end of the nineteenth century, transformed into a doctrine. In fact, there is a tension haunting the corpus of Marx's writings between a multilinear and a continual, a dialectic and a positivistic vision of history, both coexisting as two contradictory tendencies or "temptations." As his homage to Darwin in the preface to *Capital* eloquently proves, Marx did not escape the ambition to produce a "science of society," an ambition that so deeply obsessed his age.

HEGELIAN SOURCES

The Hegelian matrix of these passages of *The Communist Manifesto, A Contribution to the Critique of Political Economy*, and *Capital* is quite evident (as admitted by Marx himself in his text of 1859). In *The Philosophy of History* (1830), Hegel drew a great historical picture of humankind in which the Western world appeared as its natural accomplishment. "The Sun—the Light—rises in the East," he wrote, trying to capture in an image, through a naturalistic metaphor, "the course of the whole historical process [*der Gang der Weltgeschichte*], the great Day's work of Spirit [*das grosse Tagewerk des Geistes*]." World history, Hegel added, "travels from East to West, for Europe is absolutely the end of History, Asia is the beginning."[10] Depicted as "the childhood of History," the East was, in his eyes, incapable of any evolution. It was "unhistorical" [*geschichtlos*], condemned to perpetuate the same "majestic ruin."[11]

According to Hegel, history was the process through which Spirit became conscious of itself, and this self-realization had a double dimension concerning both space and time. Its rational character was embodied by the Western world, that is, Europe, the place where Spirit revealed itself. The cleavage separating prehistory from history was not only chronologically but also geographically recognizable, because it divided Europe (civilization) from the extra-European world (barbarism). This dichotomy was the motor of universal history that, finally, coincides with the triumph of the West over the "peoples without history." As Ranajit Guha suggests in his interpretation of Hegel, starting in the epoch of

Columbus, Europe became aware of itself—and underwent a journey of self-discovery—through a movement in which the lineages of the intercontinental space coincided with those of universal time, geography with history.[12] As telos of universal history, the West spoke in the name of the world, including it dialectically into its own movement. The state accomplished civilization, merging geography, history, and politics into a single unity. Since the East simply exhibited its immutable features, the West had integrated it into universal history. Several scholars have interpreted the Hegelian dialectic as a mimesis of colonialism: the sublation of world-historical contradictions by a movement that simultaneously removes and conserves them (*Aufhebung*) simply translates, onto a conceptual level, the movement of expropriation and incorporation displayed by the colonial conquests of Europe.[13] In short, colonialism is inscribed into the epistemic horizon of European modernity.[14]

Of course, Marx did not simply "reverse" (in materialistic rather than idealistic terms) Hegel's historicism, and his works contain many arguments against a teleological vision of history and deterministic causality. Capitalism did not appear to him as an economic mechanism generated by compelling rules, but rather as a system of social relations whose history was shaped by conflict. Its advent implied new forms of property, the commodification of work, and the dismantlement of a system of existing social practices and customs that could not occur without clashes. In other words, the rise of capitalism could not be conceived of as a "natural" transition.[15] Often cataclysmic, its history was molded by a violence that the chapter of *Capital* on primitive capitalist accumulation described with tragic accents. On the other hand, Marx defended a humanistic conception of history as a field of potentialities and possibilities, the field of class straggle, the privileged sphere of action where the future was built, far from any teleology, without being written in advance.[16] History did not follow a straight road; it was made of ruptures and bifurcations. Finally, progress was neither engendered by "natural" laws nor barely identified with the development of productive forces; it was not conceived as a goal in itself but rather as the material base for satisfying the needs of an emancipated society. Thus, many "Marxs" coexisted in the same work: an apologist of industry who admired the "revolutionary" role of the bourgeoisie, whose material achievements, according to the famous formula of *The Communist Manifesto*, went far beyond the Egyptian pyramids, the Roman aqueducts, and Gothic cathedrals; and a Romantic thinker "disenchanted" by technology, fascinated by preindustrial societies and the egalitarianism of primitive communities.[17]

EMPIRES

What matters most here is that such a romantic and antievolution- ist Marx is exactly the same Marx who wrote on colonialism and the "Orient." According to the author of *Capital,* catastrophe and progress, oppression and liberation went together, in the framework of an eco- nomic system transforming all technical and scientific progress into social regression: the proletariat alone possessed the lever for sublat- ing these contradictions and establishing an emancipated society. This revolutionary dialectics, nevertheless, remained a prerogative of the in- dustrial societies of the West. Marx thought socialism in universalistic terms but—prisoner of the idea of a "civilizing mission" so typical of the nineteenth century—he never broke with its implicit Western para- digm. It is not difficult to perceive in this historical picture the optimism of the Enlightenment as well as a typically nineteenth-century Euro- centric view. Intimately believing in the Promethean accomplishments disclosed by the advent of industrial capitalism, Marx announced the *Verbürgerlichung der Welt,* attributing to the bourgeoisie an imaginary "revolutionary" role.

Nineteenth-century Europe still remained, to a very large extent, a rural continent. It certainly experienced an epoch of modernization, but its transformations had been neither rapid nor homogeneous. For many decades, the industrial revolution was relegated to England and a few other regions of Western Europe; machines and factories were small islands in a rural landscape and industrial capitalism did not dominate the European economy until the 1880s, and in many countries only in partial and incomplete forms. On the political level, the end of the Old Regime did not create modern states provided with representative in- stitutions and controlled by emerging industrial and financial elites. In other words, the nineteenth century did not produce a new dominant bourgeois state, according to the classical Marx's definition, quickly transformed by Marxists into a canonical formula. It rather produced different hybrid forms between an ascending (but not yet ruling) bourgeoisie and an aristocracy still permeating state institutions. Absolutism was over but the Old Regime "persisted," as convincingly argued Arno J. Mayer.[18] Aristocracy remained a model for the new social and economic elites and established symbiotic relationships with them. According to Jürgen Osterhammel, the word "bourgeois" designated quite indistinctly "respectable" people—those wearing gloves—rather than a class of capitalist businessmen. Thus, any member of a liberal profession was "bourgeois."[19] The first half of the "long" nineteenth century was even, as many historians have highlighted, a kind of "golden October" for slave owners.[20] As a result of this link between bourgeoisie and aristocracy, conservative liberalism feared—not to say hated—democracy, in which it saw a form of anarchism and the "era of crowds." Far from being a natural corollary of liberalism and the market, according to the common view, democracy would be the outcome of more than a century of political struggles. Nineteenth-century "democracies" could be defined, as Domenico Losurdo insightfully suggests, as *Herrenvolk* democracies: representative assemblies reserved to a minority of lords, strictly delimited by *class, gender,* and *race* boundaries, in which laboring classes, women, and colonized peoples were rigorously excluded from any form of citizenship. In short, elections simply concerned white, male property owners.[21] The "bourgeois" classes shaped the world in their own image, but their historical role certainly had been more Thermidorian than "revolutionary."

In the twentieth century, Marxism recognized the colonized peoples as political actors, attributing to them the dialectical task of "negating" imperialism. This was not yet the perspective of Marx. He considered the colonial world as the periphery of the West, the only force that, in the last analysis, determined its evolution. It was a subjugated world whose revolt—even morally justified—was condemned to fail because of both its social weakness and its regressive or immature political orientation. The reader of the British Museum was unable to recognize the existence of historical subjects in the colonial world simply because his epistemic horizon did not allow him such a change of focus. Marx's socialism was born in a time in which the industrial proletariat of Western Europe began to act as a class for itself (*für sich*), that is, as a conscious actor in history. He lived in London, surrounded by chimneys and commodities, a place where the echoes of the Haitian Revolution seemed almost extinguished.

The intuition of the emancipatory potential of the colonized peoples sometimes arises from his correspondence, in the form of isolated observations. For instance, his writings on the American Civil War reveal an intransigent abolitionism—well testified by the letter he sent to Lincoln in 1864 in the name of the International Workingmen's Association—but they approach the question of slavery exclusively from the point of view of its ineluctable conflict with industrial capitalism. In some of his letters to Engels, on the contrary, Marx expressed his hope to see a slave rebellion—especially after the execution of John Brown—and emphasized the impact that the creation of an army of black soldiers could have had in the pursuit of war. In January 1860, he even imagined the junction between a rebellion of American slaves and a peasant uprising against Russian serfdom, a convergence that would have meant a historical turn on an international scale: "Thus, a 'social' movement has been started both in the West and in the East. Together with the impending breakdown in Central Europe, this promises great things."[22] Such expectation, nevertheless, was not fulfilled.

"PEOPLES WITHOUT HISTORY"

In many articles, Marx and Engels endorsed the Hegelian conception of the "peoples without history" (*geschichtlose Völker*). Engels explicitly quoted the German philosopher in an article written in 1849 for the *Neue Rheinische Zeitung*, the democratic newspaper led by Marx during the revolution in Germany. In his view, the Slavic nations of Southern Europe were condemned to disappear as "relics of a nation mercilessly trampled under foot in the course of history." They were, "as Hegel says, residual fragments of peoples."[23] In 1848, Engels argued that they had supported the Tsarist reaction and contrasted the historical movement of civilization going from East to West. He reaffirmed this idea in 1891, four years before his death, when he highlighted the cleavage between "Western progress" and "Eastern barbarism."[24]

A similar vision inspired Marx's articles on China and India written in the 1850s for the *New York Daily Tribune*, in which the stigmatization of the violence of colonialism did not put into question the legitimacy of British imperial conquest in the name of a superior civilization. According to Marx, "Indian society had no history at all, at least no known history" because, in the last analysis, its history corresponds to the history of its rulers, "the successive intruders who founded their empires on the passive basis of that unresisting and unchanging society."[25] In spite of its hypocrisy, its egoistic purposes, and its inhumanity, the British Empire acted in India as an "unconscious tool of history." Its mission was double, at the same time destructive and regenerative: on the one hand, it had to demolish the ancient Asiatic society and, on the other hand, it had to lay "the material foundations of Western society in Asia."[26] In very similar terms, in 1848 Engels welcomed the defeat of emir Abd el-Kader, the leader of the Arabic resistance against French colonization, arguing that, in spite of the brutal methods displayed by General Bugeaud, "the conquest of Algeria was an important and fortunate fact for the progress of civilization."[27]

Needless to say that such a vision of the "Orient"—Asia and Africa—as a world of stagnation, immutable and paralyzed by centuries of lethargy, congenitally unable to produce innovation and a cumulative development, had a large intellectual pedigree. It was a commonplace for many Enlightenment and nineteenth-century thinkers who—from Montesquieu to John Stuart Mill, passing through Adam Smith and Hegel—defended the idea of "oriental despotism."[28] As Perry Anderson has convincingly argued, the concept of the "Asiatic mode of production" forged by Marx differed little from this paradigm.[29] The main feature of Asiatic societies, the latter wrote in *Capital*, lay in their "unchangeableness" (*Unveränderlichkeit*).[30] The concept of an Asiatic mode of production gathered different elements—the lack of land property, the persistence of village communities, an autarchic rural economy, and an irrigation system managed by a centralized bureaucratic authority (the "hydraulic State")—whose correlation was not proved. It could not apprehend geographic, economic, and political contexts as different as China, India, Japan, and the Ottoman Empire. Perhaps in Marx's vision, as Harry Harootunian suggests, the Asiatic mode of production was "more a methodological device than a completed historical and empirical reality,"[31] but it remained the prism through which he interpreted both Asian history and the role of British colonialism in the nineteenth century.

As Mike Davis lucidly pointed out, Marx shared the optimism of many mid-Victorian observers concerning both the quickness and the consequences of the "railroad revolution" in India.[32] Reread more than a century and a half later, his assessments of the "Orient" appear disturbingly closer to an apologist of imperialism like David Landes than to an anti-Eurocentric anthropologist like Jack Goody. In other words, Marx inclined toward a vision of Western domination as a providential destiny.[33] The historical debate on the origins of the European *Sonderweg* is certainly not yet closed, but most scholars share the idea that nothing in Confucianism, Shintoism, or Islam prevented the rise of capitalism. Today, European hegemony appears historically transitional and relative, whereas cultural explanations of Asiatic backwardness have been abandoned in the last decades in light of the economic boom of China and India, relativizing the vision of Japanese exceptionality. The myth of an Asiatic "immutability" is perfectly symmetrical to the myth of a European *Sonderweg*, which is nothing but an old teleological pitfall. According to a world historian and Asia specialist like Christopher Bayly, Europe's transitory hegemony was the product of the accumulation of multiple elements already existing—even separately—in different parts of the world. He thinks that Europe paradoxically benefited from its historical backwardness due to the wars of the seventeenth and eighteenth centuries. Between the Thirty Years War and the Seven Years War, the continent experienced a military revolution that laid down the premises for the imperialism of the nineteenth century. Bayly synthesizes the historical change produced by weapons' destructiveness, transport routes, military logistics, and medical protection through a simple but incisive formula: "Europeans became much better at killing people."[34] There is no doubt that Marx would have shared such a statement.

VIOLENCE AND REBELLION

Of course, acting as "an unconscious tool of history" by laying in India the material basis of Western civilization (schools, rational administration, railways, and a modern system of production) did not absolve the British Empire of its crimes, and Marx condemned them with the most severe words. In 1853 he compared the "human progress" introduced by colonialism in India to a "hideous, pagan idol, who would not drink the nectar but from the skulls of the slain."[35] Two chapters of the first volume of *Capital* (31 and 33) are entirely devoted to describing the violence and brutality shaping the primitive accumulation of capital. In the wake of religious thinkers like the Quaker William Howitt, the author of *Colonization and Christianity* (1838), Marx painted an absolutely terrifying historical landscape. He enumerated the horrors of capitalism—"the discovery of gold and silver in America, the extirpation, enslavement and entombment in mines of the aboriginal population, the beginning of the conquest and looting of the East Indies, the turning of Africa into a warren for the commercial hunting of black-skins"—in which he recognized the "rosy dawn of the era of capitalist production."[36]

Today, historians depict the devastating consequences of colonialism in Asia, Africa, and the Americas, as "genocides" or "late Victorian holocausts." Even those who prefer to avoid such concepts must recognize that imperial conquest produced everywhere a "political, social, and biological destabilization," engendering in many cases a new "ecology of disease."[37] The result was an enormous demographic collapse in Asia and Africa, not to speak of the Oceanic islands. As a dialectical reverse side of "Progress," such a demographic catastrophe was the result of a colonial *governmentality*—we could say in Foucaldian terms—through which imperialism ruled territories and populations. In the wake of Karl Polanyi, Mike Davis has convincingly explained that the dozens of millions of deaths due to Indian famines in the second half of the nineteenth century were caused by the free market of grain combined with the destruction of the traditional Indian village communities.[38] Marx had understood the existence of an organic link between such a human Apocalypse and capital accumulation, but he could not explain it outside of a dialectical—and teleological—historicism.

As an inheritor of Rousseau and Kant, Marx rooted his critique of colonialism in the philosophy of Enlightenment. He radically departed from the racist vulgate of his time that, far from being limited to Gobineau and Galton, contaminated many socialist thinkers, such as Cesare Lombroso.[39] In the history of colonialism, Marx argued, humanity and morality clearly stay on the side of the ruled, but such evidence did not allow them to reverse the course of history, which was decided in Western Europe. Colonialism simply revealed, in a ruthless way, the dialectic of history: a process in which progress prevailed as a cortege of victors made of blood and oppression. This was a tragedy in which colonized peoples deserved compassion but could not pretend to be recognized as historical subjects. Their resistance too had to be viewed with a legitimate suspicion. As we have seen, Engels considered Abd el-Kader the leader of "a nation of robbers" accustomed to pillage and massacre. Marx's opinion on Simon Bolivar, the hero of Latin America's independence wars, was not much more laudatory. In an article published in 1859 by the *New American Cyclopaedia*, he described him as a caricature of Napoleon Bonaparte, "the most dastardly, most miserable and meanest of blackguards." (Such an assessment established the premises for a "missed encounter" between Marxism and Latin-American culture that lasted for almost a century.)[40] In India, the Sepoy Uprising of 1857 was the mirror of Hinduism, a religion that had cultivated the art of torture since its origins. According to Marx, the "horrid mutilations" inflicted by the rebels on the British—cutting off noses and breasts— were the consequence of a colonial violence that had established torture as a form of government (raped women, spitted children, burned villages). Such resentment and fury by the colonized people, nevertheless, were sterile and did not offer any social or political alternative.[41] The Taiping rebellion, the deepest and most extended social uprising of the nineteenth century, inspired more fear in Marx than empathy or admiration. Merging Confucianism and evangelical Christianity, this revolt arose against both traditional Chinese rule and the foreign occupation of the coasts, in the name of strong egalitarian aspirations, but it did not offer sufficient warranties to the defenders of Western progress. Even depicting it as an authentic "popular war," Marx rejected its fanaticism and despised its fighters, only capable of "producing destruction in grotesquely detestable forms, destruction without any nucleus of new construction."[42] He was very skeptical with respect to their communist tendencies, which were as far from European socialism "as Chinese philosophy [is] in relation to Hegelian philosophy." It was true that, according to Marx, the second Opium War seemed to put into question the "progressive" goal of the first one—"opening trade with China"— but that did not change his negative judgment on the revolt, a judgment in which even a generous critic like Kevin Anderson is compelled to perceive "an air of ethnocentric condescension."[43] Of course, the Taiping rebellion revealed the agony of "the oldest empire in the world," but it could not represent the dawn of "a new era for all Asia."[44] Such a task belonged to the West.

TENSIONS

As many historians have highlighted, in the 1870s the Irish question changed Marx and Engels's ideas on colonialism. In their eyes, the British rule in Ireland was the key to explaining the passivity and impotence of the English working class: a people oppressing other people cannot be free and, by consequence, the English proletariat should support the national liberation of Ireland in order to defend its own interests.[45] The authors of *The Communist Manifesto*, however, did not extend this conclusion to the extra-European world. In their anthropological studies—notably Engels's *The Origin of the Family, Private Property and the State* (1884), based on his reading of *The Ancient Society* of Lewis H. Morgan (1877), as well as Marx's *Ethnological Notebooks* (1879–82)—they nuanced their analysis of the noncapitalist world, but did not change their view on the relationship between East and West.[46] This statement does not transform Marx into a naïve or cynical apologist of Western imperialism. A simple comparison of his writings on colonialism—even the most ambiguous and problematic—with those of the representatives of classical liberalism, from John Stuart Mill to Tocqueville, eloquently shows their radical discrepancies. Marx's vision of socialism was genuinely universal and his internationalism concerned humankind as a whole. Mill opened his celebrated essay *On Liberty* (1859) warning his readers against the illusion that such a concept could be extended to "those backward states of society in which the race itself may be considered as in its nonage." Despotism, he added, was "a legitimate mode of government in dealing with barbarians."[47] Tocqueville—often considered as the subtlest theoretician of modern liberalism—opened his masterwork *Democracy in America* (1835) explaining that "the Indians occupied [the continent] without possessing it." Providence had placed them there only temporarily, "for a season," because this huge and luxuriant continent was awaiting its legitimate owners: it "seemed but an empty cradle awaiting the birth of a great nation."[48] It is obvious that Marx's Eurocentric views could not be compared to such self-satisfied apologetics of colonialism.

According to Edward Said, Marx inscribed his thought into an *orientalist* horizon like most intellectuals and scholars of his time. He certainly did not investigate the extra-European world with the aim of its conquest and submission, but contributed to the invention of an imaginary "Orient" comforting a Western prejudice. If orientalism was a "style of thought based upon an ontological and epistemological distinction" between "the Orient" and "the Occident" defined as abstract and antipodal categories—superior/inferior, civilized/barbarian, advanced/backward, rational/irrational—Said suggests that Marx could legitimately be considered as one of its representatives, in spite of his emancipatory ideas. Marx's writings, he observed, "are perfectly fitted thus to a standard orientalist undertaking, even though Marx's humanity, his sympathy for the misery of people, are clearly engaged."[49] Perhaps the case of Marx reveals the limits of orientalism conceived as a homogeneous category including indiscriminately all the representatives of Western culture, from Flaubert to Verdi, from Marx to Weber.[50] Gilbert Achcar insightfully observes that Marx's orientalism was essentially epistemic, insofar as Eurocentrism was the intellectual horizon of his time; it was not *supremacist*, since he struggled against a hierarchical, fixed, and oppressive international order.[51]

AFTERMATHS

During the second half of the nineteenth century, anti-imperialism was much more radical among anarchists than among Marxists. Sketching a kind of cultural anthropology of the radical movements opposed to the first globalization, Benedict Anderson highlights this contrast. Differently from Marxist socialism focused on the Western, urban working class, and rooted in the industrialized and Protestant countries of continental Europe—primarily Germany—anarchism extended its influence into the rural, Orthodox, and Catholic countries of Eastern and Southern Europe. Anarchists welcomed the peasant rebellions of the "backward" countries and defended the rights of the peoples "without history." Unlike Marx, who lived as an exile in London—the capital of the British Empire and the heart of capitalism—they followed the wave of transoceanic migration. Bakunin was active in Russia, Germany, France, Spain, and Italy, and his disciple Errico Malatesta did not disdain living in Argentina. It was certainly easier for a Filipino writer and nationalist like José Rizal to establish contacts with Spanish, French, and

Italian anarchists as well as with the Cuban nationalist José Marti, rather than with Marxist socialists.[52]

As a German-Jewish exile, Marx observed the world of the nineteenth century with a peculiar lens, as both an insider and an outsider. He lived in London, but remained a marginal intellectual excluded from all established institutions, including academic ones. He analyzed the expansion of capitalism throughout the world, but did not perceive the signs of coming revolts in the colonies. As we have seen, he was more than skeptical with respect to the Chinese and Indian rebellions against imperialism. In his eyes, Simon Bolivar was an epigone of Napoleon, not the inheritor of the Haitian Revolution and a symbol of the liberation movements of Latin America. In fact, Marx neglected the Haitian Revolution and failed to see the abolition of slavery as a central issue of his time. It was C. L. R. James, a West Indian black intellectual, who published the first Marxist history of the Haitian Revolution, *The Black Jacobins* (1938), a book written both outside of academic institutions and official Marxism.[53] And it is for similar reasons that the Marxists ignored for decades the Mexican Revolution (until its discovery as an object of investigation by Adolfo Gilly, a historian who had passed through the experiences of the Bolivian and Cuban revolutions).[54] If communist parties could lead peasant revolutions in China and Vietnam, it is because their leaders—mostly urban intellectuals—departed from the inherited schemes of proletarian, Western socialism. It took the end of real socialism and the crisis of Fordism to rediscover the hidden history of the seamen struggles in the age of maritime capitalism preceding the industrial revolution. The modern representations of the proletariat as a European, industrial working class occulted the first experiences of solidarity, self-organization, and self-emancipation displayed in the Atlantic by the "many-headed hydra" comprising sailors, pirates and deported slaves.[55] Living in an age of machines and factories, Marx did not consider such experiences as significant for the future.

Finding the traces of an orientalist vision in Marx's writings, nevertheless, does not mean that he should be filed into the cabinet of nineteenth-century intellectual vestiges. After his death, several currents of social democracy adopted an openly "social-imperialist" approach and justified colonialism in the name of a European "civilizing mission." In 1904, the social democrats condemned the extermination of the

Herero in Southwestern Africa because such a violence and brutality—
they argued—had demeaned the Germans to the level of savage African tribes.[56] Other Marxist currents, on the other hand, adopted radical
forms of anticolonialism. If we simply depict Marx as a reluctant apologist of colonialism, his influence on the anti-imperialist movements
and revolutions of the twentieth century inevitably becomes an obscure
enigma. From the Russian Revolution to the Vietnam War, Marxism
became the theoretical framework of decolonization.[57] Many national
liberation movements displayed a Marxist flag and even postcolonialism
recognized among its inspirers a constellation of Marxist intellectuals
as different as C. L. R. James, W. E. B. Du Bois, and Frantz Fanon. The
myth of an immaculate Marx exempt from all Eurocentric tendencies is
as naïve and sterile as the perfectly symmetrical vision of a colonialist
(white, male, and European) Marx. Today, Dipesh Chakrabarty, one of
the most severe critics of Marxist historicism, does not wish to abandon
Marx and the categories inherited from European Enlightenment, without which it would be impossible to think political modernity. His idea
of "provincializing Europe" rather means their renewal "from and for
the margins."[58]

A MISSED DIALOGUE

Now, let us go ahead several decades and compare two thinkers who
embody the legacy of Marx. Adorno depicted the "dialectic of Enlightenment," abandoning the idea of progress and extracting from Marx's
theory of reification a critique of instrumental reason. His melancholy,
analytical gaze focused on Western totalitarianism and completely ignored the colonial world. C. L. R. James, on the other hand, scrutinized
modernity as imperial domination, shifting its core from the West to the
South and emphasizing the emancipatory potentialities of the colonized
subjects. Both of them developed and enriched some premises of Marx's
theory. Western Marxism and anticolonial Marxism, nevertheless, remained two separate intellectual continents.

The name of C. L. R. James never appears in the *Gesammelte Schriften*
of Theodor W. Adorno, or the name of the Frankfurt philosopher in
the impressive work of the author of *Black Jacobins*. Thus, it is quite
surprising to discover that they met a couple of times during the 1940s.[59]

They met for lunch in New York, near the New School for Social Research—probably thanks to their common friend Herbert Marcuse—when Manhattan was a crossroads between the trajectories of German-Jewish exiles and the Black Atlantic.[60] There is no doubt that it was a failed encounter, and we can legitimately suppose that they met only to acknowledge their mutual dislike and incomprehension. We should try to explain why a dialogue between them did not take place—why it was, perhaps, impossible—adding that nevertheless this wasted opportunity was damaging for both of them. We are compelled to think in terms of counterfactual intellectual history in order to imagine the possible results of a dialogue that did not take place.

In *Representations of the Intellectual*, Edward Said highlighted the affinities between Adorno and James,[61] presenting them as two examples of exiled intellectuals who shared a similar approach to history and society. Both of them, Said explained, were "contrapuntal" thinkers who rejected conformism and escaped canonical views: they immigrated to New York in 1938, at the edge of the war, and lived in America until the advent of McCarthyism. Adorno returned to Frankfurt in 1949, where the Institute for Social Research was resettled after the creation of the German Federal Republic, and James was expelled to London in 1952 after having been deported to Ellis Island for several months. We could speak of two reversed exiles: one exiled to the United States, the other from. In fact, they shared more than a common outsider status and a similar style of thought. In spite of many crucial discrepancies—from their vision of communism to their analysis of mass culture—they separately but symmetrically elaborated a similar diagnostic of Western civilization, depicting it as a process of the "self-destruction of reason."

In 1938, Adorno devoted a seminal essay to Spengler in which he analyzed *The Decline of the West* (1918) in the light of Nazism. Against the dominant interpretation that reduced this book to a monument of "cultural despair" oriented toward the romantic idealization of a premodern golden age of culture, Adorno considered it as a fruitful contribution to the explanation of the present crisis of Europe: "Spengler is one of the theoreticians of extreme reaction," he wrote in his essay, "whose critique of liberalism proved itself superior in many respects to the progressive one."[62] Beyond his morphological and naturalistic vision of the exhaustion of a vital cycle of Western civilization, finally dying as a sick, old body, Spengler announced the advent of a totalitarian order. He understood the dialectic relating technological and industrial progress to social reification and the dehumanization of the world. Of course, Adorno rejected Spengler's nationalism and conservatism but shared some elements of his diagnostic and suggested a "progressive" use of *Kulturkritik*. In his eyes, Spengler's book proved that all complaints about decadence and all denunciations of approaching barbarism were useless and sterile if they did not put into question civilization itself, not only its latest stage of decay: "To escape the charmed circle of Spengler's morphology it is not enough to defame barbarism and rely on the health of culture. Rather, it is the barbaric element in culture itself which must be recognized."[63]

In 1980, in an interview with the *Radical History Review*, James said that he became a Marxist at the beginnings of the 1930s through the influence of two books: Trotsky's *History of the Russian Revolution* (1932) and *The Decline of the West*. What he found in Spengler's book, he added, was precisely the need for a criticism of civilization as a whole: "It took me away from the individual and the battles, and the concern with the kind of things that I had learned in conventional history."[64] In 1940, writing on the great historians of the twentieth century, James hoped that "the fog of mysticism" pervading Spengler's book would not obscure its "colossal learning, capacity for synthesis and insight."[65] Of course, James was not fascinated by the political ideas of Spengler; he was attracted by his radical criticism of Western civilization. For a young intellectual who had been educated in the positivistic and pragmatic cultural atmosphere of the British Empire, the discovery of German *Kulturpessimismus* could bring new and fresh ideas.

In 1935, James became one of the outstanding figures of Pan-Africanism and the British movement against the Ethiopian War. Whereas Adorno reviewed the *Spenglerstreit* under the impact of Hitler's rise to power, James could not read it without relating its concept of civilization to the history of imperialism. On the one hand, Adorno concluded his essay with the evocation of a vague, abstract hope: "What can oppose the decline of the west is not a resurrected culture but the utopia that is silently contained in the image of its decline."[66] On the other hand, the alternative that James opposed to the collapse of civilization was neither abstract nor silent. He simply highlighted that Spengler's "tremendous volume" was completed in 1917, the year of the Russian Revolution.[67] Adorno's essay on Spengler was published in 1938, the same year in which James's *The Black Jacobins* came out. As he explained almost forty years later, he conceived this book on the Haitian Revolution in order to show the colonized people of Africa and the Caribbean as historical subjects: "instead of being constantly the object of other peoples' exploitation and ferocity, [they] would themselves be taking action on a grand scale and shaping other people to their own needs."[68]

As we know, the concept of "self-destruction of the reason" (*Selbstzerstörung der Vernunft*) is the core of Horkheimer and Adorno's *Dialectic of Enlightenment* (1947).[69] In this book written during the Second World War, they described the "regression" of bourgeois, civilized society into barbarism, but explained that such a process should not be interpreted as the result of the attack on civilization by the external forces of barbarism; it was rather the product of the dialectic of reason itself, reason interpreted as an instrumental rationality that had transformed progress into social regression and could only display itself as a form of domination. "Reason is totalitarian," they wrote, thus suggesting that Nazism—the totalitarian epilogue of the West—was a coherent and authentic product of civilization. In a fragment of *Minima Moralia* (1951), Adorno had also formulated this concept of the "self-destruction" of reason in teleological terms: the primitive and rough violence of the most ancient past, he explained, already implied the "scientifically organized violence" of Nazism.[70]

In 1949, two years after the publication of *Dialectic of Enlightenment*, Adorno and Horkheimer came back to Frankfurt. In 1952, James was deported to Ellis Island as an "undesirable alien" and after six months of internment he was expelled toward the United Kingdom. "I was an alien. I had no human rights," he wrote in terms strikingly reminiscent of Hannah Arendt's concept of "pariah": somebody who "has no right to have rights."[71] During this period of detention, James wrote *Mariners, Renegades and Castaways* (1953), an original, provocatively "anachronistic"—we could say with Ernst Bloch "non-contemporaneous"[72]—interpretation of Moby Dick in light of the twentieth century. According to James, this novel prefigured the social conflicts generated by industrial capitalism. He presented the Pequod, the ship in which Melville's story takes place, as an allegory of modern capitalist society. The Pequod's mariners symbolized the proletariat—a multinational working class mostly comprising colonial, non-White subjects (notably Queequeg, Tashtego, and Daggoo, the three "savage" harpooners)—whereas Captain Ahab embodied the bourgeoisie, obsessed by its desire to rule the world, even at the risk of their mutual destruction. In his struggle against the whale, Ahab was ready to sacrifice his ship and the crew, just as the dominant classes had driven the world toward totalitarianism. The mariners had a harmonious relationship with nature; they knew and respected nature instead of approaching it as "something to be conquered and used"; they were themselves the "very forces of Nature" and spontaneously considered man as part of nature, "physically, intellectually, and emotionally."[73] Ahab, on the contrary, wished to control and master nature. James described him as the embodiment of a modern rationality that does not develop knowledge and technology with an emancipatory purpose but instead only with an instrumental goal. In the eyes of Ahab, the mariners were not human beings but an anonymous mass, a reified matter he called "manufactured men."[74] The brutal and ferocious armed guard that protected him irresistibly evoked the SS. According to Melville's careful description of the process of labor on the ship—the mariners dismembered and stocked the whales in a very rational way, applying simultaneously multiple fragmented tasks—the Pequod appeared as a modern factory. As James observed:

> This world is our world—the world we live in, the world of the Ruhr, of Pittsburgh, of the Black County in England. In its symbolism of men turned into devils, of an industrial civilization on fire and plunging into darkness, it is the world of massed bombers, of cities in flames, of Hiroshima and Nagasaki, the world in which we live, the world of Ahab, which he hates and which he will organize or destroy.[75]

In short, read in the middle of the twentieth century, the message of Melville's novel was the transformation of liberal society into totalitarianism: "Melville's theme is totalitarianism, its rise and fall, its power and its weakness."[76] The third chapter of *Mariners, Renegades and Castaways* is titled "Catastrophe" and describes the final destruction of the whaleboat: a self-destruction, we could say, because it results from Ahab's obsession with power that is simultaneously *Promethean* (he believes in science and technology) and *totalitarian* (he does not know anything but domination). "The voyage of the Pequod," James writes, "is the voyage of modern civilization seeking its destiny."[77]

In a famous fragment from *Minima Moralia* (1951), Adorno depicted his idea of "negative dialectic" as those robot-bombs that combined "the utmost technical perfection with complete blindness," adding that such destructive weapons were the real image of the "world-soul [*Weltgeist*], not on horseback like Napoleon in Jena but on wings and without a head."[78] Hegel had seen the "world spirit" as progress, Adorno as catastrophe. He contemplated this spectacle of decadence with resignation and stoicism, adopting the posture of the meditating damned in Michelangelo's *Universal Judgment*.[79] In *Moby-Dick*, James suggests, this is the posture of Ishmael, the "intellectual" observing the self-destruction of reason. Contrary to Adorno, however, who replaced Hegel (and Weber) in the position of the observer, James did not identify with Ishmael, "the intellectual"; he identified with the crew. Ishmael, in James's interpretation, embodies the instability and hesitation of the intellectuals. He permanently swings between Ahab and the crew, attracted by both, but finally succumbing to Ahab: "his submission to the totalitarian madness was complete."[80] In *Mariners, Renegades, and Castaways*, the cataclysm leading to totalitarianism is described from the point of view of the crew, the "anonymous crew," whose members like Queequeg, thanks to their "nobility of spirit" and harmonious relation with both nature and other human beings, "embodied the mystery of the universe and the attainment of truth."[81]

This epistemological discrepancy explains the different conclusions that Adorno and James drew from a similar diagnostic of modernity. It could eventually be related to a different reading of Hegel and Marx, their common intellectual background. The Frankfurt philosopher had virtually abandoned any hope of a possible sublation of the conflicts of modern civilization: the contradiction between productive forces and property relations could only result in a reinforcement of domination. The "revolt of nature" against instrumental reason—a theme further elaborated by Horkheimer[82]—could not break the boundaries of domination and became the ground for totalitarianism.[83] Not departing from a classical Marxist interpretation of Hegel, James believed in the role of the proletariat as the redeemer of history. Like Lukács, he stressed the "negation of the negation" in the dialectical historical process but also enlarged the definition of proletariat, including the colonized peoples.[84] Of course, this entailed a change in the historical perspective.

The German-Jewish exiles of the Frankfurt School very soon transformed Auschwitz into a metaphor of totalitarianism and the unveiled
epilogue of civilization. James considered the violence of fascism and
Nazism as the result of a transfer into Europe of a wave of systematic
destruction and oppression that had already been experimented with in
the colonial world. In the "Prologue" to the first edition of *Black Jacobins* (1938), he clearly alluded to fascism and Nazism in describing the
colonization of Haiti:

> The Spaniards, the most advanced Europeans of their day, annexed
> the island, called it Hispaniola, and took the backward natives under
> their protection. They introduced Christianity, forced labor in mines,
> murder, rape, bloodhounds, strange diseases, and the artificial famine
> (by the destruction of cultivation to starve the rebellious). These and
> other requirements of the higher civilization reduced the native popula-
> tion from an estimated half-a-million, perhaps a million, to 60,000 in
> 15 years.[85]

There is no doubt that he would have shared Fanon's description of Nazism as "the whole of Europe transformed into a veritable colony."[86]
But the process of colonization and extermination ultimately resulted in
revolution, and James clearly admitted that his book had been written
with a retrospective gaze in which the revolutions of the present enlightened those of the past. He wished to describe the Haitian Revolution
as a grandiose, artistic painting, but his own time did not allow him to
escape from politics: "The violent conflicts of our age enable our practiced vision to see into the very bones of previous revolutions more easily than heretofore. Yet for that very reason it is impossible to recollect
historical emotions in the tranquility which a great English writer, too
narrowly, associated with poetry alone."[87] In such conditions, tranquility would have been a form of philistinism.

It would be a simplification to describe the discrepancy between
Adorno and James in terms of political pessimism versus political optimism. We could find in many pages of *Mariners, Renegades and Castaways* the equivalent of Adorno's almost teleological vision of Auschwitz
as the achievement of the dialectic of Enlightenment. James was not a
naïve defender of the idea of "progress" and he never thought of socialism or liberation as the ineluctable outcome of history. He shared

Adorno's conception of a "negative universal history,"[88] as well as his attempt to save—through the critique of instrumental reason—the emancipatory potentialities of Enlightenment itself. Differently from Adorno, nevertheless, he did not conceive the dialectic of Enlightenment only as unfolded domination but also as a process of conflicts and struggles. Confronted with the reality of fascist counter-Enlightenment, he defended a form of radical Enlightenment and radical cosmopolitanism or, to put it in Marx-Hegelian terms, of "universalism from below."[89] We cannot ignore the different positions of Adorno and James at the moment of their missed dialogue, a difference that could be related to the crossroad of the opposed paths of the Jewish-German exile and the Black Atlantic. It was more than a political or a cultural difference; it was a mental, psychological, and existential difference: the Holocaust entered the historical consciousness of the West when the end of the Second World War announced a new wave of colonial revolutions. Paul Buhle elegantly synthetized the reasons for such a discrepancy: listening to the Frankfurt philosophers, James "found them interesting, but by no means compelling. They dwelt upon the collapse of the West. James sought the fragments of redemption."[90]

Adorno probably remained skeptical as well in front of his Caribbean interlocutor. Almost nothing in the cultural background of the German philosopher predisposed him to express the slimmest curiosity about a defender of popular culture such as James. As an aristocratic Marxist "mandarin" affected by an incurable phobia of images and popular music, which he always reduced to manifestations of the culture industry, if he did not interpret them—as he did with jazz—as the aesthetic dimension of the authoritarian personality, Adorno could not understand the cultural concerns of an internationally recognized specialist of cricket like C. L. R. James. James did not ignore the reified form of modern culture and warned against the alienating, dehumanizing tendencies of the culture industry, but could not accept an elitist retreat into the boundaries of the aesthetic avant-garde. As he wrote in *American Civilization* (1950), "In modern popular art, film, radio, television, comic strip, we are headed for some such artistic comprehensive integration of modern life, that the spiritual, intellectual, ideological life of modern peoples will express itself in the closest and most rapid, most complex, absolutely free relation to the actual life of the citizens tomorrow."[91] We don't know if he had read Kracauer's *Theory of Film* (1960), but he certainly approved of the idea—radically rejected by Adorno—at the core of this book, that "many a commercial film or television production is a genuine achievement besides being a commodity," and that, consequently, "germs of new beginnings may develop through a completely alienated environment."[92]

In James's view, this dialectical tension between alienation and liberation also concerned the realm of sport. In *Beyond a Boundary* (1963), he opposed the cricket practiced as an entertainment for the British elite to the cricket played by the blacks of Trinidad, which reflected their search for freedom. Two great cricket players—the Australian batsman Sir Donald Bradman and the Caribbean star Matthew Bondman, a white and a black man—embodied these different cultures. The first one had achieved his records by applying to the game the codes of a "bourgeois rationality"—we could say an "instrumental rationality"—whereas the second one played cricket as a sport expressing a moral as well as an aesthetic behavior. His way of practicing cricket revealed a different rationality related to an African culture.[93]

PARTING WAYS

Finally, we might legitimately ask whether such a missed dialogue was not the symptom of a *colonial unconscious* of classical critical theory, at least in the early Frankfurt School. Adorno's violent rejection of jazz was certainly inspired by his criticism of mass culture; nevertheless, it revealed an implicit perception of African American culture as a form of barbarism. *Dialectic of Enlightenment* interpreted universal history as a process of domination and oppression from Antiquity to the twentieth century, but did not include any reference to the history of colonialism. Colonialism does not appear in the exploration of nineteenth-century French culture of Benjamin's *Arcades Project*, or in his texts on fascism, where he quoted a pamphlet by Marinetti written as a propaganda text during the Ethiopian War.[94] And even Benjamin's article on Surrealism did not mention its anticolonial commitment, one of the principal political concerns of this avant-garde movement.[95] Benjamin's only anticolonial text is a short review of a French book on Bartolomé de Las Casas he wrote in 1929 for *Die Literarische Welt*.[96] In other words, the scholars of the Frankfurt School had not been able to break the epistemic horizon of Marx; this was the colonial unconscious of critical theory. Their antifascism rejected biological racism, whose most radical expression was anti-Semitism, but remained silent on colonialism. Only Marcuse changed his views on this matter, in the wake of the movement against the Vietnam War in the United States. In his "Political Preface" (1966) to the second edition of *Eros and Civilization*, he stressed that the opulence and illusory freedom—a form of "repressive sublimation"— of the advanced industrial societies was "transforming the earth into hell. The inferno is still concentrated in certain far away places: Vietnam, the Congo, South Africa, and in the ghettos of the 'affluent society': in Mississippi and Alabama, in Harlem. These infernal places illuminate the whole." In the same text, Marcuse compared the massacres perpetrated by the US army to the Nazi genocides, evoking the "photographs that show a row of half naked corpses laid out for the victors in Vietnam: they resemble in all details the pictures of the starved, emasculated corpses of Auschwitz and Buchenwald."[97] The idea of such a comparison never crossed the minds of Adorno and Horkheimer.

Inscribing this missed dialogue between Adorno and James into the broader question of the relationship between Marxism and the West, one could interpret it taking into account their different connections with the three dominant currents of Marxism in the 1930s and the 1940s: *classical*, *Western*, and *Black* Marxism. In the first half of the twentieth century, classical Marxism still existed as a theory of revolution embodied in a variety of tendencies (Lenin, Luxemburg, Trotsky, Pannekoek, and the like). Its exhaustion coincided with the Stalinization of the international communist movement. Its core was Europe and its cultural background was Eurocentric, but it announced, in the wake of the Russian Revolution, a new wave of struggles against imperialism. Tracing the genealogy of postcolonialism, Robert Young designates the Congress of the Peoples of the East, which took place in Baku in 1920, as one of its premises.[98] According to Perry Anderson, Western Marxism was born in the 1920s from the defeat of the revolutions that followed the Great War. It corresponded with the advent of Stalinism in the USSR and the rise of fascism in Western Europe. Skeptical with respect to the revolutionary potentialities of the laboring classes, Western Marxism neglected history, economics, and politics to withdraw into philosophy and aesthetics. Of course, we should not underestimate the very heterogeneous character of Western Marxism, in which Gramsci and Adorno coexisted, but Anderson's definition captures quite well the general orientation of the Frankfurt School.[99] Beside these two currents, there was a third, still marginal one, embodied in a variety of black intellectuals (West Indians like C. L. R. James, African Americans like W. E. B. Du Bois, those from the French Caribbean like Aimé Césaire) who reinterpreted Marxism, focusing on the question of racial and colonial oppression. In their view, race was as central as class and colonialism was as crucial as industrialism in the history of capitalism. The historian Cedric Robinson named this current *Black Marxism*, "not a variant of Western radicalism whose proponents happen to be Black," but rather a displacement of Marxist theory from *class* to *race* (from Europe to the colonial world).[100] The most significant innovation introduced by this intellectual current concerned the interpretation of slavery. Instead of considering slavery as the vestige of an archaic mode of production—eventually related to the "primitive accumulation" of capitalism, as Marx suggested in *Capital*— W. E. B. Du Bois, C. L. R. James, and Eric Williams stressed its modernity, defining slave labor as a fundamental dimension of capitalism: it accompanied the process of modernization of Europe as well as its economic expansion and the establishment of its first global hegemony. This is also the reason that they refused to consider capitalism as a "progressive" stage of human history.[101]

In this triangle, a dialogue was possible between classical and Black Marxism (James was a Trotskyist and Du Bois a member of the Communist Party), eventually between classical and Western Marxism (we could think of Gramsci, Lukács, and Korsch), but it was much more difficult between Western and Black Marxism. The obstacle to such a dialogue was the blindness of the former in front of colonialism. Thus, Western Marxism is an extremely pertinent concept, even if its original definition—formulated by Perry Anderson in the middle of the 1970s— did not refer to the Eurocentric dimension of the Frankfurt School or the French and Italian communist culture.[102]

In conclusion, we might come back to the counterfactual hypothesis formulated above: What could have produced a fruitful, rather than a missed, encounter between Adorno and James or, putting the question in broader terms, between the first generation of critical theory and Black Marxism? It probably would have changed the culture of the New Left and that of Third Worldism. The Frankfurt School would have overcome its Eurocentric boundaries and the colonial revolutions would have approached the question of development with different paradigms. Perhaps *Dialectic of Enlightenment* would have been discussed at an international conference in Havana in the 1960s. The second generation of the Frankfurt School would not have exclusively focused on topics such as public space and communicative action, but also on the critique of capitalism and globalization. Postcolonial studies, on their own, would not have reduced Marxism to a simple Eurocentric worldview and would have been more than a "critical discourse" founded on textual rather than historical bases.[103] Of course, counterfactual interpretations do not change history, but they help to see what went wrong. Several decades after this missed encounter between Adorno and James, Western Marxism and Postcolonial studies merged under the sign of defeat. The former was born from the failure of revolution in the 1930s—Stalinism and fascism—and the latter emerged on the ashes of the colonial revolutions, buried in the mass graves of Pol Pot's Cambodia. Their common field became the academy, where critical thought found a haven, far from the sound and the fury of the past century. History is made of missed encounters, of lost opportunities that leave the bitter taste of melancholia.

⑥ ADORNO AND BENJAMIN

LETTERS AT MIDNIGHT IN THE CENTURY

TESTIMONIES

DEEPLY shaped by the presentiment of an impending catastrophe, the dialogue between Adorno and Benjamin depicts a melancholy constellation. In a previous chapter, we have already observed the ambivalent assessments of Benjamin on melancholy, as they appear in both his book on the German tragic drama and his strongly critical review of Erich Kästner's novels. Now, it is important to emphasize the melancholic character of Benjamin himself. According to many witnesses, melancholy was his deepest disposition; it also explains his fascination with *Angelus Novus*, the Paul Klee painting that he acquired in Munich at the beginning of the 1920s, which inspired his famous ninth thesis on the concept of history, where the past is depicted as a landscape of ruins.[1] Adorno, for his part, considered Benjamin's "melancholy gaze" a sort of methodology, an incurable "sadness" (*Trauer*) combining Jewish apocalyptic visions with "the antiquarian tendency to see the present transformed into the ancient past, as if by enchantment."[2] And Benjamin himself, in a highly enigmatic fragment written in Ibiza in August

1933, "Agesilaus Santander," stressed "the fact that [he] was born under the sign of Saturn—the planet of slow revolution, the star of hesitation and delay."[3] He drew his melancholy all over the years of his Paris exile, until his suicide in Port Bou, in September 1940.

Adorno's melancholy gaze, on the other hand, was neither antiquarian nor apocalyptical. Rather than in his letters to Benjamin, it came out in his postwar works, where he contemplated with sadness and resignation a catastrophe that had already taken place. It was the melancholy of a critical mind in front of a world irremediably wounded by violence. In 1950, he gathered his "reflections from damaged life" under the sign of a "melancholy science" (*traurige Wissenshaft*) that searched for "the good life" beyond the deep layers of reification:

> What philosophy once called life, has turned into the sphere of the private and then merely of consumption, which is dragged along as an addendum of the material production-process, without autonomy and without its own substance. Whoever wishes to experience the truth of immediate life, must investigate its alienated form, the objective powers, which determine the individual existence into its innermost recesses.[4]

The correspondence between Adorno and Benjamin is a human and intellectual testimony to the collapse of Europe in the first half of the twentieth century,[5] the age in which critical thought described the "dialectic of Enlightenment"—the tendency of Western rationality to become totalitarian[6]—and recognized that "there is not a document of civilization which is not at the same time a document of barbarism."[7] Their correspondence is a faithful mirror of this troubled age. It deserves multiple readings as a reservoir of ideas, evocations, and critical remarks on culture, art, and history. Apparently absent, politics remains in the background as a silent, overwhelming, menacing presence. These letters are an open window on the intellectual workshops of two philosophers who shaped the culture of the twentieth century as well as a touching testimony to the greatness, distress, and melancholy of the Jewish-German émigrés from Nazi Germany at the edge of the deluge that would submerge Europe. Finally, they are the epitaphs of a tormented intellectual friendship: they tell the story of the encounter, the dialogue, the reciprocal influences, the discrepancies and incomprehension that both united and distanced two great minds. These conflictive affinities intimately intertwined their personalities and thoughts. We need to connect the threads of this friendship.[8]

The age of this correspondence is at the same time very close and very distant from us. It is close, because many friends of Benjamin have died only in recent years, after having diffusely spoken and written about him, and many disciples of Adorno are still active. It is distant for reasons going beyond the obvious fact that Hitler and fascist Europe are a finished, remote past. It is distant from us also because it belongs to a different intellectual and mental landscape: these letters witness the importance—with its related pleasure—of epistolary exchange in a time in which the telephone still had a limited diffusion and the Internet did not exist even in science fiction.

Adorno observed that Benjamin was a passionate writer of letters, an activity to which he devoted a significant part of his time. Writing was for him a source of pleasure that he could not renounce, a pleasure he cultivated as an art carefully accomplished in minute detail. His typed letters were quite rare and his handwritten pages display a painstaking calligraphy made of regular, very small characters that create a harmonious unity. Writing letters did not mean only the communication and formulation of thoughts; it was also an exercise in aesthetic creation with an impact both intellectual and visual. Benjamin thought the act of writing of great importance and it seems that, even in exile, his friend Alfred Cohn provided him with his preferred letter paper. Such customs—possibly a "pattern of ritual" inherited from Stefan George[9]—were extremely peculiar, even for a generation born at the end of the nineteenth century. As Adorno suggests, interpreting Benjamin's epistolary style in light of his theory of *Trauerspiel*, the German baroque drama, letters were to him "natural history illustrations of what survives the ruin of time."[10] Younger than Benjamin by eleven years, Adorno mostly typed his letters, often adding some handwritten corrections. This is an interesting detail: the pitiless critic of administered society and universal reification could easily accommodate the constraints of mass society. He quite comfortably settled in the United States—it is doubtful that Benjamin could have—where he quickly started to work for the radio, a medium in which he saw (and heard) nothing but the historical tendency of "the regression of listening." A picture from the 1960s, the epoch in which he led the Institute of Social Research reinstalled in Frankfurt, shows him in his office speaking on the phone as an ordinary businessman.[11] It would be very difficult to imagine a similar picture of Benjamin. Of course, times had changed. Nobody wrote in such a way after the war and this probably explains the fascination with Benjamin's calligraphy. Many years after the death of his friend, Adorno described his letters as an archeological vestige, as a precious remain of a finished age, when writing letters was not yet an obsolete form of communication, when letters still possessed an "aura."

CONSTELLATION

This correspondence deals mostly with the years of exile. Concerning the Weimar period, only Benjamin's letters have survived. Those of Adorno remained in Berlin when their recipient left for Paris in 1933 and were lost. Both philosophers had met several times in Germany, in Frankfurt and in Berlin, where in 1929 they had extensively debated the "Arcades Project," just outlined by Benjamin. Their letters kept contact rather than nourishing a dialogue that could take place quite frequently through face-to-face conversation. Benjamin's epistemological method, explained in the introduction to his *Trauerspielbuch*, inspired Adorno's PhD thesis (*Habilitationschrift*) on Kierkegaard (a work to which Benjamin devoted a favorable review when it was published in 1933 with the title *Kierkegaard: The Construction of Aesthetics*).[12] This book, he wrote, belonged to the category of "those rare first books in which inspiration manifests itself in the guise of criticism."[13] Thus, during the Weimar years Adorno and Benjamin constructed the basis for a dialogue that would be developed outside Germany. Since 1934, their correspondence became much more constant and resulted in an extremely intense intellectual exchange. It is the exile that, putting them in similar conditions as outsiders, made them closer to each other and reinforced their intellectual community. Their letters became the realm of a debate henceforth impossible in Germany and replaced a public space that had been destroyed. In their exchange, the correspondents analyzed and discussed manuscripts that risked not being published or, in the best cases, published only by journals and small publishers, unable to reach a significant audience.

But to go back to the beginning, when did Adorno and Benjamin's friendship begin? They met in Frankfurt in 1923 at Café Westend,

Opernplatz, one of the privileged places for the city's intelligentsia during the Weimar Republic. At the origins of their encounter lay Siegfried Kracauer, a common friend whose crucial role in the intellectual trajectory of both of them is not adequately mirrored in their correspondence. Chief editor of the feuilleton of the *Frankfurter Zeitung*, the most prestigious German newspaper of the 1920s, Kracauer had been the spiritual father of Adorno, whom he met as an adolescent and introduced to the study of philosophy during the First World War. He was also a friend of Benjamin, who regularly contributed to his newspaper. But Kracauer was a simple mediator. Philosophy, literary criticism, aesthetics, Marxism, theology, and mass culture were the elements of a vast Jewish-German intellectual constellation in which we must locate their friendship and whose capitals were Frankfurt and above all Berlin.

In spite of their affection and mutual esteem—a feeling that grew over the years—their friendship was obviously neither unique nor the most important in their lives. For more than a decade, they adopted with each other a respectful and formal tone: Lieber Herr Benjamin, Lieber Herr Wiesengrund. The significant eleven-year age difference within the same generation—which was shaped by the First World War, even if it would be inappropriate to qualify them as representatives of the *Frontgeneration*, neither of them having experienced the trenches[14]—probably had an influence on keeping such a distance in their relationship. Twenty years old in 1923, Adorno played the role, according to his own words, of "the recipient" (*Nehmenden*).[15] He wrote that when he met Benjamin he had the feeling of discovering philosophy itself. According to numerous testimonies, Adorno was deeply sensitive to Benjamin's personality and natural authority, in spite of the aristocratic arrogance he precociously manifested. We can imagine their conversation at the Café Westend conducted by Kracauer, the inevitable mediator, who stuttered throughout his life.

Some years before this meeting, inspired by his affection (and attraction) for the young Adorno, Kracauer wrote a remarkable essay on friendship, whose core he grasped in "consonance between personalities" and whose possible form was a "spiritualized erotic love" (*durch geistige Sinnenliebe*).[16] In 1923, Adorno wrote to Leo Löwenthal that, after reading Goethe's *Elective Affinities*, he felt "in spiritual union with Friedel" (the nickname of Kracauer).[17] The correspondence between Adorno and Kracauer in the first half of the 1920s reveals a passionate,

tormented, and finally broken love story. Of course, the friendship between Adorno and Benjamin was very different. Their meeting certainly
was not a turning point in the life of the latter, whose personal and
spiritual trajectory had already been shaped, almost ten years earlier, by
his encounter with Gershom Scholem. This Jewish scholar of the Kabala
who immigrated to Palestine in 1925 was and remained his best friend
and his first interlocutor. Even when after a meeting in Paris in 1936
they began to call each other by their first names—Lieber Walter, Lieber Teddie—Adorno and Benjamin continued to use the *Sie* form. In
other words, for many years their correspondence kept a formal, staid
character. That certainly mirrored their epoch as well as the customs
of their social milieu, but it also reflected a distance they did not have
with other friends. Thus, it is astonishing to observe the intimacy of the
correspondence between Benjamin and Grete Karplus, Adorno's wife,
whom Walter knew in Berlin in the middle of the 1920s and who would
help him (even financially) in the following decade. They used the *Du*
form and addressed each other with the nicknames of Detlef and Felizitas, exchanging sentences charged with affection and sympathy that
appear as transgressions of the formal, aesthetic rules established by
Teddie. In 1938, when they immigrated to New York and the Institute
for Social Research began to think about a possible transfer of Benjamin
across the Atlantic, Gretel tried to convince him by letters, describing
the "surrealist" character of the American metropolis, where he could
feel as at home as among his Parisian "arcades."[18] In turn, Detlef wrote
to Felizitas that he had seen Katharine Hepburn for the first time and
had been shocked by their resemblance. The limited place reserved for
humor in his correspondence with Adorno did not allow Benjamin to
congratulate an inflexible critic of cultural industry like his friend for
having married a Hollywood beauty.[19]

HIERARCHIES

Such a distance—progressively reduced but never completely erased—
between the two correspondents also lay in a paradoxical aspect of their
relationship: after 1933 Adorno, the younger, "the recipient," quickly
achieved a dominant position from a material and "institutional" point
of view. The work of Benjamin developed in the 1920s and 1930s, from

his book on German tragic drama to the aphorismatic *One-Way Street*, from his seminal essay on mass culture to "On the Concept of History," from his literary essays to his unfinished book on Paris in the nineteenth century. At that time, the work of Adorno had just begun to take shape. He would publish his major books only in the postwar years, and one should not forget that this correspondence occurred between one of the most reputed German literary critics of the Weimar Republic and the future author of *Dialectic of Enlightenment* (1947), *Minima Moralia* (1951), *Negative Dialectics* (1966), and *Aesthetic Theory* (1970). In 1940, at the moment of Benjamin's death, Adorno had just published a book on Kierkegaard and some remarkable articles of music criticism. Some of his writings were clearly inspired by the theoretical insights of "The Work of Art in the Age of Its Technological Reproducibility," as Adorno himself openly recognized. Benjamin was a source of inspiration to him, but the reversal was certainly not true. Over the years, Adorno became a careful, sharp, insightful, and often severe reader of Benjamin's writings, eventually being recognized as a privileged, to many extents irreplaceable critic, but never as an inspirer.

The paradox lies in the fact that the "recipient" no longer accepted such a role. Aware of being an indispensable mediator between his friend and the Frankfurt School in exile, he willingly adopted, far beyond the posture of a fraternal critic, that of a patron, a protector, and, even more distastefully, a censor. What were the arcane reasons for such a nonegalitarian relationship, in which Benjamin's intellectual supremacy was dialectically upturned onto material submission, with many unpleasant consequences? How could the "recipient" transform himself into an examiner, a kind of judge whose sentences decided the future of his friend and whose letters were awaited with anxiety and fear because they could announce safety or catastrophe? It would probably be shortsighted to explain such a paradox in purely psychological terms, as a conscious strategy of domination pursued by Adorno. This nonegalitarian relationship lay primarily in an objective situation created by a context they had not chosen: the rise of National Socialism in 1933. Many material and psychological consequences of this major turn affected their friendship: transforming and reinforcing but also reshaping it on the basis of a new "hierarchy." Of course, Adorno did not create this situation, but he seemed to be quite comfortable in dealing with it. In order to measure such a metamorphosis, one could compare Benjamin's letter of July 17,

1931, with those he wrote after 1933. In the first, he elegantly but steadily expressed his discontent with Adorno's lighthearted use of his own ideas without being quoted during his inaugural course at the University of Frankfurt.[20] He politely asked him to apologize for such an unpleasant attitude and ultimately accepted a dedication in his book in the guise of compensation. Such self-confidence would be unimaginable in the letters of 1937–40, where a much more friendly and intimate tone often hid undisclosed discrepancies and where he carefully abstained from criticizing the articles of his correspondent.

The material basis of their relationship deserves a more insightful scrutiny. Both of them came out from the German-Jewish bourgeois elite: Adorno was the son of a rich wine trader from Frankfurt (his mother, with Genoese and Corsican origins, was a Catholic); Benjamin was the son of an art merchant.[21] Both of them faced the conservatism of the German university, pervaded by anti-Semitism. Benjamin quickly realized that there was no place for him in the German academic institutions; thanks to Paul Tillich, Adorno quickly became a *Privatdozent*, that is, a nontenured and nonremunerated teacher: the highest position that, with few exceptions, a young Jewish intellectual could reach in the humanities. Adorno, however, could benefit from his family's financial support at least until 1938, whereas Benjamin was compelled to earn his own living as a literary critic after the death of his father in 1926, what he always considered an insupportable burden. From 1933 onward, he lived in Paris as an exile in miserable conditions, relying upon the sporadic assistance of some Jewish institutions like the Alliance Israélite Universelle and the help of some friends. His former wife, Dora, who managed a small guesthouse in San Remo, Italy, and Bertolt Brecht, who received him in Denmark, allowed him to overcome the most difficult moments. Starting in 1937, the small monthly grant ($80) he received from the Institute for Social Research (the Frankfurt School transferred to New York and hosted by Columbia University) became an irreplaceable condition for survival in both material and psychological terms. Adorno started his collaboration with the Institute in 1934 and officially became one of its members in the spring of 1938, when he immigrated to New York, but he very soon achieved the position of mediator between Benjamin and Max Horkheimer, the scientific and financial director of the Institute. It was Adorno who pleaded for Benjamin with Horkheimer, prepared their meeting in Paris, informed him about the Institute's decision to finance his research (The "Arcades Project"), and ultimately, after the outbreak of the war and the French defeat of 1940, tried to save him by bringing him to New York. In other words, the history of their friendship is the chronicle of Adorno's growing power over Benjamin. In a letter to Scholem from February 1935, Benjamin evoked, through a vague allusion to Kafka's *Trial*, the Institute for Social Research, "among whose rafters . . . my exceedingly battered mortal thread is becoming lost."[22] In March 1939, when his essay on Baudelaire was severely criticized by Adorno and finally rejected by the journal of the Institute, *Zeitschrift für Sozialforschung*, he wrote to his friend in Jerusalem with a "heavy heart," evoking the possibility that Horkheimer would decide to suspend the financial support of the Institute, with catastrophic consequences for his life and work.[23] Hannah Arendt, who regularly visited Benjamin in Paris during their exile years, witnessed his anxiety as he permanently confronted the Institute's sword of Damocles. She probably exaggerated when she put his whole relationship with Adorno under the sign of "fear," a fear related to both timidity and "dependence," but her observation—based on her knowledge of both men—certainly grasped the core of the problem.[24]

EXILE

This correspondence tells the history of two different exiles. Benjamin was among the first intellectuals to leave Germany in 1933. In mid-March, he settled in Paris. His letters to Scholem—even more Scholem's letters to him—witness a clear and sharp awareness of the historical dimension of the turn that had occurred.[25] As a reputed Jewish and left-oriented literary critic, Benjamin knew that any opportunity for work in radio, newspapers, and magazines—his main sources of income for years— was wiped out. Since he never had been a member of the Communist Party, he did not fear an immediate arrest, but his German career was abruptly interrupted. All his contracts had been canceled. On February 28, he wrote to Scholem "the air [was] hardly fit to breath" in Berlin and he was facing a sort of economic strangulation.[26] Their brothers— Georg Benjamin, a leader of the Communist Party, and Werner Sholem, a former Reichstag deputy who was responsible for the Trotskyist opposition—had been arrested and tortured. Both of them would be deported and killed in the Nazi concentration camps. In April, Scholem measured the width of the "catastrophe," comparing the defeat of the workers movement with the end of German Judaism.[27] Now, Benjamin wrote to him a few days later, "the emancipation of the Jews stands in a new light."[28] In the curriculum vitae he wrote some years later in applying for an American visa, he stressed that his intellectual itinerary was divided "quite naturally into two periods, before and after 1933."[29]

The *Gleichhaltung*—Josef Goebbels's "coordination" for Nazifying the German cultural institutions—compelled Benjamin to leave a country where there was no place for him. His belonging to the German "homeless" left—he had no party affiliation—inevitably reinforced his isolation in exile, where he was excluded from the solidarity network of German antifascism. "Life among the émigrés," he wrote to Scholem in December 1933, "is unbearable, life alone is no more bearable, and a life among the French cannot be brought about. So only work remains, but nothing endangers it more than the recognition that it is so obviously the final inner mental resource."[30] Benjamin attended the International Congress in Defense of Culture, the first great international antifascist meeting, which took place in Paris in 1935, but he did not belong to the list of speakers. In short, exile deprived him of any solid economic base and threw him into a condition of extreme precariousness. He quickly realized he could not publish even under a pseudonym (for a while, he signed as Detlef Holz). His autobiographical essay "Berlin Childhood" was not published (it would be only posthumously); *Deutsche Menschen*, a collection of letters by German classical writers he published in Switzerland in 1936, had a very limited impact; the accomplishment of his most ambitious project, a book on Paris as the cultural capital of the nineteenth century, depended on the mood of the director of the Institute for Social Research. In January 1940, he wrote a letter to Scholem that was a description of both the world situation and his emigration years: "Every line we succeed in publishing today—no matter how uncertain the future to which we entrust it—is a victory wrenched from the powers of darkness."[31] His library—which he had enriched over the years as a work of art, with a collector's passion—remained in Berlin; he could recuperate a part of it in Paris, through Denmark, but finally he was compelled to abandon it again with the German occupation in the springtime of 1940. Between 1933 and 1940, he changed addresses many times in the French capital, mostly because of his difficulties in paying for a rental.

In contrast, Adorno never considered himself an exile, properly speaking, before 1938, when he settled in New York.[32] Of course, Hitler's rise to power wiped out his academic ambitions in Germany, but the fact of not being listed by the Jüdische Gemeinde (he had been baptized as a Catholic, his mother's religion, then inscribed within the Protestant community) as well as the significant financial means of his family saved him from the "economic strangulation" described by Benjamin in his letters to Scholem. He was admitted to Oxford's Merton College as an "advanced student" and began to imagine an academic career in the United Kingdom. However, such a perspective did not enchant him and in 1938 he was happy to accept Horkheimer's offer to join the Institute for Social Research in New York. From 1933 to 1938, Adorno regularly traveled between Oxford and Frankfurt, where his family lived, particularly his beloved mother and aunt, a singer and a pianist who had oriented him toward music. Such relative economic comfort and freedom of movement explain why Adorno did not experience the turn of 1933 as a trauma. Otherwise, it would be difficult to understand the ingenuousness with which, in a letter of April 1934, he suggested that Benjamin apply for the Literary Writers' Association (Reichschriftumskammer) created by Goebbels, which did not yet include an "Aryan paragraph."[33] It goes without saying that Benjamin did not follow his advice and that his own application was rejected one year later. It would also be difficult to understand his article—more indecent than naïve—published in June 1934 in *Die Musik*: a laudatory review of the work of the composer Herbert Müntzel inspired by the poems of the Nazi leader Baldur von Schirach. In his review, Adorno welcomed the advent of "the image of a new romanticism . . . perhaps analogous to what Goebbels called 'realistic romanticism.' "[34] We should remember this text—he later will define it as a mistake—in order to better appreciate the self-assurance with which, in 1937, he demolished Kracauer's book on Jacques Offenbach in his letters. According to Adorno, this historical essay was simply "shameless and idiotic," inspired by commercial purposes and distastefully "apologetic."[35] Of course, after such an intellectual crime, the Institute for Social Research had to revise its relationship with Kracauer, and he was proud of rejecting an article by him on Nazi propaganda for the *Zeitschrift für Sozialforschung*. In other words, Adorno did not seem to have experienced the difficulties of emigration. His correspondence with Benjamin evokes them only once, in 1936, just a year after the promulgation of the Nuremberg Laws, when he asked him to discretely explore the chance he had of achieving French citizenship through the Corsican origins of his mother (this project failed, as well as Benjamin's application).[36]

In 1939, when war broke out in Europe, the Institute for Social Research started serious efforts to save Benjamin. It offered him a stable position in the United States and he abandoned his hesitations in leaving Europe. His possible emigration to America had been previously mentioned without any concrete step being taken. A similar project—sometimes discussed with Scholem—concerned Palestine, but it faced even bigger obstacles, both material (the University of Jerusalem could not offer him a permanent position) and intellectual (it would have been almost impossible to carry on his "Arcades Project" in Palestine) in nature. Many of Benjamin's letters mention his desire to learn English and Hebrew, but this always remained wishful thinking. His attempts to leave France actually began in 1939, especially after his short internment in a camp for "enemy aliens" during the fall and, more dramatically, after the French defeat of June 1940, when he left Paris and traveled to Marseille. The Institute spared no efforts to help him; Adorno canceled his vacations in order to follow the rescue of his friend. Nevertheless, his attempt was unsuccessful and probably could not have been more effective. Two of Benjamin's friends, Arendt and Kracauer, reached New York. If he did not, this was not because of insufficient help, but rather because of his exhaustion, despair, and misfortune. He committed suicide at Portbou, after having been arrested on the Spanish frontier and threatened with being delivered to the French authorities (and consequently to the Gestapo), but his traveling companions ultimately would be able to cross the border, reach Lisbon, and embark to New York. He lacked the energy for such a trip and probably worried about his life in America, where he was afraid of feeling himself a museum piece, "the last European."[37] His suicide was an act of despair as well as a testimony against fascism, when any chance of escape seemed lost.

POLITICS

The silence of Adorno's and Benjamin's letters on the major political events of their time is quite astonishing. The rise of fascism and the deepening of the European crisis until the outbreak of the war constituted the background of their exchange, but it was rarely analyzed or commented upon. Unlike Benjamin's correspondence with Brecht and Scholem, the letters he exchanged with Adorno do not have any appraisal of the Moscow trials (except for a vague allusion by Adorno to Trotsky's *Revolution Betrayed*),[38] Nazi repression, the Spanish Civil War, the French Popular Front or the Munich treaty. Of course, neither Adorno nor Benjamin were political analysts, but their interpretations of fascism did not completely coincide, and the latter probably preferred to not charge their delicate relationship with a political discrepancy.

In Benjamin's eyes, fascism had a historical and political form—that of German National Socialism—and was a concrete threat constantly evoked, when he wrote his theses "On the Concept of History," by the gas mask that hung in his room, which looked to him "like a disconcerting replica of the skulls with which studious monks decorated their cells."[39] In his theses, where it appears under the metaphoric form of "Antichrist," fascism was a danger for humanity as a whole. Nothing could survive its victory, neither the hope of a future liberation nor the memory of the lost struggles: "even the dead will not be safe from the enemy if he wins."[40] In contrast, Adorno's awareness of the historical catastrophe embodied by National Socialism came later. It was only during the war that, under the impact of the extermination of the Jews, he interpreted totalitarianism as the result of a process of "the self-destruction of enlightenment."[41] From 1944 onward, Auschwitz became a central dimension of his thought and work. Until the Second World War, however, he viewed fascism as the accidental expression of a general tendency toward an "administered society" and the reification of human relations. He found in totalitarianism the standardization of life and thinking, the rejection of otherness, and the suppression of "nonidentity" (*Nichtidentisch*), what he called "ticket mentality."[42] Consequently, not a single line of his writings referred to the means of fighting against fascism. Unlike Benjamin, he did not pay attention to the politics of official communism and social democracy, whose passivity and sectarianism had had catastrophic aftermaths. In his commentaries on Horkheimer's essay "The Jews and Europe" (1939), Benjamin severely criticized "the self-satisfied optimism of our left-wing leaders" and his melancholic view of history did not ignore the autonomy of politics as subjective intervention and revolutionary action as the art of "now-time" (*Jetztzeit*).[43] Auguste Blanqui, whose purpose was "to do away from present injustice" and "to snatch humanity at the last moment from the catastrophe looming at every turn," remained to his eyes the paradigm of such a revolutionary politics.[44] According to Adorno, who conflated Hegel's dialectic with Weber's diagnostic of modernity, history was a linear movement toward the triumph of the West—like Hegel's Absolute Spirit—but its epilogue was the "iron cage" of totalitarianism. Fascism was omnipresent, invading and intrinsically related to modernity where, he wrote in an essay on Aldous Huxley from 1938, the only utopia still conceivable was "total collectivization" and "total domination."[45]

The tragic experiences mirrored by this correspondence doubtless found a powerful echo in the pages of *Minima Moralia* (1951) devoted to the intellectuals in exile. One of these fragments—written in 1944— deserves a large quotation:

> Every intellectual in emigration is, without exception, mutilated, and does well to acknowledge it to himself, if he wishes to avoid being cruelly apprised of it behind the tightly-closed doors of his self-esteem. He lives in an environment that must remain incomprehensible to him, however flawless his knowledge of trade-union organizations or the automobile industry may be; he is always astray. Between the reproduction of his own existence under the monopoly of mass culture, and impartial, responsible work, yawns an irreconcilable breach. His language has been expropriated, and the historical dimension that nourished his knowledge, sapped. The isolation is made worse by the formation of closed and politically controlled groups, mistrustful of their members, hostile to those branded different. The share of the social product that falls to aliens is insufficient, and forces them into a hopeless second struggle within the general competition. All this leaves no individual unmarked. Even the man spared the ignominy of direct co-ordination bears, as his special mark, this very exemption, an illusory, unreal existence, in the life process of society. Relations between outcasts are

even more poisoned than between long-standing residents. All empha-
ses are wrong, perspectives disrupted. Private life asserts itself unduly,
hectically, vampire-like, trying convulsively, because it really no longer
exists, to prove it is alive. Public life is reduced to an unspoken oath of
allegiance to the platform. . . . The eye for possible advantages is the
mortal enemy of all human relationships; from these solidarity and loyalty can ensue, but never from thoughts of practical ends.[46]

These words doubtless brought a part of lived experience. Retrospectively observed, exile does not lack nobility, but is always endured with
a feeling of irreparable loss, material impoverishment, and spiritual
"mutilation." Very few exiles in Paris, Prague, London, or New York felt
themselves enriched by the epistemological privileges of the "stranger,"
which Georg Simmel lucidly described at the beginning of the twentieth century:[47] exile is sad and miserable. An autobiographic taste is
also recognizable in Adorno's affirmation that the language of exiles
"has been expropriated." Proud of writing in an "untranslatable" language—Arthur Lovejoy qualified his style as the "metaphysical pathos
of darkness"[48]—Adorno never accepted replacing German with English,
as Arendt, Kracauer, and Marcuse did. Sharing the opinion of his com-
patriot Werner Sombart, he probably considered the language of Shake-
speare much more adapted to "merchant nations" (*Händlervölker*) than
to philosophical thinking. Other autobiographic evocations were his
references to the "poisoned" relationships between exiles, as well as to
conformism becoming a survival condition. This evokes the censorship
he and Horkheimer imposed on the Institute's journal: *Zeitschrift für
Sozialforschung* was systematically purged of any word with a radical
connotation. In the revised version of Benjamin's article on the German
socialist collector Eduard Fuchs, fascism became "totalitarian doctrine"
and "human constructive forces" replaced the word "communism." The
purpose of such semantic euphemisms was—as Horkheimer explained
in 1938—to not pronounce a single word "that could be interpreted
politically."[49]

Adorno's allusion to the isolation of the exiles in a foreign and often
hostile context was also autobiographical. In fact, their lives in the 1930s
did not exceed a narrow universe of mostly Jewish-German émigrés. In
Oxford, Adorno had the feeling of leading "the life of a medieval scholar
in 'Cap and Gown.'"[50] He did not keep a good recollection of this ex-

perience (nor did he leave good reminiscences, according to Isaiah Berlin).[51] His letters did not mention any contact with the United Kingdom, a country whose philosophical tradition he was not interested in. Only the work of Karl Mannheim, a Jewish-Hungarian émigré and a former assistant at the University of Frankfurt, deserved his attention (he wrote a critical review of *Ideology and Utopia*). In New York, except for the first years in which he contributed to the Princeton Radio Research Project led by Paul Lazarfeld, his life was almost completely circumscribed by the boundaries of the Institute for Social Research, where his privileged interlocutor was Horkheimer.[52] In a letter he mentions a dinner with another Frankfurt exile, the Christian philosopher Paul Tillich. The only significant personality he met in New York, according to his letters, was Meyer Shapiro, a Marxist art historian from Columbia University who spoke German and was familiar with many antifascist émigrés (at that time he was a sympathizer of Leon Trotsky).

In Paris, Benjamin was extremely isolated. This resulted from the great suspicion of the French toward the German exiles, as he stressed in a letter to Scholem in which he quoted a popular aphorism: "the émigrés are worse than the Krauts [*boches*]."[53] According to Hannah Arendt, Benjamin loved France, a country where he felt as "at home" as in Berlin. He was fascinated by this city that had "offered itself to all homeless people like a second home ever since the middle of the last century." But what most attracted him to Paris, she added, was the past: "the trip from Berlin to Paris was tantamount to a trip in time—not from one country to another, but from the twentieth back to the nineteenth century."[54] In the eyes of Benjamin, Paris was the city of Baudelaire, a city whose atmosphere he had particularly liked since his first journey in 1913 and to which he later devoted his "Arcades Project." The entire city, one could say, appeared to him as a gigantic realm of memory: its past was engraved in its buildings and its streets as a living exhibition. In his essay on Eduard Fuchs he summarized in a few lines his image of the French capital: "the ground of three great revolutions, the home of exiles, the source of utopian socialism, the fatherland of haters of tyranny such as Michelet and Quinet, and finally the soil in which the Communards are buried."[55] It was only several decades after his death that French culture discovered this émigré who had translated Baudelaire and Proust and introduced Surrealism to the readers of the *Literarische Welt*. He met Gide and Valéry, to whom he had devoted reviews and who each wrote statements in order to support his application for French citizenship, but their relationships were not intimate. In 1935, Jean Paulhan rejected an essay on Bachofen he had written for *NRF*, the most prestigious literary journal in Paris, and only a few articles were published in French during his lifetime. First of all, Benjamin's Paris was the Bibliothèque Nationale—a famous photograph by Gisele Freund shows him working in the catalogue room—where he spent several years, interrupted by his frequent trips to San Remo, Svendborg, and Ibiza, where he was invited to by his ex-wife, Brecht, and Jean Selz. The only French person he was familiar with was Adrienne Monnier, the owner of a Latin Quarter bookshop; in the fall of 1939, she mobilized all her energies in order to liberate him from Nevers's camp for "enemy aliens."[56]

Much more complex and probably shaped by a reciprocal incomprehension was Benjamin's relationship with the Collège de Sociologie, whose ideas were spread by journals like *Contre-Attaque* and *Acéphale*. In 1936, he met Pierre Klossowski, the translator of "The Work of Art in the Age of Its Technological Reproducibility," and Georges Bataille, curator at the Bibliothèque Nationale, who introduced him to the Collège. The last avant-garde movement of the interwar period, this association gathered a group of intellectuals led by Bataille, Michel Leiris, and Roger Caillois. Some of them had participated in Surrealism but decided to distance themselves from André Breton and to abandon Marx in order to reactivate the legacy of Durkheim's sociology and Mauss's anthropology. Benjamin was fascinated and at the same time frightened by their antibourgeois radicalism and their new approach to the "sacred." His skepticism was reinforced by Adorno, who observed in Caillois's writings a "faith in nature which is hostile to all and indeed crypto-fascistic," not dissimilar from the mysticism of Gustav Jung and Ludwig Klages, not to speak of the Nazi conception of *Volksgemeinschaft*.[57] Many years later, Klossowski remembered an anecdote that illustrates the incomprehension that existed between the German exiles and the intellectuals of the Collège de Sociologie. Questioned by Adorno about the activities of his association, Bataille answered: "Inventing new taboos." Astonished, Adorno replied, "Have we not enough taboos?" whereas Benjamin nodded his head in agreement.[58] According to Klossowski, Benjamin attended the meetings of the Collège with both curiosity and consternation, considering the "metaphysical and political excess" of its members as an unforgivable mistake. The German experience had clearly proved that such a dangerous game could create "a field psychologically favorable to fascism."[59] He confirmed his criticism in reviewing in *Zeitschrift für Sozialforschung* a novel of Caillois, *L'aridité*, but he signed his article with a pseudonym in order to avoid conflicts with Bataille, who helped him at the Bibliothèque Nationale (notably protecting some of his manuscripts).

SURREALISM

In spite of their shared skepticism with respect to Bataille and the Collège de Sociologie, Adorno and Benjamin significantly disagreed in their interpretations of Surrealism. Surrealism was a crucial element of the latter's fascination with France at least since his reading of Louis Aragon's novel *Paris Peasant* (1926), some excerpts of which he translated for the *Literarische Welt*. In a substantial article written in 1929, Benjamin described Surrealism as the first avant-garde movement that reintroduced to Europe "a radical concept of freedom" whose traces had been lost since Bakunin.[60] "To win the energies of intoxication for the revolution": such was the project of Surrealism, a movement that tried to conciliate freedom and human emancipation. It used magic and dreams in order to transfigure reality and to "anticipate" liberation: not only the end of exploitation but also the accomplishment of bodies, imagination, art, and minds. Benjamin highlighted the disruptive potentialities of this "anarchic" component of Surrealism but, at the same time, he criticized its indifference to "the methodical and disciplinary preparation for revolution."[61] In short, Surrealism accomplished the *pars destruens* of revolution, not its *pars construens*. As Michael Löwy and Margaret Cohen have pointed out, Benjamin shared with Breton a "Gothic" interpretation of Marxism that was fascinated by the magical dimension of the past and found in enchantment and the marvelous the sources of its utopian imagination.[62] Like Surrealist creations, Benjamin's aphorismatic, fragmentary, and "micrologic" style invented "profane illuminations" that sketched the image of a liberated society. There was an evident affinity between the Surrealistic practice of "free associations" and the deconstruction of capitalist rules, inspiring the art of wondering embodied by the figure of *flâneur*: transforming modernity into a realm of aesthetic pleasure and avoiding simultaneously both commodity reification and productive, utilitarian rationalization of time. The Surrealist theory of the dream stimulated Benjamin's interest in Freud and gave him an essential key to interpreting Paris and the nineteenth century. In *The Arcades Project*, "awakening" (*Erwachen*) was defined as "the great exemplar of memory" (*des Erinners*).[63] The modern city, with its condensation of the past in architecture and landscape, was a privileged field for such an exercise of memory reactivation. Combining the remnants of a past destroyed by industrial capitalism and the phantasmagoria of the commodity universe produced by modernity, the big city engendered "lived experiences" and "electrical shocks"—in Baudelaire's sense—that established a dialectical relationship with the past. In *The Arcades Project*, this fruitful articulation between dream and reminiscence was identified with Surrealism: "The nineteenth century—to borrow the Surrealists' term—is the set of noises that invades our dream, and which we interpret on awaking."[64]

According to Benjamin, a fundamental feature of modernity lay in the exhaustion of transmissible experience (*Erfahrung*) and the primacy of lived, ephemeral, fragmentary experience (*Erlebnis*). The past ceased to live in the present—where it subsisted as "a secularized relic"[65]—because it could not be appropriated through a process of spontaneous and almost natural transmission from one generation to another. In his essay on the figure of the storyteller, Benjamin symbolically dated the crucial moment of the end of transmissible experience to the Great War. The industrial massacre of 1914–18 broke the natural rhythms of existence of millions of human beings, throwing their "tiny, fragile" bodies into the middle of "a force field of destructive torrents and explosions": such a traumatic suffering suddenly made obsolete and useless their previous experiences.[66] From this moment onward, the past needed a trigger or a fuse in order to be reactivated. In the aesthetic field, Surrealism was the most interesting and ambitious attempt to fill this gap between the fugitive instant, shock, and memory.

According to Adorno, however, neither reminiscence nor utopian images could fill such a dichotomy between *Erlebnis* and *Erfahrung*, whose ineluctable result—as he wrote to Benjamin in February 1940—was a "dialectical theory of forgetting," that is, "a theory of reification."[67] The vanishing of memory in modern societies coherently followed a historical process displayed under the sign of domination. Benjamin viewed reminiscence as an intellectual instrument for preserving the dream of a classless society. In the eyes of Adorno, this was romanticism: the idealization of the past naïvely transformed into a "golden age." In his essay "Paris, Capital of the Nineteenth Century" from 1935, Benjamin used memory as a "mythical and archaic category" and risked formulating a theory dangerously close to reactionary visions such as Jung's "collective unconscious" and Klages's myth.[68] In Benjamin's essay "The Paris of the Second Empire in Baudelaire"—finally rejected by *Zeitschrift für Sozialforschung*—Adorno saw a form of "immediate," "almost anthropological" materialism that reduced the concept of phantasmagoria to bohemian behavior and resulted in a deadlock, "at the crossroads between magic and positivism."[69] In other words, the magic of the *flâneur* and the positivism of a historical reconstitution of bohemianism, a pitfall he compared to Georg Simmel's writings on the city and to Kracauer's book on Offenbach, where the boulevard became the core of the nineteenth century. Benjamin analyzed the literary figures of Baudelaire's poetry (the *flâneur*, the bohemian, and the dandy) as both products of the phantasmagoria of a "reified" society (he borrowed this concept from Marx and Lukács) and an attempt to escape reification. He related Baudelaire's work to the advent of mass society with innovations such as gaslights, supermarkets, feuilleton, photography, arcades, and boulevards as well as the emergence of crowds and new social figures such as journalists, detectives, policemen, conspirators, and professional revolutionaries. The "shocks" that—mirroring the life of a big city—produce the rhythm of Baudelaire's poetry were perfectly symmetrical to Blanqui's insurrections, in which Benjamin saw the most important barricade leader.[70] Both of them belonged to the modern city and rejected the philosophy of progress with its positivistic faith in industrial society. Finally, it was this "practical" critique of capitalism—the common core of Surrealist aesthetic and Blanquist politics—that exasperated Adorno. He expressed his hostility to Surrealism in many of his writings, from *Philosophy of New Music* to an article from 1956 included in *Notes on Literature*. In the latter, he stressed the impotence of Surrealism in front of reification and suggested that its fascination with dream objects was a form of fetishism close to pornography.[71]

After the war, Adorno gave an exact definition of Benjamin's style qualifying his aphorismatic and fragmentary texts as "thought-images" (*Denkbilder*).[72] Benjamin analyzed concepts as images, not as representations but as separate entities susceptible to being observed as spiritual objects. Adorno did not share this method and indicated the limit of Benjamin's thought in a "philosophy of fragmentation [that] remained itself fragmentary." In short, his "micrological and discontinuous method never entirely integrated the idea of universal mediation";[73] the result was its incapability to attain the dialectical totality in the sense of Hegel and Marx. These discrepancies explain the contradictory attitude of Adorno: on the one hand, he tried to convince Horkheimer to support Benjamin's "Arcades Project" (he described it as a "really extraordinary contribution to theory" and as "a masterpiece");[74] on the other hand, he could not hide his negative assessment of Benjamin's essay on Baudelaire, ultimately using his power of censorship. Friendship, admiration, inspiration, contrasting views, and, above all, an incontestable "hierarchical" superiority within the Institute for Social Research: these were the elements that oriented the attitude of Adorno toward Benjamin.

MASS CULTURE

An additional discrepancy discussed in their correspondence was related to art in mass society. The famous essay of Benjamin "The Work of Art in the Age of Its Technological Reproducibility"—first published in French by *Zeitschrift für Sozialforschung* in 1936—aroused the enthusiasm of the young philosopher of music. Adorno found this aesthetic theory that postulated the loss of aura as the peculiar feature of the culture industry to be deep and illuminating. Nevertheless, his enthusiasm resulted from a very unilateral reading of this text. Whereas Benjamin indicated two main consequences of the advent of a technically reproducible art—on the one hand, the end of its irreducible uniqueness (aura) and, on the other hand, the new potentialities of its dissemination (including its democratization)—Adorno saw nothing but a reflection on "the 'liquidation' of art."[75] Whereas Benjamin highlighted that, for the first time in history, the work of art conceived of as reproducible—for instance, the movie—emancipated itself "from the service of ritual," thus "increasing the opportunities for exhibiting its products,"[76] Adorno saw nothing but a new illustration of "bourgeois sadism" overwhelming the mass audience.[77] According to Benjamin, the art of mass society could have an emancipatory dimension that dialectically compensated for the decline of aura; according to Adorno, it meant the end of artistic creation through universal reification. Benjamin merged multiple influences in a new, original theory: Brecht's epic theatre, Soviet constructivism (discovered thanks to Asja Lacis), and Kracauer's theory of "the mass ornament";[78] Adorno's criticism combined aesthetic aristocratism with cultural pessimism. Many years later, he would describe in psychoanalytical terms this essay of Benjamin as a typical "identification with the aggressor."[79]

"The Work of Art in the Age of Its Technological Reproducibility" deeply influenced two essays by Adorno—the first on jazz and the second on the "fetish-character" in music—published in 1936 and 1938 by the journal of the Institute for Social Research. In his opinion, he wrote to Benjamin, the so-called progressive elements of jazz were nothing but a façade that hid something "in truth utterly reactionary."[80] The core of jazz was a regressive violence susceptible to reinforcing the chains of domination, exactly like Horkheimer's interpretation of fascism as the expression of the "revolt of nature." Functioning as an outlet for the masses of an alienated society, jazz awakened the destructive potential of instrumental rationality.[81] In his eyes, the monotone excitation of jazz combined an act of revolt with the despair of submission, thus revealing a "sado-masochistic" component.[82] Its fainting rhythms were reminiscent of military parades in a way that perfectly epitomized the totalitarian tendencies of mass society. In his essay on the fetish-character in music, he compared the American bandleaders of the swing age to the fascist Führer.[83] Reformulating the concept of the decline of aura in terms of "regression of listening," Adorno's article finished with a radical criticism of mass music as a form of art that thoroughly expressed the masochism of listening, general alienation, and identification with the authority. As many later writings of Adorno clearly suggest, his answer to the decline of aura was the atonalism of Schoenberg. Such music, he pointed out, did not wish to be "decorative" but "truthful": abandoning harmonic consonances, he tried to attain the authentic expression of an intimate suffering, of the anxiety of human beings facing the violence of a reified world.[84] In a letter of 1936, Adorno described Vienna as his "second home":[85] Paris was the capital of the nineteenth century's revolutions, Vienna the core of the crisis of bourgeois world and subjective identity.

Starting from a similar statement—the birth of an art without aura in modern capitalism—Benjamin and Adorno drew opposed conclusions.

The former prescribed the *politicization of art*—favored by its new technical bases—as a necessary answer to "the aestheticizing of politics as practiced by fascism";[86] the latter withdrew into a form of resigned romanticism coupled with a purely *contemplative criticism.* This discrepancy simply reflected two different forms of left melancholy, both romantic but politically divergent: the former in favor of radical agency, the latter resigned and passive. Thereafter, how are we to explain the letter of Benjamin that, commenting on Adorno's essay on jazz, expressed his idea of a "profound and spontaneous inner communication between our thoughts"?[87] Why did he not observe that Adorno had simply applied to music his theory of the loss of aura? Of course, the émigré in Paris was neither familiar with jazz nor interested in searching for the "fascist" unconscious of Duke Ellington. His "enthusiasm" probably depended on different reasons: his "fear" of a man to whom he was materially submitted, the "poisoned relationships" between the exiled, and the dissimulation that followed. In his letters, Benjamin simply did not dare criticize Adorno.

REDEMPTION

In the spring of 1938, Scholem was lecturing in New York and met Adorno, who had just arrived in America. In a letter to Walter, Teddie's extensive (and positive) comments on this meeting became the pretext for explaining their different views on Jewish theology (a discrepancy discussed two years earlier in San Remo). To the method of Scholem, whose attempt to "save theology" seemed to him "strangely linear and romantic," he opposed Benjamin's approach, in his eyes clearly "superior," which tried "to mobilize the power of theological experience anonymously within the realm of the profane."[88] Such an approach, he wrote, was close to his own and distant from Brecht's orthodox materialism (rapidly evoked as a "philosopher's stone, and rock of offence, currently living in Denmark").[89] He reaffirmed this judgment in 1950, in an article that presented Benjamin's thought as an attempt to introduce Jewish mysticism into the *Aufklärung.* The result was not a quest for transcendence, but rather a singular hermeneutic that consisted in interpreting profane literature as if it were a sacred text and trying to preserve the legacy of theology through its violation: "he looked to radical profanation as the only chance for the theological heritage which squandered itself in profanity."[90] It is an extremely sharp observation that lucidly grasps the project of Benjamin. Unlike Brecht, for whom "On the Concept of History" was a superb revolutionary manifesto written in a cryptic mystical style,[91] or Scholem, for whom Benjamin was a metaphysical thinker unfortunately disguised as a materialist,[92] Adorno understood that his Paris friend was at the same time a *Marxist* and a *theologian*. Politics and religion, Marxism and messianic Judaism coexisted in his thought without disappearing. Following the rationalistic reading of Brecht or the religious interpretation of Scholem, many critics have considered such an attempt at merging Marxism and Jewish theology to be an inexorable failure. Nevertheless, Benjamin tried neither to "theologize" Marxism nor to "secularize" messianic Judaism into historical materialism. According to Michael Löwy, he grasped them as two complementary elements: "There is, in Benjamin, a relation of reciprocal reversibility, of mutual translation between the religious and the political that cannot be unilaterally reduced: in a system of communicating vessels, the fluid is necessarily present in all the arms simultaneously."[93] In other words, theology (transcendence) and Marxism (history) needed each other to be effective; otherwise, the former would become positivism, like most Marxism of Benjamin's time, and the latter a form of mysticism.[94]

Such an original articulation between religious and profane, messianic and secular thought finally results in a new vision of history and revolution. In his theses of 1940 — transmitted to Adorno by Arendt and published by the Institute one year after Benjamin's death — this new vision turns dark and apocalyptic. The most famous thesis — the ninth — puts history under the frightened gaze of an Angel who, pushed toward the sky by a storm, observes a landscape of ruins in front of him: the past is a chain of defeats and oppression that only mistakenly was called progress. In *Dialectics of Enlightenment*, their masterpiece published at the end of the Second World War, Horkheimer and Adorno evoked this *Denkbild* in connection to their own vision of totalitarianism as the epilogue of the trajectory of Western civilization.[95] According to Benjamin, nonetheless, history is not entirely contained in this cortege of victors celebrated by historicism as a linear, chronological, homogeneous, and empty time of "progress." History holds in itself the memory of the vanquished, the recollection of suffered defeats, and the promise of future redemption. According to the Jewish tradition, "every second was the small gateway in time through which the Messiah might enter."[96] To the historicist vision of the past, Benjamin opposed a messianic conception of revolution: the advent of a new age that, in breaking the enchainment of downfalls, interrupted the continuity of history. Instead of "advancing" history, revolution should "stop" it. Unlike Marx, who defined revolutions as the locomotives of history, Benjamin considered them as the "emergency brakes" for stopping the train's course toward catastrophe.[97] It is precisely in such a sudden breakout of historical time that he introduced a messianic dimension: as a redemptive force, revolution did not accomplish history; its goal was rather exiting from history.

In Benjamin's view, revolutions also fulfilled a demand of memory. The revolutions of the nineteenth century brought "wish images" (*Wunschbilder*) that exhumed an ancestral past:

> Corresponding to the form of the new means of production, which in the beginning is still ruled by the form of the old (Marx), are images in the collective consciousness in which the new is permeated with the old. These images are wish images. . . . In the dream in which each epoch entertains images of its successor, the latter appears wedded to elements of primal history [*Urgeschichte*]—that is, to elements of a classless society. And the experiences of such a society—as stored in the unconscious of the collective—engender, through interpenetration with what is new, the utopia that has left its trace in a thousand configurations of life, from enduring edifices to passing fashions.[98]

In this passage, remembering brings a utopian tension that, between the poles of Surrealism and messianic Judaism, creates Benjamin's version of historical materialism.[99]

Adorno had very well understood the inspirations of Benjamin's thought but he did not accept his revolutionary conclusions. Like Brecht, Lukács, and Korsch, Benjamin considered "the subject of historical knowledge [to be] the struggling, oppressed class itself."[100] In the eyes of Adorno, such a vision simply revealed Brecht's deleterious influence on his friend. His own Marxism, in contrast, was purely aesthetic and completely indifferent—not to say hostile—to any idea of class struggle. In the Marxist conception, he thought, the proletariat was a kind of abstract and useless deus ex machina. If Benjamin wished to remain a member of the Institute for Social Research—Adorno warned him—he should abandon such a political style of thinking. "Precisely here, there is a limit," he wrote in 1935, explaining the reasons for Institute's censorship on his essay "Paris, the Capital of the Nineteenth Century."[101]

Their discrepancy was as deep as it was unavoidable: Adorno rejected any idea of political commitment whereas Benjamin considered any critique of capitalism limited to the aesthetic sphere to be sterile and worthless. In the conclusion of "The Author as Producer"—a very Brechtian text that he did not send to Adorno—he wrote that the final struggle would not oppose capitalism to "spirit," as a fight between metaphysical entities, but capitalism and the proletariat as two antagonistic social forces.[102]

It was perhaps thanks to such a peculiar articulation between communism and theology that Benjamin tried to escape the deadlocks of the dominant versions of historical materialism: Stalinism, social democracy, and Western Marxism, that is, bureaucratic authoritarianism, evolutionary reformism, and a withdrawal into aesthetics.[103] Locking himself in the latter, Adorno always refused to give a political dimension to his critical theory. The roots of his discrepancy with Benjamin were the same as those of his conflict with Marcuse, whose interpretation of "On the Concept of History" was much more radical than his own.[104] In 1969, the author of *One-Dimensional Man* accused Adorno, the director of the Institute for Social Research, of betraying critical theory with his conformism and conservatism (he had called the police in order to evacuate the Institute occupied by rebellious Frankfurt students).[105]

This dialogue—born in 1923, just after the first chaotic and troubled years of the Weimar Republic—was tragically broken in September 1940, in Portbou, at the beginning of a new historical catastrophe. It is to Adorno that Benjamin wrote, in French, his last words, when he found himself in "a situation without escape."[106] They were the last words of a friendship and an unaccomplished dialogue. Their letters remain as the melancholic epitaph of the richest and at the same time the most tragic period of European history, when it was midnight in the century.

7 SYNCHRONIC TIMES

WALTER BENJAMIN AND DANIEL BENSAÏD

PORTBOU

PORTBOU is the Catalan small town where Benjamin committed suicide in September 1940, when he tried to escape from France (figure 7.1). He feared being arrested by the Vichy police and delivered to the Gestapo, as already happened with many other German-Jewish émigrés. In Marseille, he had obtained an American visa thanks to his friends from the Frankfurt School exiled in New York, and he had tried to cross the Spanish border to get to Lisbon, where he might have embarked for the United States. After a perilous journey through the mountain paths, the Guardia Civil had stopped him at Portbou, menacingly saying that they would deliver him to the French authorities. Won over by despair and exhaustion, he took his own life. The following day, his travel companions were allowed to pursue their journey to Lisbon (among them the writer Lisa Fittko and the photographer Henny Gurland, the future wife of Erich Fromm).[1]

Today, Portbou is internationally known as the place of Benjamin's death and has been transformed into a "realm of memory." Since 1990,

7.1. Portbou in the 1930s, Postcard. Archives Marian Roman.

the year in which a famous memorial by the Israeli sculptor Dani
Karavan was inaugurated, the village has become a place of pilgrimage
(figure 7.2). The myth of Portbou lies in the beauty of the site as well
as in the mystery of Benjamin's grave, which has never been found.
In fact, it does not exist, in spite of many official documents attest-
ing to both his death and his burial. In 1940, his remains had been in-
humed in a small leased niche with a simple number (563); five years
later, they were moved to a common burial ground.[2] The search for
the grave began two months after his death, when, leaving France for
New York, Hannah Arendt stopped at Portbou. On October 21, she
wrote a letter to Gershom Scholem, their common friend in Jerusalem,
describing her visit with these words: "The cemetery faces a small bay
directly looking over the Mediterranean; it is carved in stone in ter-
races; the coffins are also pushed into such stone walls. It is by far one

7.2. *Memorial Passatges*, by Dani Karavan (1994). Museu Memorial del Exili, La Jonquera.

of the most fantastic and most beautiful spots I have ever seen in my life" (figure 7.3).[3]

In 1990, Karavan's memorial compensated for this absent grave. Today, this work of art—a kind of tunnel going down from the hill toward the sea—is not only a pilgrimage site but also the main tourist attraction of the Catalonian town. The town is full of panels related to Benjamin and hotel halls are decorated with posters of him (figure 7.4). The city council regularly organizes conferences devoted to the German critic and recently decided to create a "Casa Benjamin" for hosting exiled artists and writers.

Actually, Portbou is a crucible of memories. Beyond the sepulture of Walter Benjamin, it is a realm of memory of the German exiled, thousands of whom crossed the Spanish border to escape from Nazi persecution in Europe. It is also a realm of memory of the Spanish Civil War. In February 1939, Portbou was one of the main transit places during the exodus of the Spanish Republicans to France after the fall of Barcelona and Franco's victory. Hundred of thousands of Spanish exiles passed through the same frontier, although in the opposite direction (figure 7.5). In France, they were interned in refugee camps that, after the Ger-

7.3. Portbou, cemetery (2014). Museu Memorial del Exili, La Jonquera.

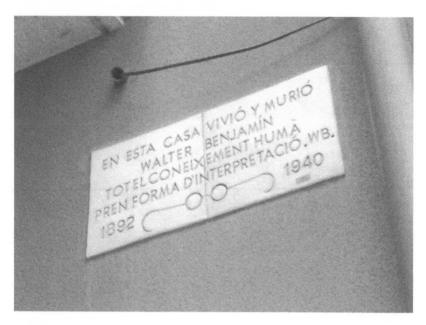

7.4. Commemorative plaque in the building of the former Hostal Francia, where Walter Benjamin committed suicide in 1940. © Joan Gubert, Portbou 2016.

7.5. Portbou, Spanish Republican exiles, end of January 1939. © Manuel Moros, Peneff Collection.

man occupation in 1940, were transformed into transit sites leading toward the concentration camps of the Third Reich.[4] All over this path, visitors find landmarks evoking the steps of the Spanish Republican exile. Today, nevertheless, this Benjamin Memorial overlooking the Mediterranean inevitably calls to mind other exiles; it summons people who tried to escape from other suffering places, often dictatorships and persecutions. In the last two decades, many thousand people have lost their lives trying to reach the coasts of Italy, Greece, and Spain, the doors of the European Union.

There is an astonishing entanglement between Benjamin, the philosopher of memory; Portbou, the village where he died, the site of his materially inexistent but symbolically overwhelming grave; and the present situation of Europe as a destination for contemporary refugees. There, the ghost of Benjamin encounters the memories of both European and postcolonial exiles. In many respects, this kind of short circuit illustrates the clash between past and present at the heart of Benjamin's vision of history.

PARIS

And now, let us jump forward to Paris, several decades later. During the 1970s, Daniel Bensaïd was known as an actor in May '68 and a leader of the French radical left. In those "street fighting years," militant politics absorbed all his psychic and intellectual energies. It is at the end of the following decade—a "Thermidorian age," as he used to define it—that his critical thought took shape. The 1980s had been a crossing of the desert, when Paris became, according to Perry Anderson, "the capital of the European reaction."[5] All changed at the end of this decade. In 1991, Bensaïd made this lucid assessment:

> The left no longer recognizes its own memory. General amnesia. Too many tricks gobbled up, too many promises unfilled. Too many affairs poorly classified, with corpses in the closet. One does not even drink to forget anymore; one manages. The French Revolution? Dissolved in the apotheosis of the bicentennial. The Commune? The latest utopian foolishness of archaic proletarians. The Russian Revolution? Buried with the Stalinist counterrevolution. The Resistance? Not too clean when we

look at it carefully. There are no other founding events, no birth, no landmarks.[6]

The end of communism—the historical turn of the twenty-first century—had a strong impact on Daniel Bensaïd's intellectual and political trajectory. No longer obsessed with the defense of a revolutionary tradition belonging to a concluded past, he tried to grasp and interpret the features of the new world that was emerging and scrutinized the horizon for the premises of a new resistance. He did not reject his "Bolshevik" past, but was aware that it could not provide an answer to the questions of the present and that it was time to invent new critical tools and to explore new forms of action. His writings were not directed exclusively to the reduced audience of political activists but to a wider readership. In this way, he could satisfy a literary vocation previously self-censured. His writings took an aesthetic form that expressed a fruitful freedom as well as the search for a personal style of thinking. Disposed to dialectical, if not to paradoxical, formulas, he introduced himself as a partisan of a very peculiar genre: "Libertarian Leninism."[7] Thus, he wrote in quick succession several works in which past and present met, conflating history with philosophy, literature, and politics. In *Moi, la révolution*, he cast scorn upon a "comtemptible bicentenary"—the burial of 1789 celebrated by François Furet—anthropomorphizing the Revolution and allowing it to speak in the first person: breaking the framework of the official commemorations, she claimed her place in the history of oppressed uprisings and reaffirmed her still-unfulfilled emancipatory project.[8] In *Jeanne de guerre lasse*, it was Joan of Arc who, depicted as a feminist fighter *ante litteram*, denounced the confiscation of her memory by any sort of nationalism or conservatism.[9]

In the 1990s, Bensaïd became in several respects a *border crosser* (figures 7.6–7). First of all, he was a border crosser between different political traditions, because he succeeded in liberating Trotskyism from the defense of a revolutionary heritage already codified into scholasticism.[10] Thus, between questions and reappraisals, he started a fecund dialogue with Alain Badiou, Jacques Derrida, and Toni Negri, the representatives of philosophical and political traditions previously neglected. This *Aufhebung* of classical Marxism was an attempt at salvation that inscribed it into a new reality and conflated it with other political cultures

7.6. Daniel Bensaïd, early 1970s. Association Daniel Bensaïd, Paris.

7.7. Daniel Bensaïd, 1989. Association Daniel Bensaïd, Paris.

(which had earlier been observed with hostility or contempt). He tried to overcome the gap—already detected by Perry Anderson one decade before—between Trotskyism, which mostly focused on economics and politics, and Western Marxism, which traditionally retreated into philosophy and aesthetics.[11] Thanks to Bensaïd, Trotskyism began to merge with other currents of critical thought, from Bourdieu's sociology to the Frankfurt School. Second, he became a border crosser between different generations of activists, allowing the survivors of May '68 to meet a new generation that had discovered politics and radical commitment within the "antiglobalization" movement of the 1990s. He created the journal *Contretemps*, a discreet and fraternal left forum without partisan links, whose pages hosted the contributions of many young people coming from different traditions and political experiences (including non-Marxist). In this exchange between ages and ideas, his role has been irreplaceable. Finally, he was a border crosser between the left movements of several countries and continents. As a leading member of the Fourth International—a kind of "bonsai Komintern," as he affectionately and self-ironically defined it[12]—he had many friends in both Europe and

Latin America. He was fluent in Spanish and in Portuguese as well. Neither doctrinal nor abstract, but rather nourished by a living experience of the diversity of cultures and human beings, such internationalism was a sort of anthropological background to his activism. Thus, he shook the prejudices of a French left too often the prisoner of a narrow national memory. Familiar with Latin America, he met several activists who died in combat, during the tragic experience of the guerrillas of the 1970s. The remembrance of these fallen revolutionaries certainly helped him to master the trauma of AIDS twenty years later: "Used to meeting specters and ghosts," he wrote in his autobiography, "I had been pushed on their side by the ordeal of sickness."[13]

Bensaïd introduced himself as a simple activist and his peculiar position was quite unclassifiable. Gramsci's concept of "organic intellectual" did not scare him, in spite of the inglorious trajectory of many communist "fellow travellers" and he was flattered to be accused of being an "organic intellectual" of the French LCR (Revolutionary Communist League). In other words, his commitment was antipodal to that of many media "intellectuals" fabricated by the cultural industry. To these champions of political conformism so often admired by magazines and TV shows, he devoted the sharp and ironical criticism of his *Fragments mécréants* as well as a demolishing portrait of Bernard-Henry Lévy (BHL), one of the most prized export commodities of the French media.[14] Nor was Bensaïd an intellectual in the Sartrean sense of the word, a writer or a scholar denouncing injustice or even, as a kind of "legislator," establishing some ethical and political norms. He preferred the posture of the activist who, not exposed to the temptation of elitism, never abandoned a "healthy principle of reality" both modest ("we speak and think in a community of equals") and responsible ("differently from the media oracle, the militant takes into account the possible consequences of his words"). Finally, Bensaïd was not a "specific" intellectual in a Foucauldian sense: he never pretended to be an "expert" or to affirm scientific truths. This explains his marginal position inside the academic world, which finally accepted him—he became a professor of philosophy at the University of Paris 8—in spite of his obstinate refusal to submit himself to its codes and rituals. The activist and the scholar are not always interchangeable figures; he always "kept out of the conferences of philosophical brotherhood, seminars and academic high masses."[15]

It was just after the historical turn of 1989 that he was diagnosed with AIDS, the disease that would kill him twenty years later. He always remained very discreet about his sickness and suffering. This modesty—which was never occultation or public denial—probably lay in his refusal to be defined by the disease, thus becoming a prisoner of an identity assigned by public recognition: he did not fear stigmatization, but rather refused to appear as a victim. Such behavior was neither evasion nor denial, neither exemplar nor heroic. More prosaically, it was a condition for preserving his intellectual independence. In the middle of the 1990s, he came very close to death. In his book on Joan of Arc, written just after discovering his illness, he attributed to her this meaningful meditation: "I learned to live what remained of my life, day after day, minute after minute, to defend those precious moments against the overwhelming idea of the last time, of the last fall and the last colors on the roof tiles, of the last winter and the last snow in my small window, of the last spring and the last blossoming. I learned to defend each fragment of the day against the poison of regret."[16]

His sudden recovery thanks to new providential therapies was followed by a frenetic series of travels, lectures, public debates, polemics, essays, and theoretical works. It was such an impressive acceleration that his readers were unable to follow the rhythm of his publications. Probably, some of his books were written too rapidly and published when they were not yet mature, like mirrors of a lavish thought that did not find the time to be sculpted into an accomplished form. Sometimes, the brilliance of his style seemed to fill the holes of a hurried thought. The fact is that AIDS forbade him any long-term project; he worked frenetically because nothing could wait or be postponed. The books he wrote after 1989—from *La discordance des temps* (1995) to *Marx for Our Times* (1995), from *Les Dépossédés* (2007) to *Eloge de la politique profane* (2008)—remain the fragments of an extremely ambitious but unaccomplished work, prematurely interrupted. That was the ransom of an announced death. On the other hand, he probably tried to reach—like a negative privilege linked to his disease—an existential plenitude quite rare in an ordinary life. As he wrote, the awareness of being close to death modifies "proportions and temporal perspectives. . . . We try to seize the day, following our inspirations and desires."[17] From this point of view, he was the opposite of Marx, his tutelary figure, who spent his life writing and rewriting *Capital*, without accomplishing it before his death.

REREADING MARX

Marx remains the common thread running through Bensaïd's works, from his first book written with Henri Weber during the summer of 1968 while hidden in the Parisian flat of Marguerite Duras (*Mai 68, une repetition générale*),[18] until his last texts of political theory. Doubtless Bensaïd was a Marxist reader of Marx, insofar as he recognized himself within the intellectual tradition inaugurated by the eleventh thesis on Feuerbach: interpreting the world in order to transform it. His Marxism, nevertheless, was neither apologetic nor conservative. His aim was not to restore an "authentic" Marx against the deformations, incomprehension, or falsifications accumulated in more than a century of exegesis. In *Marx for Our Times* (1995) he analyzed a work whose richness is made of its internal tensions and that is open to multiple interpretations: there is not one but *many* Marxisms. He convincingly argued that the attempts to assimilate Marx to Comte are highly debatable, but at the same time recognized that both Karl Kautsky and Walter Benjamin legitimately belonged to the Marxist tradition. In other words, social Darwinism and positivistic historical materialism as well as messianic utopias could find valuable reasons for claiming the heritage of the author of *Capital*. Marx's work reveals an intimate conflict, deeply rooted in the culture of its century, between a positivistic model (the discovery of the driving laws of capitalism) and a vision of history as the result of the conflicts engendered by the totality of social relations. Thus, Marx's work is the mirror of a "double temptation" typical of his time: on the one hand, his desire to elaborate a "science," as proved by his homage to Darwin in the preface to *Capital*; on the other hand, his umbilical link with Hegelian dialectic, which pushed him to see in the class struggle the motor of history.[19] Facing such a dilemma, Bensaïd's Marxism claimed both pluralism and historicism.

At the end of a century of controversies, Bensaïd decided to approach Marx's thought negatively, emphasizing what in his eyes it no longer should be. It should not be a philosophy of history, that is, the

construction of a universal history—in Hegel's sense—in which socialism appeared as the ineluctable, teleological result of the contradictions
of capitalist society. In short, history did not provide a guaranteed happy
ending or automatic progress: Marx did not conceive history, according
to a positivistic paradigm, as a linear progression along a chronological
axis, shaped by the quantitative accumulation of productive forces. Of
course, he considered—especially in the *Grundrisse*—the development
of productive forces as a necessary premise for reducing work time and
liberating the creative potentialities of human beings, but this did not
mean a "productivistic," utilitarian vision of socialism as a kind of industrial Moloch. On the other hand, Marx's categories could be helpful
in order to think the transformation of productive forces into destructive ones, a metamorphosis that reached its paroxysm in the twentieth
century. Progress is not a linear process but a dialectical movement that
produces its own negation. Progress and regression, we could say, adopting Bensaïd's metaphorical image, went forward together, embraced
by the phantasmagorical dance—spectacular and infernal—of commodities' world. Their relationship could not be understood by a lineal conception of temporality because the rhythm of history is kairotic,
discordant, permanently open to the irruption of events. In the wake
of Blanqui, Trotsky, and Benjamin, Bensaïd thought history as a force
field made of uncertainties and possibilities, as a highly heterogeneous
movement pushed on by discordant and fragmented times, shaped by
crises, wars, revolutions, and counterrevolutions. In his eyes, history was
a challenge, a crossing open to multiple exits, a process built through
permanent "bifurcations" and consequently forged by the choices of its
actors. No salvation is assured in advance, and the maintaining of class
domination is not ineluctable. In order to synthetize this critical vision
of history as a process demanding political understanding and strategic
thinking, he liked to quote Gramsci: "In reality, one can 'scientifically'
foresee only the struggle."[20]

Finally, Bensaïd did not consider Marxism as a variant of empirical
sociology. Seeing the unaccomplished chapter on social classes in the
third volume of *Capital* as evidence of a theoretical gap meant not understanding the "antisociology" of Marx, a thinker for whom classes are
not abstract sociological categories but living historical subjects. Classes
do not exist out of their relationships with other classes; they are not
"things"—as Durkheim's "social facts"—but subjects that forge them-

selves in the frame of social relations. That is why the field in which Marxism produced its most fruitful analysis of class conflicts was historiography (notably E. P. Thompson) instead of political economy. Bensaïd tried to be truthful to such a Marx—the thinker of reification and commodity fetishism, the analyst *ante litteram* of capitalist globalization, and the defender of proletarian self-emancipation—sometimes diminishing his own innovations or trying to give an "orthodox" taste to his personal inclinations. In *La discordance des temps* he not only admitted his passion for Charles Péguy—a peculiar figure of a Dreyfusard and nationalist republican of fin-de-siècle France—but felt it necessary to claim his "Péguyism" in peremptory terms: "Péguyist not in spite of Marxism but Péguyist because of Marxism."[21]

In a time in which the historical dialectics between memory and utopia seemed broken, Bensaïd rediscovered a Marx for whom "revolutions never run on time"[22] and the hidden tradition of a historical materialism *à contretemps*, that is, as a theory of nonsynchronous times or noncontemporaneity.

SYNCHRONIC TIMES

The fall of the Berlin Wall almost coincided with the anniversary of the death of Walter Benjamin. It is precisely during the months separating the historical event from the anniversary that Bensaïd wrote a brilliant essay on the German-Jewish philosopher.[23] The year 1990 was the starting point of a wave of commemoration: between the fiftieth anniversary of his death in Portbou (in 1940) and the centenary of his birth in Berlin (in 1892), Walter Benjamin has been canonized in German culture and beyond. In the avalanche of symposiums, books, and celebrations of those two years, the essay of Bensaïd occupies a very peculiar place. Reread today, it appears as a significant attempt to renew the ideas of the left through its confrontation with the thought of a German-Jewish thinker who had been almost completely neglected before, but its place in the field of Benjamin studies remains modest, almost intrusive. Bensaïd was not a Benjamin philologist, a "Benjaminologue." In spite of his erudition and the abundance of his literary and philosophical references, his exegesis was anything but conventional. He defined his book as a "necessary passage" occurring in a crucial moment of his life, when he discovered the first symptoms of the disease that would kill him twenty years later.[24] But this existential turn had also an intellectual dimension. This book on Benjamin revealed a new direction in his thought at a crucial moment of history that we are used to considering, in the wake of Eric Hobsbawm, as a turn of the century.

Bensaïd's book was certainly a book *on* Benjamin, but it was also, first and foremost, a dialogue *with* Benjamin, inspired by worries, interrogations, and dilemmas arising from an extremely unstable present, which, in suddenly closing the twentieth century, received its legacy of defeats and needed a reappraisal. What Bensaïd was looking for, in the work of Benjamin, was the help of another "border crosser" in front of a "rebellious history." His purpose was not to unveil the secrets of a complex and often hermetic body of work, but rather to build, through its critical assimilation, "a principle of intelligibility, of orientation in the labyrinths of history."[25]

Practicing criticism as a creative work, Bensaïd was much more faithful to Benjamin than the army of his accredited exegetes. First of all, he fruitfully departed from the consolidated reception of the German philosopher that, for decades, focused hugely, if not exclusively, on the aesthetic dimension of his work, and he discovered a *political* Benjamin. Committed from the early 1920s to a difficult but stimulating dialogue with the Marxist tradition, Benjamin did not dissociate his aesthetic criticism from politics, and opposed the "politicization of art" to the "aestheticizing of politics" accomplished by the regimes of Mussolini and Hitler.[26] Toward the end of his life, the struggle against fascism became a central dimension of his writings, framing a new vision of history deeply shaped by messianic hopes. This is the red thread connecting Benjamin to Bensaïd.[27] In short, Bensaïd's book was conceived of as a reflection starting from Benjamin. In the large corpus of his writings, the former focused mostly on *The Arcades Project* and the theses "On the Concept of History," rereading them in the present, updating and actualizing them.

The crucial link between the theses of 1940 and their rereading in 1990 was not a vague "elective affinity" between their authors due to their Jewishness, their communism, or their shared "heretical" inclinations; it was rather a dialectical constellation between *two epochs:* the beginning of the Second World War and the end of the twentieth century. In spite of their obvious, incommensurable differences, these two moments are meaningfully similar landmarks and bifurcations of history. Benjamin wrote his theses at the beginning of 1940, only a few months before his suicide in Portbou, on the Spanish border, in a literally cataclysmic historical context shaped by the Republican defeat in the Spanish Civil War, the German-Soviet nonaggression treaty, and the outbreak of the Second World War, just before the Nazi occupation of France. Written as a sort of intellectual testament, his text mirrors an epoch dominated by Nazism and Stalinism. His life was just finishing in France, the country where he had lived in exile, and he did not reach the United States, where his friends Adorno and Horkheimer awaited him and where he imagined himself to be a vestige of an engulfed world, "the last European."[28] The theological dimension of his last texts is all the more pronounced and profound as the European left appeared defeated, abandoned by its leaders and crushed by the inexorable advance of Nazism, which, with the complicity of the USSR, dominated the continent (the "Great Patriotic War" would start only one year later, after Benjamin's death). In such a context, thinking emancipation and revolution became a *wager*, an act of faith. Theology appeared as an indispensable ally of Marxism, unable to reawaken a disoriented antifascism and to reinvent a new idea of communism that would no longer be a prisoner of the illusions of Progress but would be inspired by the will of redeeming the vanquished of history. Nourished by a permanent dialogue with Gershom Scholem, a historian of the Kabbalah, Benjamin's messianic impulse was powerfully reinforced by this cataclysmic context.

The turn of 1989 has certainly been less tragic than that of 1940. The fall of the Berlin Wall was experienced as a happy ending and even engendered, for an ephemeral moment, the myth of the "end of History": the ineluctable and definitive triumph of market capitalism and democratic liberalism, both presented as the best order that humankind might wish for. However, it is also incontestable that the feeling of a historical defeat of the left and the workers movement had never been as deep or as overwhelming, since the rise of Hitler to power in 1933, the victory of Franco, and the German-Soviet pact in 1939, as at the moment of the end of the Soviet Union. People understood that this event meant much more than the implosion of a tyrannical regime, because it unveiled the shipwreck of the hopes of a century of emancipatory struggles. This assessment quickly became evident in the eyes of everyone, even those who, like Bensaïd, had always struggled against Stalinism. Trotskyism did not exit undamaged from this defeat. "Our universe of thinking did not collapse," he wrote in his autobiography, "yet it was deeply shaken. The crisis was threefold: a theoretical crisis of Marxism, a strategic crisis of our revolutionary project, and a social crisis of the subject of universal emancipation."[29] The history of communism and the Marxist tradition as a whole were put into question. The task of rethinking a revolutionary project, its social forces, its organizational instruments, its alliances, and its strategy became unavoidable. Perceived as a "messianic sentinel," Benjamin offered him a compass for resisting in the middle of the storm. Since history seemed fixed on the stable tracks of the linear, "homogeneous, and empty" time of triumphant liberalism, communism could only survive in a messianic form, as the promise of a redemption to come, as the testimony of a fidelity to the vanquished, as an act of faith in a possible (but certainly not ineluctable) interruption of the course of history.

In the 1980s, sometimes at the price of doubtful interpretations, Hannah Arendt was the emergency exit for a generation that had abandoned Marxism and joined the ranks of "antitotalitarian" republicanism, a group less and less radical, more and more inclined to embrace the tradition of classical liberalism. At the beginning of the 1990s, Benjamin was, for those who discovered the political dimension of his thought, a useful tool for resisting this conservative wave. He became a kind of "Ark"—borrowing the image he suggested in *Deutsche Menschen* (1934)—allowing the transfer of critical thought into the new century.[30] Conceived of as a necessary shift before coming back to the question of Marx and Marxism—a task he would accomplish a few years later with *Marx for Our Times*—Bensaïd's book on Benjamin disoriented many readers. Discovering Benjamin, he seemed to dismiss Ernest Mandel, the theoretician of the Trotskyist movement during the previous decades. "Inheritor of the Enlightenment and believing in the emancipatory virtues of productive forces, the liberating power of science, and the historical logic of progress," Mandel was "a typical example of frantic optimism";[31] the leader of the Fourth International was the embodiment of a classical Marxism that, until the end of the 1970s, had seemed fit to provide a key for deciphering the dynamic of the world but appeared now as irremediably overwhelmed by the last historical turn. "An enigma is irreducibly attached to the event, at the same time origin and bifurcation," Bensaïd wrote under the impact of 1989.[32] In such a historical conjuncture, the rediscovery of a messianic thought excavating the memory of the century could be more profitable than the conventional schemes positing the conflict between forces and relations of production and more insightful than the "long view" of structural history, with its superposed layers and its tectonic movements reducing events to a pure superficial agitation. The twentieth century was an age of sudden, unexpected, and shocking ruptures that escaped any deterministic causality; it created many "now-times" (*Jetzt-zeit*) in which the present met the past and reactivated it. Its end took the form of a condensation of memories in which its wounds reopened and history met its lived experience. Bensaïd described this encounter in an almost baroque style: "the water tables of collective memory" conflated "the symbolic sparkle of the historical event."[33]

Writing as an internationalist and a global activist very familiar with the Latin-American world, he enriched the concept of memory with an enlarged typology. Beside the German couple of *Andenken*, a word that surrounds memory, "prowling around it," and *Eingedenken*, "which is return and penetration, going down and fecundation," he paid attention to their Portuguese and Spanish equivalents: *lembranças*, ephemeral, superficial, "cheap recollections," and *memorias*, "obstinately melancholic," filled with *saudades*, sad for the nostalgia of a loss past; *recuerdos*, personal and fragile, open to forgetfulness, and *memoria*, "haunted by ghosts."[34] He regretted that a beautiful word like "remembrance," much more intense than "reminiscence," had almost disappeared in the French language, where it joins the concept of *remémoration*. A continent of revolutions such as Latin America was a gigantic reservoir of popular memories. He evoked that of the peasants of Cuautla, who, since the Mexican Revolution, have impeded the transfer of the mortal remains of Emiliano Zapata to the capital. They know, Bensaïd explained, "that their entry in a Pantheon where victors and vanquished cohabit would be a second death."[35] It was precisely against the embalming of the French Revolution, pompously celebrated in 1989, that Bensaïd wrote *Moi, la révolution*. Officiating the burial of 1789, Furet could not understand Michelet or Charles Péguy, two authors whose interpretation of the revolution was based on remembrance instead of commemoration.[36]

HISTORICISM

Benjamin's conception of history is radically opposed to what he called historicism, that is, a positivistic historiography that, in "On the Concept of History" (1940), he identified with nineteenth-century scholars such as Leopold Ranke and Numa Denis Fustel de Coulanges. For them, history was a closed continent, a definitively finished process. The past of historicism was nothing but cold, dead matter ready to be archived or put into a museum. A rigorous, scientific exploitation of sources allowed scholars to reestablish the concatenation of events and the roles played by actors; the meaning of history mechanically came out of their careful chronological reconstruction. To this conception—well synthesized by the formula "once upon a time"—Benjamin opposed a different vision of history as an *open time*. According to him, the past never abandons the present; it haunts the present and cannot be separated from it. The past remains with us and, consequently, can be reactivated. Nothing is definitely lost, although everything belonging to the past— material objects as well as individual and collective recollections—is constantly menaced.

Benjamin identified historicism with a form of history writing that accepts as ineluctable the victory of the rulers, a form of "empathy with the victors" based on the "indolence of the heart" (thesis 7).[37] His conception of history was the opposite. Working through the contradictions of the present is the condition of reactivating the past. Benjamin called this reawakening of what has happened "recollection" or "remembrance" (*Eingedenken*), and described his approach to the past as an attempt to accomplish this process. To remember means to salvage, but rescuing the past does not mean trying to reappropriate or repeat what has occurred and vanished; rather, it means to *change the present*. The transformation of the present carries a possible "redemption" of what has passed. In other words, in order to rescue the past we have to give birth again to the hopes of the vanquished, we need to give a new life to the unfulfilled hopes of the generations that preceded us. As Benjamin writes:

> The past carries with it a temporal index by which it is referred to redemption. There is a secret agreement between past generations and the

present one. Our coming was expected on earth. Like every generation
that preceded us, we have been endowed with a weak Messianic power,
a power to which the past has a claim. . . . To be sure, only a redeemed
mankind receives the fullness of its past.[38]

Historicism means *khronos*: a purely linear, quantitative, and chronological vision of history as an ensemble of events put on the plane of a
measurable, elapsed time. Historicism views history as a closed experience, as a "homogeneous and empty time," susceptible to being filled
with a succession of dates and events clearly recognizable in the columns
of a calendar.[39] According to Benjamin, on the contrary, history belongs
to *kairos* and history writing implies a qualitative conception of time
as an open and unfinished process. But the reawakening of the past—
which means "to reawaken the dead," establishing with them a fruitful
relationship and recognizing their haunting presence in our societies—
is not an easy task. Remembrance needs particular, exceptional historical constellations. In order to reactivate the past we have to change the
present, which is a political task. Benjamin does not consider history
writing as a work of abstract reconstruction, but rather as the intellectual dimension of a political transformation of the present. Historical
knowledge is a revolutionary act that cannot be confused with mere
scholarship. The methodic, peaceful investigation in the archives—the
places where the past is conserved and protected from disturbing in-
terferences by the living world—is the procedure of historicism. "To
articulate the past historically," Benjamin thinks, means rather "to seize
hold of a memory as it flashes up at a moment of danger."[40]

In other words, far from being sealed and frozen, the image of the past
emerges from the conflicts of the present. Benjamin calls "now-time"
(*Jetzt-Zeit*) this particular moment in which the past clashes with the
present and reemerges in it: "what has been [*Gewesene*] comes together
in a flash with the now [*Jetzt*] to form a constellation."[41] "Now-time"
is the dialectic link between the unaccomplished past and the utopian
future. It is the sudden irruption of the past into the present, breaking
up the continuum of a purely chronological time. This is why, according
to Benjamin, history is not only a "science" but also, and perhaps first of
all, "a form of recollection" (*Eingedenken*). In a passage of *The Arcades
Project*, he compares this approach to "the process of splitting the atom"
in order to "liberate the enormous energies of history that are bound

up in the 'once upon a time.'"[42] This means a break, an interruption of historical time, a suspension of time that he illustrated, in a famous passage of his theses, through the image of the revolutionaries of July 1830 firing at the clock towers in Paris.[43]

In other words, history asked to reactivate an unaccomplished past, listening to its demand of "redemption." Of course, this approach is problematic—in his correspondence with Benjamin, Max Horkheimer emphasized that a conception of history as an "unfinished process" inevitably implied a theological dimension—but it can also be epistemologically fruitful. Theology, instead of science, recognizes and realizes the potentialities of memory. "What science has 'determined,' remembrance can modify," he wrote in *The Arcades Project*, adding that such mindfulness could "make the incomplete (happiness) into something complete, and the complete (suffering) into something incomplete. That is theology; but in remembrance we have an experience that forbids us to conceive of history as fundamentally a-theological, little as it may be granted us to try to write it with immediately theological concepts."[44] In her commentaries on *The Arcades Project*, Susan Buck-Morss clarifies this point, explaining that theology (transcendence) and Marxism (history) need each other to be effective; otherwise, the former would become a form of mysticism, and the latter of positivism, like most Marxism of Benjamin's time.[45] This conception of history results in its representation through images. "Now-time" becomes a "thought-image" (*Denkbild*) and history writing results in a montage of dialectic images rather than the linear narrative typical of historicism.[46] In other words, the concepts of "now-time" and "recollection" suppose a vision of history as a coexistence of different historical times, or as a symbiotic relationship between past and present, history and memory.

The kind of historicism with which Daniel Bensaïd was confronted was different from the positivistic school of Fustel de Coulanges. In the 1970s, it was a Marxist historicism that postulated a linear continuity from the French Revolution to the Left Union (Union de la Gauche), passing through the Popular Front of 1936 and the Resistance in 1944. The PCF defended a form of national communism—sometimes turning to communist chauvinism—that integrated Marxism into a national, republican tradition. It viewed socialism as the accomplishment of a French historical destiny whose universal dimension included not only 1789 and 1793, the Rights of Man and the Terror, but also the "civilizing mission" of colonialism, basically accepted for more than twenty years, between the Popular Front and the Algerian War. French Stalinism, nevertheless, reproduced some features of classical historicism—a linear vision of history as the uninterrupted growth of productive forces, a naïve conception of progress as purely economic and technical advance, the certainty of final victory—for which Benjamin severely reproached German social democracy in his theses of 1940.

From the 1980s onward, historicism became a feature of liberalism, embodied by François Furet, the historian of both the French Revolution and communism. The years between the celebration of the bicentenary of the storming of the Bastille and the publication of *The Passing of an Illusion* (1995) were the time of Furet's canonization as the harbinger of liberal democracy, the final and hopeful result of civilization. Announced in 1789 and achieved in 1989, after two insane centuries of "revolutionary passions," the end of communism sealed the triumph of liberalism. According to Bensaïd, Furet was a conservative scholar who, merging a "Thermidorian" and a Cold War taste, revisited the history of communism as a satisfied apologist of the established order. The failure of communism proved the virtues of its ideological enemy and the task of the historian was precisely to explain why history could not have a different conclusion. Furet, he sarcastically observed, wrote history as a "notary of the accomplished fact," as a "strategist of the battles whose results are already known," as a scholar who, in the classical tradition of historicism, reduced history to chronology and celebrated its results by applauding the victors.[47] This teleological vision—history as an ineluctable path to liberalism—finished with a self-complacent stoicism that recalled to mind Fustel de Coulanges: "Here we are, condemned to live in the world as it is."[48]

What is interesting to observe, however, is the source of Bensaïd's critique of historicism and the singular way that led him to Benjamin. This very peculiar source was Charles Péguy, a Catholic poet and writer of the end of the nineteenth century, the founder of *Cahiers de la Quinzaine*. In spite of his commitment in defense of Captain Dreyfus and his youthful socialism, Péguy was a figure banned from the left tradition because of his mysticism and his nationalist turn in 1914, the year of his death. His posthumous transformation into a minor fascist icon had definitely transformed him into a forbidden author. Bensaïd observed in Benjamin a strong and fascinating "resonance" of Péguy: they shared the same radical rejection of positivism and historicism. In their wake, he found a "modest" but fruitful path for rediscovering Marx.[49]

This "frame of affinities" concerned some crucial elements: the rejection of a unilateral conception of universal history, the definition of event, and the empathy with the vanquished. Péguy identified the idea of universal history with the work of Ernest Renan, the most respected scholar of the Second Empire and the beginning of the Third Republic. In the wake of Auguste Comte, the founder of positivism, Renan depicted history as a "horizontal" progress, measured by a purely quantitative growth, which could be compared, adopting the spirit of natural sciences, to the biological process of evolution of a human body: the history of humanity had to pass through successive steps as a human being goes from childhood to adulthood. Such a vision of a "lineal and indefinite progress, perpetually pursued, perpetually pushed, perpetually achieved and stored, perpetually consolidated" inevitably corresponded to a conception of the past as dead matter, ready to be archived and conserved.[50] And this excluded, Bensaïd added, to any form of "reminiscence and reviving."[51] This rejection of lineal history led Péguy to redefine the event, against any idea of fatalism and objectivism, as "irruption" and "intercalary gush."[52] Events are unpredictable and shape history as abrupt breaks, changes, and "bifurcations." Péguy opposed the radiance of the event to the "geometrical" time of positivism: history was not a regular, straight movement; it was a tree with multiple branches. "Arborescence," Bensaïd wrote, "is the modality of historical exuberance. Its temporality is not slack; it is broken and rhapsodic, made of contradictions and stretching."[53] Finally, this conception of history belonged to the vanquished, a category in which Péguy had enrolled himself with pride, as he announced to the subscribers of the *Cahiers de la Quinzaine*, emphasizing that his defeat was probably more honorable than many ominous victories achieved through prevarication, opportunism, and betrayal.

REVOLUTION

In the wake of Marx, Ernest Mandel never doubted that revolutions were the "locomotives of history." In a fragment of *One-Way Street* (1926) titled "Fire Alarm," Benjamin defined them, in contrast, as the "emergency brake" stopping the train's rush toward catastrophe: "Before the spark reaches the dynamite, the lighted fuse must be cut."[54] In *The Arcades Project*, he announced a radically antipositivistic historical materialism that would have "annihilated in itself the idea of progress": its "founding concept was not progress but actualization."[55] By adopting this idea, Daniel Bensaïd introduced a considerable shift in the radical left. In a text titled "The Mole and the Locomotive," he recognized that "the train of progress" had derailed: "in the railways' saga, the sinister wagons [of Auschwitz] have eclipsed the steel horse." Digging its underground rut, "the mole wins over the locomotive." In this passage, the mole becomes an allegorical figure—as those described by Benjamin in *The Origins of German Tragic Drama* (1925)—evoking the memory of the defeated revolutions of the twentieth century.[56]

Between "Critique of Violence" (1921) and "On the Concept of History" (1940), Benjamin elaborated an idea of revolution that merged Marxism with Jewish messianism. Far from being "natural," this encounter provokes many questions and controversies. Between those who, like Brecht, considered Benjamin as a Marxist incapable of liberating himself from a troublesome and useless religious legacy, and those who, in the wake of Scholem, depicted him as a Jewish theologian disguised with a Marxist mask, the disagreement was almost insuperable. The theses of 1940 are an attempt to think revolution (and the struggle against fascism) as an emancipatory act susceptible to breaking the continuity of history (the triumphant cortege of the victors) and redeeming the memory of the vanquished. Marxism (the revolution made by a historical subject) and messianism (the advent of a new era) could not be dissociated. In order to merge Marxism and Jewish messianic hope, Benjamin reinterpreted both of them in a very heterodox, heretical way. Some critics have depicted him as a thinker "between two stools," torn between Moscow and Jerusalem.[57] Borrowing this metaphor, Bensaïd described the Jewish-German philosopher as a "Marrano" communist.[58] Benjamin's journey to the Soviet capital in 1926 had been a terrible deception, extensively related in his diary and his conversations with Brecht in 1938.[59] During the 1930s, Benjamin expressed in several letters sympathy for Trotsky and his interest in Surrealism—to which he devoted a brilliant article in 1929—which testifies to the libertarian taste of his communism.[60] Jerusalem, the city where his friend Scholem had settled in 1923, was never a real option in his eyes, in spite of his efforts to learn Hebrew. He never considered Judaism as a national identity—Zionism seemed to him a caricature of the *völkisch* ideology—because he could not separate it from Diaspora, its true vocation. The destiny of Judaism could not be dissociated from the European future.

Definitively, Benjamin's Judaism was as heretical as his communism. He thought the revolution in messianic terms—the descent of history into the apocalypse, the crucial moment in which the fall transforms itself into redemption—but his messianism was not conceived of as the passive waiting for a divine intervention, that is, a deliverance coming from outside. According to Scholem, Jewish messianism was born as a "waiting for historical cataclysms," because its most important role consisted in announcing "revolutions, the catastrophes coming with the passage from the time of present history to the future messianic times."[61] Benjamin completed this vision with a fundamental addendum: instead of *awaiting* the Messiah, human beings had to *provoke* a messianic interruption of the course of the world, and such human action was social and political revolution. This was the core of his heretical approach to the biblical tradition. In an essay written in 1964, Herbert Marcuse stressed this feature of Benjamin's thought: "Since the revolution becomes messianic, it could no longer orient itself toward the continuum. Nevertheless, that does not mean a simple waiting for the Messiah. The latter lies only in the will and action of the oppressed, of those suffering in the present or, according to Benjamin, in the class struggle."[62]

Benjamin defended a peculiar position within antifascism. The fight against the "Antichrist"—as he defined the Nazi dictatorship in his theses of 1940—implied the abandonment of the vision of history that had inspired the culture of antifascism.[63] Dominated by the idea of progress, antifascism wished to defend civilization against barbarism. Benjamin did not share this perspective: following Blanqui, he considered progress to be a dangerous myth that acted on the proletariat as a powerful narcotic, weakened its strength, and finally demobilized it. Far from opposing civilization to barbarism, he considered fascist barbarism an outcome and a face of civilization itself. It was not enough to defend the legacy of the Enlightenment against fascism, because an effective struggle should recognize the links connecting fascism to modern rationality itself. Technical, industrial, and scientific progress could transform itself into a source of human and social regression. The development of productive forces could reinforce domination and its means of destruction, as the Great War had clearly proved. Fascism was neither a reaction against modernity nor a new fall of civilization into barbarism; it was rather a peculiar synthesis of the counter-Enlightenment—the rejection of a universal idea of humankind—and a blind cult of modern technology. We could not fight against this form of *reactionary modernism* in the name of a progress "conceived as a historical norm."[64] Benjamin, nevertheless, was not a conservative romantic. He did not oppose technology—his writings on mass culture and his aesthetic discrepancies with Adorno rather inscribe him among modernists—but he warned against the totalitarian potentialities of modernity. Adopting a brilliant formula, he wished for a communism able to transform technology into "a key to happiness," instead of the fascism that had transformed it into a "fetish of decadence."[65]

Bensaïd stressed the revolutionary dimension of Benjamin's messianic thought. Departing from a linear conception of time, he recognized the *kairotic* rhythm of history, that is, an asynchronic, "discordant" rhythm, permanently opened to the irruption of event. He did not believe in historical teleology and, as we have seen, he considered struggle to be the only predictable thing.[66] With a clear exaggeration, he added that, behind his "peaceful gentleness," Benjamin hid an "armed Messiah."[67] We do not need to quote the testimonies of his friends and the assessments of his biographers in order to recall how much the German philosopher was intimately reluctant to participate in any form of political activism (in spite of his critique of Surrealism, which he reproached, with a certain effrontery, as "completely neglecting the methodic and disciplined preparation of revolution").

To grasp in Benjamin's messianic aspirations the features of a "strategic reason" is audacious to say the least. In fact, such an imaginary portrait of Benjamin evokes two opposed trajectories—that of a literary and art critic attracted by the Bolshevik Revolution and that of a revolutionary activist fascinated by literature—that mirror rather Bensaïd's own intellectual journey.[68] Bensaïd had the temperament of a novelist; he renounced literature to devote himself to politics and all his books possess a literary taste; on the contrary, it would be very difficult to imagine Benjamin metamorphosed into an activist or a political leader.

In his book, Bensaïd sketched the profile of a critical and subversive thinker, but he made a mistake presenting the aphorisms of Benjamin on politics as the expression of a *secularized* messianism, that is, a conception of politics able to transcend its "theological and philosophical prehistory."[69] In his first thesis of 1940, Benjamin theorized the alliance between historical materialism and theology, not their reciprocal dissolution in an atheistic politics. Always "wizened" and "out of sight," theology hid itself in the costume of a puppet, of an automaton, but still existed. Its survival was even the necessary condition for rescuing historical materialism. Similarly, in the eighteenth thesis, "the strait gate through which the Messiah might enter"[70] was not a simple metaphor but alluded to a Jewish tradition that he wished to reactivate in the present. Secularization, on the contrary, could take different forms. It had also contributed to weaken the workers movement through the social-democratic consecration of secular fetishes like technique, work, and progress and the Stalinist sanctification of industry, charismatic leadership, and socialist fatherland. Benjamin's revolutionary messianism took the form of a *political theology*—sometimes in a symmetrical confrontation with Carl Schmitt[71]—which is certainly controversial but impossible to neglect or reject as a simple stylistic procedure. Differently from Bensaïd, Benjamin did not believe in a "secular" Messiah. Since his writings from the beginning of the 1920s, in which he theorized a "divine violence," nihilistic and "law-destroying,"[72] until his theses of 1940, Benjamin conceived revolution as a material and human action (notably after his discovery of Marx) as well as a spiritual movement of redemption, salvation, and restoration of the past (*restitutio in integrum*).[73] Only a religious experience might bring to revolution the élan it needed as an act of social and political emancipation. Of course, he did not conceive of its goal as the establishment of a theocracy, but its task was simultaneously secular and religious. Stéphane Moses has highlighted the continuity of Benjamin's thought, depicting it as *stratification* in which three paradigms—theological, aesthetic, and political—superposed and intertwined with one another without rejecting or neutralizing reciprocally.[74]

This attempt to secularize Benjamin's messianic thought led Bensaïd to sketch a strange genealogy in which Scholem is astonishingly absent, but in which instead appear Uriel da Costa and Spinoza, two heretical Marranos to whom he felt very close but who are almost unnoticed in the writings of Benjamin. The category forged by Isaac Deutscher of the "non-Jewish Jew,"[75] the heretical Jew who belongs to a Jewish tradition of overcoming and rejecting Judaism itself, might perfectly be applied to Bensaïd, not to Benjamin. The former fiercely claimed, evoking the "betrayal of Spinoza," "the Jewish anti-Zionism of the secular Jew";[76] the latter, who knew neither the Holocaust (even if he intuited the catastrophe) nor Israel (though he expressed reservations toward Zionism), never rejected Judaism, in spite of his difficult and critical relationship with the Jewish tradition.

The conclusion of Bensaïd's book is a plea for a junction between "the sharp ax of messianic reason" and "the hammer of critical materialism," or, in other words, for a reconciliation between memory and history. At the end of his book, he staged an imaginary dialogue between them, in which they mistreat each other: History treats Memory as a "novelist" and the latter replies, "parvenu!"; History reproaches Memory for Penelope's "dark holes" and the latter despises the coldness of Clio's archives. At the end, however, they recognize that it had been a mistake to divide their paths. Politics could have connected them and a politics based on the alliance between history and memory would have been different from the politics we have known.[77]

UTOPIA

The "messianic reason" defended by Bensaïd tried to merge history and memory but could not depart from the trauma of the event. In 1990, the historical dialectic between the experience of the past and the utopic projection toward the future was broken. The horizon was removed from sight and the past became a saturated memory of wars, totalitarianism, and genocides. The angel of history reappeared with his frightened sight contemplating a new defeat. In this context, Bensaïd recognized that "today the alliance between the utopic legacy and the revolutionary project has fallen apart."[78] This was probably the fundamental reason for his radically *antiutopic* statement. Differently from prophecy that "elaborates a critical and polemical image of tradition," utopia carried in his eyes "a lingering smell of bad secularized afterworld [*un relent rancide d'au-delà mal sécularisé*]."[79] His conclusion was irrevocable: "There is no utopic prophecy." In a posterior essay, he criticized Ernst Bloch, the philosopher of expectation and the principle of hope, opposing him to Walter Benjamin, for whom "the utopia disappears in favor of the Messiah."[80]

Such an assessment is quite debatable. Scholem devoted many illuminating pages to the utopia lying at the core of the messianic tradition: "Although their advent is astonishing and fearful, messianic times are depicted even under a utopic light. Utopia always mobilizes the past for stimulating the hopes of restoration," that is, the realization of the kingdom of God on earth. This announcement of redeemed humankind represented "the prophetic legacy of messianic utopianism," Scholem wrote, adding that, in times of darkness and persecution, it allowed the Jews to overcome humiliations and oppression.[81]

Utopia also fills the work of Benjamin, as proved by his fascination with Fourier, his writings on Bachofen, and also, in a broader sense, his cultural archeology of Paris as a gigantic reservoir of "dialectical images," crossing points between memory and the dream of a liberated society. The most famous among these passages—already quoted in the previous chapter—evokes the desires and hopes haunting the imagination of Baudelaire, Blanqui, and the Commune in Paris: the shift from an image deposed in the collective unconscious to the utopia of a classless society.[82] In Benjamin's works, messianism, romanticism, and utopia merge without excluding one another; they are gathered by the "now-time," which connects the remembrance of the past with the utopia of the future. In his theses of 1940, he formulates this idea through the image of a "secret heliotropism" of history.[83] In such a vision of history, Stéphane Moses observed, "utopia appears in the very heart of the present," as "a hope lived in the mode of today."[84] Marx himself, seen by Benjamin as a prophet of catastrophes rather than as the oracle of a radiant future, paid tribute in *The Communist Manifesto* to the utopian socialists, the first ones who elaborated "the fantastic pictures of future society."[85]

The antiutopic assessments of Bensaïd resulted from the turn of 1989, the symbolic moment of crystallization of a cumulative cycle of defeats. It was the outcome of an internalized shipwreck that produced a blooming of memories; it had nothing to do with the commonplace that identifies utopia with totalitarianism. Nor was it nostalgia for the clichés about the passage of socialism "from utopia to science." Probably there was also, for an intellectual who had been one of the actors of May '68, the will to oppose a generation that had quietly passed from Maoism to the rejection of communism as a totalitarian ideology. Twenty years after May '68, the "utopia in power" designated a considerable number of former rebels ultimately well installed in the institutions of the Fifth Republic, where they occupied parliamentary seats and ministerial offices. Benjamin's time was saturated with utopias (not only those of the Russian soviets but also those of the "Thousand-Year Reich," with their respective "new men"); Bensaïd's time experienced their fall, whose outcome was the melancholy of a century of defeated revolutions. In *Moi, la révolution*, he expressed this deep melancholic feeling through the words of the revolution itself:

> He fell into an infinite sadness that rendered him speechless. That digs a deep intimate emptiness as if one suddenly parted from ones' self. I know what I'm talking about; it is a deep plunge into melancholy, the classical melancholia of Saint-Just and Blanqui, more austere than the romantic and disenchanted melancholy of Baudelaire or Mallarmé. This type has the lucidity of catastrophe dressed against the sacred homilies of progress. I ran into it in 1794. I found it once more after June 1848. It was still there in the aftermath of the Commune, that melancholic eternity of mankind under the stars . . . that caused Blanqui to totter on the threshold of madness.[86]

In one of the most beautiful pages of his book on Benjamin—another possible effect of this dialectical reverberation of 1940 in 1990—Bensaïd evoked his "melancholic galaxy" in which he put four very different figures: Baudelaire, Blanqui, Sorel, and Péguy.[87] The first two certainly belonged to the universe of the German philosopher, the second two to his own. Then he inscribed Benjamin into another genealogy, beside Saint-Just, Rosa Luxemburg, Gramsci, Trotsky, and Che Guevara. There is no doubt that Bensaïd shared the spirit of Benjamin, for whom struggles "are nourished by the image of enslaved ancestors."[88] In *Le pari mélancholique* (1997), he reformulated this intuition—borrowed from Blanqui—using a famous essay of Lucien Goldmann on Pascal: revolution is a *bet*.[89] The twentieth century had accentuated the tragic dimension of the great revolutionaries whose actions always were inspired by the hope of a future liberation as well as by the recollection of defeated revolutions and broken dreams, by the debt tacitly inherited from the vanquished of history. Such a melancholic dimension dealt with the awareness that nothing is won in advance, that "the enemy has never ceased to be victorious" (Benjamin) and that, "in the balance of probabilities, barbarism does not have fewer chances than socialism" (Bensaïd). In other words, the transformation of the world was a melancholic bet, neither hazardous nor foolish, nourished by memory, voluntarist but also based on reason, a mixture of "strategic hypothesis and regulating horizon."[90] Ernst Bloch would have defined it through a formula that Bensaïd disliked: "a concrete (and possible) utopia."

NOTES

INTRODUCTION

1. Rainhart Koselleck, "Historia Magistra Vitae: The Dissolution of the Topos Into the Perspective of a Modernized Historical Process" (1967), in *Futures Past: On the Semantics of Historical Time*, ed. Keith Tribe (New York: Columbia University Press, 2004), 26–42.
2. Francis Fukuyama, "The End of History?," *National Interest*, Summer 1989, 3–18; Fukuyama, *The End of History and the Last Man* (New York: Free Press, 1992); on this debate, see Perry Anderson, "The Ends of History," in *A Zone of Engagement* (London: Verso, 1992), 279–375; and Josep Fontana, *La Historia después del fin da la Historia* (Barcelona: Crítica, 1992).
3. Perry Anderson, "Renewals," *New Left Review* 1 (2000): 13.
4. Eric Hobsbawm, *Age of Extremes: A History of the World, 1914–1991* (New York: Vintage, 1995).
5. Christa Wolf, *City of Angels or the Overcoat of Dr. Freud* (New York: Farrar, Straus and Giroux, 2010).
6. Reinhart Koselleck, "Einleitung," in *Geschichtliche Grundbegriffe: Historisches Lexikon zur politisch-sozialen Sprache in Deutschland*, ed. Otto Brunner,

Werner Conze, and Reinhart Koselleck, 8 vols. (Stuttgar: Klett-Cotta, 1972), 1:xv. See also Gabriel Motzkin, "On the Notion of Historical (Dis)continuity: Reinhart Koselleck's Construction of the *Sattelzeit*," *Contributions to the History of Concepts* 1, no. 2 (2005): 145–58. On the emergence of a new concept of history, cf. Reinhart Koselleck, "*Geschichte, Historie,*" in *Geschichtliche Grundbegriffe*, 2:593–717.

7. For the analytical description of this historical change, see Pierre Dardot and Christian Laval, *The New Way of the World: On Neoliberal Society* (London: Verso, 2014).

8. On this debate, opened by François Furet, *Interpreting the French Revolution* (New York: Cambridge University Press, 1981), see Steven Kaplan, *Farewell Revolution: The Historians' Feud, France, 1789–1989* (Ithaca: Cornell University Press, 1996).

9. Quoted by Anna Bravo, *A colpi di cuore* (Rome-Bari: Laterza, 2008), 220.

10. Wendy Brown, "Women's Unbound: Revolution, Mourning, Politics," *Parallax* 9, no. 2 (2003): 13.

11. Reinhart Koselleck, "Historical Criteria of the Modern Concept of Revolution" (1969), in *Futures Past*, 43–57.

12. Martin Malia, *History's Locomotives: Revolutions and the Making of the Modern World* (New Haven: Yale University Press, 2006).

13. François Furet, *Passing of an Illusion: The Idea of Communism in the Twentieth Century* (Chicago: University of Chicago Press, 1999), 502.

14. Frederic Jameson, "Future City," *New Left Review* 21 (2003): 76.

15. Ernst Bloch, *The Principle of Hope*, 3 vols. (Cambridge: MIT Press, 1986); Hans Jonas, *The Imperative of Responsibility: In Search of an Ethics for the Technological Age* (Chicago: University of Chicago Press, 1985).

16. Reinhart Koselleck, "'Space of Experience' and 'Horizon of Expectation': Two Historical Categories," in *Futures Past*, 258–59.

17. Bloch, *The Principle of Hope*. See also Ruth Levitas, "Educated Hope: Ernst Bloch on Abstract and Concrete Utopia," *Utopian Studies* 1, no. 2 (1990): 13–26.

18. Peter Thompson, "Introduction: The Privatization of Hope and the Crisis of Negation," in *The Privatization of Hope: Ernst Bloch and the Future of Utopia*, ed. Peter Thompson and Slavoj Žižek (Durham: Duke University Press, 2013), 1–20.

19. François Hartog, *Régimes d'historicité: Présentisme et experiences du temps* (Paris: Éditions du Seuil, 2003), 119–27.

20. Reinhart Koselleck, "History, Histories, and Formal Time Structures," in *Futures Past*, 95.

21. According to the famous formula coined by Ernst Nolte during the German *Historikerstreit* of the 1980s.

22. T. J. Clark, "For a Left with No Future," *New Left Review* 74 (2012): 75, followed by the cogent criticism of Susan Watkins, "Presentism? A Reply to T. J. Clark," 77–102.

23. Thompson, "Introduction: The Privatization of Hope and the Crisis of Negation," 15.

24. See Annette Wieviorka, *The Era of the Witness* (Ithaca: Cornell University Press, 2006).

25. Tony Judt, *Postwar: A History of Europe Since 1945* (London: Penguin, 2005), 802–33.

26. Walter Benjamin, "On the Concept of History," in *Selected Writings*, ed. Howard Eiland and Michael W. Jennings, 4 vols. (Cambridge: Harvard University Press, 2003–06), 4:392–93, 395.

27. Adolfo Gilly, "Mil Novecientos Ochenta y Nueve" (1990), in *El siglo del relampago: Siete Ensayos Sobre el Siglo XX* (Mexico: La Jornada Ediciones, 2002), 118. He implicitly referred to the novel of Victor Serge, *Midnight in the Century* (London: Writers and Readers, 1982).

28. Siegfried Kracauer, *History: The Last Things Before the Last*, ed. Paul Oskar Kristeller (Princeton: Markus Wiener, 1995), 83–84. See also Georg Simmel, "The Stranger," in *The Sociology of Georg Simmel*, ed. K. H. Wolff (New York: Free Press, 1950), 402–8.

29. Saul Friedländer, "Trauma, Transference and Working-Through," *History and Memory* 1, no. 4 (1992): 39–55.

30. Ernest Mandel, *Revolutionary Marxism Today* (London: New Left Books, 1979).

31. www.musicaememoria.com/loradelfucile.htm.

32. Jean-Paul Sartre and Arlette Elkaïm-Sartre, *On Genocide: A Summary of the Evidence and the Judgments of the International War Crimes Tribunal* (Boston: Beacon, 1968); John Duffett, ed., *Against the Crime of Silence: Proceedings of the Russell International War Crimes Tribunal* (New York: Bertrand Russell Peace Foundation, 1968).

33. See Berthold Molden, "Genozid in Vietnam: 1968 als Schlüsselereignis in der Globalisierung des Holocaust-diskurses," in *Weltwende 1968? Ein Jahr aus globalgeschichtlicher Perspektive*, ed. Jens Kastner and David Mayer (Vienna: Mandelbaum Verlag, 2008), 83–97.

34. Michael Rothberg, *Multidirectional Memory: Remembering the Holocaust in the Age of Decolonization* (Stanford: Stanford University Press, 2009), chap. 3; Aimé Césaire, *Discourse on Colonialism* (New York: Monthly Review Press, 2000).

35. See Kristin Ross, *May '68 and Its Afterlives* (Chicago: University of Chicago Press, 2002).

36. See Giovanni De Luna, *Le ragioni di un decennio, 1969–1979: Militanza, violenza, sconfitta, memoria* (Milano: Feltrinelli, 2009).

37. Among others Götz Aly, *Unser kampf 1968: ein irritierter Blick zurück* (Frankfurt: Fischer, 2008).

38. Dan Diner, *Gegenläufige Gedächtnisse: Über Geltung und Wirkung des Holocaust* (Tübingen: Vandenhoeck und Ruprecht, 2007). On the commemorations of May 8, 1945, see Rudolf von Thadden and Steffen Kudelka, eds., *Erinnerung und Geschichte: 60 Jahre nach dem 8. Mai 1945* (Göttingen: Wallstein, 2006).

39. Peter Novick, *The Holocaust in American Life* (New York: Houghton Mifflin, 1999), 11, 198–99. On the concept of "civil religion," see Emilio Gentile, *Politics as Religion* (Princeton: Princeton University Press, 2006). On the Holocaust's memory as a foundation of the present discourse on the Rights of Man, see Daniel Levy and Natan Sznaider, *The Holocaust and Memory in the Global Age* (Philadelphia: Temple University Press, 2006).

40. Peter Reichel, *Vergangenheitsbewältigung in Deutschland: Die Auseinandersetzung mit der NS-Diktatur von 1945 bis heute* (Munich: C. H. Beck, 2007); Régine Robin, *Berlin chantiers* (Paris: Stock, 2000).

41. See, in particular, Santos Juliá, "Memoria, historia y política de un pasado de guerra y dictadura," in *Memoria de la guerra y del franquismo*, ed. Santos Juliá (Madrid: Taurus, 2006), 15–26.

42. See, for instance, Paul Preston, *The Spanish Holocaust: Inquisition and Extermination in Twentieth Century Spain* (New York: Norton, 2013).

43. Milan Kundera, "L'Occident kidnappé ou la tragédie de l'Europe centrale," *Le Débat* 27 (1983): 3–22.

44. Tatiana Zhurzhenko, "The Geopolitics of Memory," May 10, 2007, *www.eurozine.com*.

45. Judt, *Postwar*, 803.

46. Jürgen Habermas, "Bestialität und Humanität," *Die Zeit* 18 (April 29, 1999): 6–7.

47. On Sétif, see Yves Benot, *Massacres coloniaux* (Paris: La Découverte, 2001), 9–35.

48. Theodor W. Adorno, "The Meaning of Working Through the Past," in *Critical Models: Interventions and Catchwords* (New York: Columbia University Press, 1998), 89.

49. Giorgio Agamben, "On the Uses and Disadvantages of Living Among Specters," in *Nudities* (Stanford: Stanford University Press, 2011), 39–40.

50. Jacques Derrida, *Specters of Marx: The State of the Debt, the Work of Mourning, and the New International* (London: Routledge, 1994), 101.

51. Erri De Luca, "Notizie su Euridice," *Il Manifesto*, November 7, 2013.
52. Judith Butler, "Violence, Mourning, Politics," in *Precarious Life: The Powers of Mourning and Violence* (London: Verso, 2004), 21.
53. Douglas Crimp, "Mourning and Militancy," *October* 51 (1989): 18.

1. THE CULTURE OF DEFEAT

1. Alexander Mitscherlich and Margarete Mitscherlich, *The Inability to Mourn: Principles of Collective Behavior* (New York: Grove, 1975).
2. Mario Vargas Llosa, *The Storyteller* (New York: Farrar, Straus and Giroux, 1989).
3. Roger Bartra, "Arabs, Jews, and the Enigma of Spanish Imperial Melancholy," *Discourse* 22, no. 3 (2000): 64–72.
4. Quoted by Josef Hayim Yerushalmi, *From the Spanish Court to the Italian Ghetto: Isaac Cardoso: A Study in Seventeenth Century Marranism and Jewish Apologetics* (New York: Columbia University Press, 1971), 437.
5. Raymond Klibansky, Erwin Panofsky, and Fritz Saxl, *Saturn and Melancholy: Studies in the History of Natural Philosophy, Religion and Art* (London: Nelson, 1964).
6. Chateaubriand, *The Genius of Christianity* (Philadelphia: Lippincott, 1856), 153.
7. Hans Blumenberg, *Shipwreck with Spectator: Paradigm of a Metaphor for Existence* (Cambridge: MIT Press, 1997).
8. Lucretius, *De Rerum Natura*, book 2, trans. Charles Stuart Calverley (Oxford: Clarendon, 1912).
9. Pascal, *Pensées*, ed. Philippe Sellier (Paris: Garnier, 1976), 69.
10. Siegfried Kracauer, *Theory of Film: The Redemption of Physical Reality*, ed. Miriam Bratu Hansen (Princeton: Princeton University Press, 1997), 17.
11. Reinhart Koselleck, "Transformations of Experience and Methodological Change: A Historical-Anthropological Essay," in *The Practice of Conceptual History*, ed. Todd Samuel Presner (Stanford: Stanford University Press, 2002), 76.
12. Ibid., 77.
13. Ibid., 82. Koselleck's sensitivity to the condition and spirit of the vanquished probably resulted from his experience as a German soldier on the Eastern front during the Second World War. On his intellectual and existential trajectory, see Niklas Olsen, *History in the Plural: An Introduction to the Work of Reinhart Koselleck* (New York: Berghahn, 2012), 281, who stresses his use of the couple victors/vanquished as "counter-concepts."

14. Walter Benjamin, "On the Concept of History" (1940), in *Selected Writings*, ed. Howard Eiland and Michael W. Jennings, 4 vols. (Cambridge: Harvard University Press, 2003–06), 4:391.

15. Edward P. Thompson, *The Making of the English Working Class* (1963; Harmondsworth, UK: Penguin, 1984); Ranajit Guha, "On Some Aspects of the Historiography of Colonial India," in *Selected Subaltern Studies*, ed. Ranajit Guha and Gayatri Chakravorty Spivak (New York: Oxford University Press, 1988), 37–44.

16. Carl Schmitt, "Historiographie in nuce: Alexis de Tocqueville" (1946), in *Ex Captivitate Salus: Erfahrungen der Zeit 1945/47* (Berlin: Duncker und Humblot, 2002), 25–33.

17. Alexis de Tocqueville, *The Old Regime and the Revolution* (New York: Anchor, 1955).

18. Ibid., 31.

19. On the concept of *Katechon*, see, in particular, Massimo Cacciari, *Il potere che frena: Saggio di teologia politica* (Milan: Adelphi, 2013). Schmitt developed this concept in *Der Nomos der Erde im Völkerrecht der Jus Publicum Europaeum* (1950; Berlin: Duncker und Humblot, 1997), 28–32. On the uses of this concept by Schmitt, see the fourth section of Raphael Gross, *Carl Schmitt and the Jews: The "Jewish Question," the Holocaust, and the German Legal Theory* (Madison: University of Wisconsin Press, 2004).

20. Benjamin, "On the Concept of History," 391.

21. Theodor W. Adorno, *Negative Dialectics* (New York: Herder and Herder, 1973).

22. Schmitt, *Ex Captivitate Salus*, 31–32. This Guizot's sentence is quoted by A.-C. Saint-Beuve, *Nouveaux lundis* (Paris: Michel Lévy Frères, 1868), 306.

23. Auguste Blanqui, "The Eternity According to the Stars" (1872), *CR: The New Centennial Review* 9, no. 3 (2010): 59.

24. Walter Benjamin, "Paris, Capital of the Nineteenth Century: Exposé of 1939," in *The Arcades Project*, ed. Howard Eiland (Cambridge: Harvard University Press, 1999), 25–26.

25. Miguel Abensour, *Les Passages Blanqui: Walter Benjamin entre mélancolie et révolution* (Paris: Sens et Tonka, 2013), 56.

26. Eric Hobsbawm, "Histoire et illusion," *Le Débat* 89 (1996): 138.

27. Cf. Perry Anderson, "The Vanquished Left: Eric Hobsbawm," in *Spectrum: From Right to Left in the World of Ideas* (London: Verso, 2005), 277–320.

28. Cf. Eric Hobsbawm, *Age of Extremes, 1914–1991* (New York: Pantheon, 1995); François Furet, *The Passing of an Illusion: The Idea of Communism in the Twentieth Century* (Chicago: University of Chicago Press, 1999). I have developed this comparison in "Fin de siècle: le xxᵉ siècle d'Eric Hobsbawm,"

in *L'Histoire comme champ de bataille: Interpréter les violences du xxe siècle* (Paris: La Découverte, 2010), 27–58.

29. Hobsbawm, *Age of Extremes*, 7–8.

30. Ibid., 498.

31. Ibid., 380.

32. Ibid.

33. Eric Hobsbawm, *Interesting Times: A Twentieth-Century Life* (London: Allen Lane, 2002), 56.

34. Jacques Derrida, *Specters of Marx: The State of the Debt, the Work of Mourning, and the New International* (New York: Routledge, 1994), 37. See, on this point, Terry Eagleton, "Marxism Without Marxism," in *Ghostly Demarcations: A Symposium on Jacques Derrida's Specters of Marx*, by Jacques Derrida, Terry Eagleton, Fredric Jameson, and Antonio Negri (London: Verso, 2008), 86–87; and Elías José Palti, *Verdades y saberes del marxismo: Reacciones de una tradición politica ante su "crisis"* (Buenos Aires: Fondo de Cultura Economica, 2005), chap. 4.

35. Lucio Magri, *Il sarto di Ulm: Una possibile storia del PCI* (Milan: Il Saggiatore, 2009), 13; translated as *The Tailor of Ulm: A History of Communism* (London: Verso, 2011). See Bertolt Brecht, "Der Schneider von Ulm," in *Gedichte IV* (Frankfurt: Suhrkamp, 1961), 204–5.

36. Evgeny Preobrazhensky, *The Crisis of Soviet Industrialization: Selected Essays* (White Plains, N.Y.: M. E. Sharpe, 1979).

37. Arno J. Mayer, *The Persistence of the Old Regime: Europe to the Great War* (New York: Pantheon, 1981).

38. Magri, *Il sarto di Ulm*, 28.

39. Perry Anderson, "The Ends of History," in *A Zone of Engagement* (London: Verso, 1992), 367–68.

40. Karl Marx, *The Eighteenth Brumaire of Louis Bonaparte* (1852), in *Collected Works*, by Karl Marx and Friedrich Engels, 50 vols. (New York: International, 1979), 11:107.

41. Ibid.

42. Ibid., 147.

43. Karl Marx, *The Civil War in France* (1871), in *Collected Works*, 22:356.

44. See Robert Tombs, *The War Against Paris 1871* (New York: Cambridge University Press, 1981); and John Merriman, *Massacre: The Life and Death of the Paris Commune* (New York: Basic, 2014), 253.

45. Jules Vallès, *L'insurgé* (Paris: Le Livre de Poche, 1986), 4; Vallès, *The Insurrectionist* (Englewood Cliffs, NJ: Prentice-Hall, 1971), xxi.

46. Ibid., 431; 228. On Jules Vallès's melancholy of defeat, see Scott McCracken, "The Mood of Defeat," *New Formations* 82 (2014): 64–81 (I keep also his better English translation).

47. Louise Michel, *The Red Virgin: Memoirs of Louise Michel*, ed. Bullitt Lowry and Elisabeth Ellington Gunter (Alabama: University of Alabama Press, 1981), 68. See also Sidonie Verhaeghe, "Les Victimes furent sans nom et sans nombre: Louise Michel et la mémoire des morts de la Commune de Paris," *Mots* 100 (2012): 31–42.

48. See Kristin Ross, *Communal Luxury: The Political Imaginary of the Commune* (London: Verso, 2015).

49. Rosa Luxemburg, "Order Prevails in Berlin" (1919), in *Socialism or Barbarism: The Selected Writings of Rosa Luxemburg*, ed. Helen C. Scott and Paul Le Blanc (London: Pluto, 2010), 267.

50. Rosa Luxemburg, "The Crisis of Social Democracy" (1915), in *Socialism or Barbarism*, 204. See Michael Löwy, "Rosa Luxemburg Conception of 'Socialism' or 'Barbarism,'" in *On Changing the World: Essays in Political Philosophy, from Karl Marx to Walter Benjamin* (Atlantic Highlands, N.J.: Humanities, 1993), 91–99.

51. Leon Trotsky, "The USSR in War" (1939), in *In Defense of Marxism* (New York: Pathfinder, 1970). On this dark hypothesis foreseen by Trotsky, see Isaac Deutscher, *The Prophet Outcast: Trotsky, 1929–1940* (London: Verso, 2003), 379.

52. Leon Trotsky, "The Lessons of Spain: The Last Warning," in *The Spanish Revolution, 1931–1939* (New York: Pathfinder, 1973).

53. Isabelle Tombs, "'Morituri Vos Salutant': Szmul Zygielbojm's Suicide in 1943 and the International Socialist Community in London," *Holocaust and Genocide Studies* 14, no. 2 (2000): 242.

54. Ibid. Cf. also Henri Minczeles, *Histoire générale du Bund: Un mouvement révolutionnaire juif* (Paris: Austral, 1995), 418–20.

55. Benjamin, "On the Concept of History," 391.

56. Ibid., 395.

57. Paco Ignacio Taibo, *Guevara, Also Known as Che* (New York: Macmillan, 1999), 558.

58. Salvador Allende, "Last Words Transmitted by Radio Magallanes (September 11, 1973)," in *Salvador Allende Reader: Chile's Voice of Democracy*, ed. James D. Cockroft (Melbourne: Ocean, 2000), 240.

59. Pablo Milanés, "Yo pisaré las calles nuevamente" (1974). Both Allende's speech and Milanés's song are easily available on Youtube.

60. Tommaso Campanella, "The City of the Sun," in *Rousseau's Social Contract, More's Utopia, Bacon's New Atlantis, Campanella's City of the Sun* (New York: Walter Dunne, 1901), 305. On Campanella, see Marek Bienczyk, *Melancolía* (Barcelona: Acxantilado, 2014), 49–50.

61. For a history of the concept of melancholy, see Jean Starobinski, *L'encre de la mélancholie* (Paris: Seuil, 2012). On the antithesis between melancholia

and utopia, see Wolf Lepenies, *Melancholy and Society* (Cambridge: Harvard University Press, 1992).

62. On the history of the pictorial representation of melancholy, see Jean Clair, ed., *Mélancolie: Génie et folie en Occident* (Paris: Réunion des Musées nationaux, Gallimard, 2005).

63. On the genesis of this woodcut, see Martha Kearns, *Käthe Köllwitz: Woman and Artist* (New York: CUNY Press, 1976), 161–63.

64. See Jorge Castañeda, *The Life and Death of Che Guevara* (New York: Knopf, 1997), chap. 11.

65. Régis Debray, *Praised Be Our Lords: A Political Education* (London: Verso, 2007), 103.

66. Aby Warburg, *Heidnisch-antike Weissagung in Wort und Bild zu Luthers Zeit* (Heidelberg: Carl Winter Universitätsbuchhandlung, 1920); on this debate, see Peter-Klaus Schuster, *Melencolia I: Dürers Bild*, 2 vols. (Berlin: Mann, 1991), summarized in Peter-Klaus Schuster, "Melancolia I: Dürer et sa postérité," in Clair, *Mélancolie*, 90–105.

67. See Ernst Gombrich, *Aby Warburg: An Intellectual Biography* (Chicago: University of Chicago Press, 1986), 249.

68. Erwin Panofsky and Fritz Saxl, "Dürers 'Melancolia I': Eine quellen- und typengeschichtliche Untersuchung," in *Studien der Warburg Institut 2* (Leipzig, 1922), today included in Raymond Klibansky, Erwin Panofsky, and Fritz Saxl, *Saturn and Melancholy: Studies in the History of Natural Philosophy, Religion, and Art* (New York: Basic, 1963). This study influenced Walter Benjamin's vision of melancholy in *The Origin of German Tragic Drama* (London: Verso, 1977), 140, 157. The members of the Warburg Institute, nevertheless, did not return this admiration; see Max Pensky, *Melancholy Dialectics: Walter Benjamin and the Play of Mourning* (Amherst: University of Massachusetts Press, 1993), 263–64.

69. Lucien Goldmann, *The Hidden God: A Study of Tragic Vision in the Pensées of Pascal and the Tragedies of Racine* (London: Routledge, 1964).

70. Alois Riegl, "The Modern Cult of Monuments: Its Character and its Origin" (1903), *Oppositions* 25 (1982). See also Michael Ann Holly, *The Melancholy Art* (Princeton: Princeton University Press, 2013), 9–10.

71. Anderson, "The Ends of History," 368.

72. Sigmund Freud, "Mourning and Melancholia" (1915), in *Complete Psychological Works*, ed. J. Strachey (London: Hogarth, 1957), 14:244. Giorgio Agamben stresses the continuity of Freud's vision of melancholy with the classical tradition in the first section ("The Phantasms of Eros") of *Stanzas: Word and Phantasm in Western Culture* (Minneapolis: University of Minnesota Press, 1993), 3–29.

73. Ibid., 250.

74. See Robert Hertz, *Death and the Right Hand* (1907; New York: Glencoe, 1960).

75. Wendy Brown, "Resisting Left Melancholia," in *Loss: The Politics of Mourning*, ed. David L. Eng and David Kazanjian (Berkeley: University of California Press, 2003), 458–65; for an informed critique of Brown's thesis, see Jodi Dean, "Communist Desire," in *The Idea of Communism 2: The New York Conference*, ed. Slavoj Žižek (London: Verso, 2013), 77–102.

76. Judith Butler, *The Psychic Life of Power: Theories in Subjection* (Stanford: Stanford University Press, 1997), 170. See also Michael P. Steinberg, "Music and Melancholy," *Critical Inquiry* 40, no. 2 (2014): 288–310.

77. Benjamin, "On the Concept of History," 391.

78. Siegrfied Kracauer, *The Salaried Masses: Duty and Distraction in Weimar Germany* (London: Verso, 1998). Benjamin wrote an enthusiastic review of this essay: Benjamin, "An Outsider Makes His Mark," in *Selected Writings*, 2:1:305–11. On the influence of Kracauer's essay on Benjamin's critique of the New Objectivity, see Howard Eiland and Michael W. Jennings, *Walter Benjamin: A Critical Life* (Cambridge: Harvard University Press, 2014), 340–41.

79. Benjamin, "Left-Wing Melancholy" (1931), in *Selected Writings*, 2:2:426.

80. Kracauer, *The Salaried Masses*, 88; he implicitly referred to Lukács's concept of "transcendental homelessness" (*transzendentale Obdachlosigkeit*); see Georg Lukács, *The Theory of the Novel* (London: Merlin, 1971), 61.

81. Cf. Roger Bartra, *Cultura y Mélancolía: Las infermedades del alma en la España del Siglo de Oro* (Barcelona: Anagrama, 2001), 157–61, 225–26.

82. Benjamin, *The Origin of German Tragic Drama*, 142.

83. Benjamin, "Agesilaus Santander" (1931), in *Selected Writings*, 2:2:713, 715 (two versions). According to Max Pensky, melancholy would be the connector between the "messianic" and the "materialistic" dimensions of Benjamin's thought; see Max Pensky, *Melancholy Dialectics: Walter Benjamin and the Play of Mourning* (Amherst: University of Massachusetts Press, 1993), 16. On Benjamin's melancholic character, see Gershom Scholem, "Walter Benjamin and His Angel," in *On Walter Benjamin: Critical Essays and Recollections* (Cambridge: MIT Press, 1988), 58–59. On Benjamin's concept of melancholy, see Beatrice Hansen, "Portrait of Melancholy (Benjamin, Warburg, Panofsky)," *MLN* 114, no. 5 (1999): 991–1013; and Françoise Meltzer, "Acedia and Melancholia," in *Walter Benjamin and the Demands of History*, ed. Michael P. Steinberg (Ithaca: Cornell University Press, 1996), 141–63.

84. Benjamin, *The Origin of German Tragic Drama*, 140.

85. Hanssen, "Portrait of Melancholy," 1003.

86. Benjamin, "An Outsider Makes His Mark," 2:2:310.

87. Jonathan Flately, *Affective Mapping: Melancholia and the Politics of Modernism* (Cambridge: Harvard University Press, 2008), 65.

88. See the photographic documentation of this funeral by Mario Carnicelli, *25.8.1964: C'era Togliatti* (Ravenna: Danilo Montanari Editore, 2014).

89. Charles Péguy, "A nos amis, à nos abonnés" (1909), in *Œuvres en prose* (Paris: Gallimard, 1968), 2:1273; Daniel Bensaïd, "L'inglorieux vertical: Péguy critique de la raison historique," in *La Discordance des temps: Essais sur les crises, les classes, l'histoire* (Paris: Les Editions de la Passion, 1995), 196.

90. Raymond Williams, *Marxism and Literature* (Oxford: Oxford University Press, 1977), 128–35. For an interesting approach to both Heidegger and Williams, see Jonathan Flatley, *Affective Mapping*, notably the preliminary "glossary," 11–27.

91. Jean Améry, *At the Mind's Limits* (1966; Bloomington: Indiana University Press, 1980), 12–13.

92. Ibid., 14.

93. Primo Levi, *The Drowned and the Saved* (New York: Simon and Schuster, 1988), 146.

94. Slavoj Žižek, "Melancholy and the Act," *Critical Inquiry* 26, no. 4 (2000): 657–81.

95. Raymond Willians, *Modern Tragedy* (London: Chatto and Windus, 1966), 64.

96. Goldmann, *The Hidden God*, 301.

97. Ibid. On Goldmann's vision of the socialist "wager," see Mitchell Cohen, *The Wager of Lucien Goldmann: Tragedy, Dialectics, and a Hidden God* (Princeton: Princeton University Press, 1994); and Michael Löwy, "Lucienn Goldmann or the Communitarian Wager," *Socialism and Democracy* 11, no. 1 (1997): 25–35.

98. See Antonio Gramsci, *Quaderni del Carcere*, ed. Valentino Gerratana, 4 vols. (Torino: Einaudi, 1975), 2:1403.

2. MARXISM AND MEMORY

1. Leon Trotsky, *History of the Russian Revolution*, 2 vols. (Chicago: Haymarket, 2007), 1:xvii.

2. Leon Trotsky, *My Life* (New York: Scribner's, 1930), xvi.

3. Good examples are Jeffrey J. Olick, ed., *The Collective Memory Reader* (New York: Oxford University Press, 2011); Michael Rossington and Anne Whitehead, eds., *Theories of Memory: A Reader* (Baltimore: Johns Hopkins University Press, 2007); and Astrid Erll and Ansgar Nünning, eds., *Cultural*

Memories Studies: An International and Interdisciplinary Handbook (Berlin: Walter de Gruyter, 2008).

4. Cf. Perry Anderson, *In the Tracks of Historical Materialism* (London: Verso, 1983).

5. Cf. Dan Diner, "Von 'Gesellschaft' zu 'Gedächtnis': Über historische Paradigmenwechsel," in *Gedächtniszeiten: Über jüdische und andere Geschichten* (Munich: C. H. Beck, 2003), 7–15; in a similar way, other scholars stressed a parallel shift from "class" to "identity": see Carlos Forcadell, "La Historia social, de la 'clase' a la 'identidad,'" in *Sobre la Historia actual*, ed. Helena Hernández Sandoica and Alicia Langa (Madrid: Abada Editores, 2005), 15–35.

6. Reinhart Koselleck, "'Space of Experience' and 'Horizon of Expectation': Two Historical Categories," *Futures Past: On the Semantics of Historical Time*, ed. Keith Tribe (Cambridge: MIT Press 1985), 235–75.

7. Annette Wieviorka, *The Age of the Witness* (Ithaca: Cornell University Press, 2006).

8. Cf. Régine Robin, *Berlin chantiers* (Paris: Stock, 2001).

9. Cf. *Materialen zum Denkmal für die ermordeten Juden Europas*, ed. Stiftung Denkmal für die ermordeten Juden Europas (Berlin: Nicolai, 2005).

10. Karl Marx, *The Eighteenth Brumaire of Louis Bonaparte*, in *Collected Works*, by Karl Marx and Friedrich Engels, 50 vols. (New York: International, 1975–2005), 14:ii.

11. Ibid.

12. Ibid. All this debate is analyzed in a further chapter.

13. Cf. Casey Harison, "The Paris Commune of 1871, the Russian Revolution of 1905, and the Shifting of the Revolutionary Tradition," *History and Memory* 17, no. 2 (2007): 5–42.

14. Vladimir I. Lenin, *The State and the Revolution* (New York: International, 1932).

15. Albert Mathiez, *Le bolchévisme et le jacobinisme* (Paris: Librairie de l'Humanité, 1920).

16. Cf. Daniel Bensaïd and Henri Weber, *Mai 68: Une répétition générale* (Paris: Maspero 1968).

17. Eric Hobsbawm, "The Influence of Marxism, 1945–83," in *How to Change the World: Tales of Marx and Marxism* (London: Little, Brown, 2011), 362.

18. Victor Serge, *Memoirs of a Revolutionary* (New York: New York Review of Books, 2012), 103; and Serge, "La ville en danger" (1924), in *Mémoires d'un révolutionnaires et autres écrits politiques* (Paris: Laffont, 2001), 79.

19. Raphael Samuel, *Theatres of Memory* (London: Verso, 1994), 27.

20. Cf. Michele Nani, "'Dalle viscere del popolo': Pellizza, il *Quarto Stato* e il socialismo," in *Il Quarto Stato di Pellizza da Volpedo tra cultura e politica*, by

Michele Nani, Liliana Ellena, and Marco Scavino (Turin: Istituto Salvemini, 2002), 13–54.

21. Friedrich Engels, "Introduction to Karl Marx's *The Class Struggles in France 1848 to 1850*," in Marx and Engels, *Collected Works*, 27:518, 513.

22. Ibid.

23. Claudia Verhoeven, "Time of Terror, Terror of Time: On the Impatience of Russian Revolutionary Terrorism (Early 1860s–Early 1880s)," *Jahrbücher für Geschichte Osteuropa* 58, no. 2 (2010): 254–72.

24. Svetlana Boym, "Ruins of the Avant-Garde: From Tatlin's Tower to Paper Architecture," in *Ruins of Modernity*, ed. Julia Hell and Andreas Schönle (Durham: Duke University Press, 2010), 58–85.

25. On the genesis and abandonment of this project, see Marie Bouchard, " 'Un monument au travail': The Projects of Meunier, Dalou, Rodin, and Bouchard," *Oxford Art Journal* 8, no. 2 (1981): 28–35.

26. See Norbert Lynton, *Tatlin's Tower: Monument to Revolution* (New Heaven: Yale University Press, 2009); and Pamela Kachurin, "Working (for) the State: Vladimir Tatlin's Career in Early Soviet Russia and the Origins of *The Monument to the Third International*," *Modernism/Modernity* 19, no. 1 (2012): 19–41. Finally, Tatlin's project was not realized because of the opposition of Anatoly Lunacharsky, the Commissar of Enlightenment. See Sheila Fitzpatrick, *The Commissariat of Enlightenment: Soviet Organization of Education and the Arts Under Lunacharsky, October 1917–1921* (Cambridge: Cambridge University Press, 2002).

27. Cf. Susan Buck-Morss, *Dreamworld and Catastrophe: The Passing of Mass Utopia in East and West* (Cambridge: MIT Press, 2002), 43–44; and Margit Rowell, "Vladimir Tatlin: Form/Faktura," *October* 7 (1978): 83–108.

28. Cf. Buck-Morss, *Dreamworld and Catastrophe*, 174–76.

29. This secularized messianism cannot be assimilated to the popular language of advertising analyzed by Carlo Ginzburg in his essay on the famous poster of Lord Kitchener, which includes an interesting genealogy of the stretched finger; cf. Carlo Ginzburg, " 'Your Country Needs You': A Case Study in Political Iconography," *History Workshop Journal* 52 (2001): 1–22.

30. Karl Marx, "Towards the Critique of Hegel's *Philosophy of Right*" (1844), in *Basic Writings on Politics and Philosophy*, by Karl Marx and Friedrich Engels, ed. Fritz J. Raddatz (London: Fontana, 1969), 304. The "double character" of Marx's interpretation of religion is pointed out in Michael Löwy, *The War of Gods: Religion and Politics in Latin America* (London: Verso, 1996), 4–18.

31. Boris Groys, *The Total Art of Stalinism: Avant-Garde, Aesthetic Dictatorship, and Beyond* (London: Verso, 2011), 113.

32. See notably Rivera's *Epopeya del Pueblo Mexicano* (1929–51) illustrating the steps of the Mexican National Palace.

33. Ernst Bloch, *The Principle of Hope*, 3 vols. (Cambridge: MIT Press 1995), 3:1354 ("Karl Marx and Humanity: Stuff of Hope"). See Arno Münster, *Tagträume vom aufrechten Gang: Sechs Interviews mit Ernst Bloch* (Frankfurt: Suhrkamp, 1977); and Vincent Geoghegan, *Utopianism and Marxism* (London: Methuen, 1987), chap. 6.

34. Herbert Marcuse, *Eros and Civilization* (London: Sphere, 1970), 33.

35. Ibid., 163.

36. Ibid., 109.

37. Herbert Marcuse, "The End of Utopia," in *Five Lectures* (London: Allen Lane, 1970), 63.

38. Vincent Veoghegan, "Remembering the Future," *Utopian Studies* 1, no. 2 (1990): 52–68.

39. Ugo Tommei, "Aboliamo la storia," *Italia Futurista*, May 7, 1917, quoted by Emilio Gentile, *"La nostra sfida alle stelle": Futuristi in Politica* (Rome: Laterza, 2009), 26.

40. Leon Trotsky, *Literature and Revolution* (Chicago: Haymarket, 2005), 115.

41. Ibid.

42. Trotsky, *History of the Russian Revolution*, 2:702.

43. Trotsky, *Literature and Revolution*, 204–5.

44. Alexander Bogdanov, *Red Star: The First Bolshevik Utopia* (Bloomington: Indiana University Press, 1984). See also K. M. Jensen, "Red Star: Bogdanov Builds a Utopia," *Studies in Soviet Thought* 23, no. 1 (1982): 1–34.

45. Isaac Deutscher, *The Prophet Outcast* (London: Verso, 2003), 189.

46. See Jeffrey Herf, *Reactionary Modernism: Technology, Culture, and Politics in Weimar and the Third Reich* (New York: Cambridge University Press, 1984).

47. See Romke Visser. "Fascist Doctrine and the Cult of the Romanità," *Journal of Contemporary History* 27, no. 1 (1992): 5–22; Marla Stone, "A Flexible Rome: Fascism and the Cult of *Romanità*," in *Roman Presences: Receptions of Rome in European Culture, 1789–1945*, ed. Catharine Edwards (New York: Cambridge University Press 1999), 205–20.

48. Johann Chapoutot, *Le national-socialisme et l'Antiquité* (Paris: Presses Universitaires de France 2008), 484.

49. Walter Benjamin, "On the Concept of History," in *Selected Writings*, ed. Howard Eiland and Michael W. Jennings, 4 vols. (Cambridge: Harvard University Press, 2003–06), 4:394.

50. José Rabasa, *Without History: Subaltern Studies, the Zapatistas Insurgency, and the Specter of History* (Pittsburgh: University of Pittsburgh Press, 2010), 138–47.

51. Bruno Bosteels, *The Actuality of Communism* (London: Verso, 2011).

52. Quoted by Jérôme Bachet, "L'histoire face au present perpetuel: Quelques

Remarques sur la relation passé/futur," in *Les usages politiques du passé*, ed. François Hartog and Jacques Revel (Paris: Éditions de l'EHESS 2001), 65.

53. Hans Mayer, *Der Turm von Babel: Erinnerungen an eine Deutsche Demokratische Republik* (Frankfurt: Suhrkamp, 1991), 15–16.

54. Johannes R. Becher, "Der Turm von Babel," in *Gesammelte Werke*, ed. Akademie der Künste, 18 vols. (Berlin: Aufbau, 1966–81), 6:40; Mayer, *Der Turm von Babel*, 11.

55. Buck-Morss, *Dreamworld and Catastrophe*, 67–69. Such a painting is reminiscent of the correspondence between Gershom Scholem and Walter Benjamin concerning the interpretation of a passage of Kafka's *Trial* depicting young Jewish students reading Kabbalistic texts. According to Scholem, the problem wasn't the loss of the texts themselves, but their incapacity to decipher them: see Walter Benjamin and Gershom Scholem, *Correspondance, 1933–1940*, ed. Gary Smith (Cambridge: Harvard University Press, 1992), 126–27.

56. Reinhart Koselleck,"Modernity and the Planes of Historicity," in *Futures Past*, 11.

57. Marcelo Brodsky, *Buena Memoria* (Ostfildern: Hatje Cantz, 2003).

58. Ibid., 95.

59. Juan-José Saer, *El rio sin orillas* (Barcelona: Seix Barral, 2003).

60. Paul Celan, "Todesfuge/Deathfugue," in *Selected Poems and Prose*, ed. John Felstiner (New York: Norton, 2001), 33.

61. Walter Benjamin, "Paralipomena to 'On the Concept of History,'" in *Selected Writings*, 4:404–7; and Gerhard Richter, *Thought-Images: Frankfurt School Writers' Reflections from Damaged Life* (Stanford: Stanford University Press, 2007), chaps. 1, pp. 43–71. On the dialectical images in Brodsky, see Nora Rabotnikov Maskivker, "El angel de la mémoria," in *La Mirada del Angel: En torno a las Tesis sobre la Historia de Walter Benjamin*, ed. Bolívar Echeverría (Mexico: Era, 2005), 155–70.

3. MELANCHOLY IMAGES

1. Emir Kusturica, "Souvenirs de bord," in *Il était une fois . . . Underground*, by Serge Grunberg and Emir Kusturica (Paris: Editions des Cahiers du Cinéma, 1995), 11–12; quoted in Antoine De Baecque, *Camera Historica: The Century in Cinema* (New York: Columbia University Press, 2012), 253.

2. Giorgio Agamben, "L'élégie de Sokourov," *Cahiers du Cinéma* 586 (2004): 49.

3. Cf. Richard Porton and Lee Ellickson, "Comedy, Communism, and Pastry: An Interview With Nanni Moretti," *Cineaste* 21, nos. 1–2 (1995): 11–15.

4. Guido Bonsaver, "The Egocentric Cassandra of the Left: Representations of Politics in the Films of Nanni Moretti," *Italianist* 21–22 (2001–02): 158–83.

5. De Baecque, *Camera historica*, 3; and Hayden White, "Historiography and Historiophoty," *American Historical Review* 93, no. 5 (1988): 1193. For a general approach to this controversial question, see Robert A. Rosenstone, *Visions of the Past: The Challenge of Film to Our Idea of History* (Cambridge: Harvard University Press, 1995).

6. Natalie Zemon Davis, *Slaves on Screen: Film and Historical Vision* (Cambridge: Harvard University Press, 2000), 14.

7. Paul Ginsborg, *A History of Contemporary Italy, 1943–1980* (London: Penguin, 2003), 139.

8. It was included in *Giorni di Gloria* (1945), a documentary on the Resistance directed by Mario Serandrei and Giuseppe De Santis, see Gianni Rondolino, *Luchino Visconti* (Torino: UTET, 2003), 162–64.

9. On the history of *La terra trema*, see Lino Micciché, *Visconti e il neorealismo* (Venezia: Marsilio, 1990), 76–85; and Gianni Rondolino, *Luchino Visconti*, 195–200.

10. Giovanni Verga, *The House by the Medlar-Tree* (New York: Harper, 1980).

11. Quoted in Rondolino, *Luchino Visconti*, 201.

12. Ibid., 205.

13. Luchino Visconti, "Oltre il fato dei Malavoglia," *Vie Nuove*, October 22, 1960, 26–27.

14. Antonio Gramsci, "La questione meridionale" (1926), *Rinascita* 2 (1945): 33–42; "Some Aspects of the Southern Question," in *The Gramsci Reader: Selected Writings, 1916–1935*, ed. David Forgcas (New York: New York University Press, 2000), 171–85.

15. Lino Micciché qualifies *La terra trema* as "the only great Marxist film of neorealism," see *Visconti e il neorealismo*, 185.

16. Cf. Lara Pucci, " 'Terra Italia': The Peasant Subject as Site of National and Socialist Identities in the Works of Renato Guttuso and Giuseppe De Santis," *Journal of the Warburg and Courtlaud Institutes* 71 (2008): 315–34.

17. See Nello Aiello, *Intellettuali e PCI 1944–1958* (Roma: Laterza, 1979).

18. Leo Tolstoy, *Divine and Human, and Other Stories* (Evanston, Ill.: Northwestern University Press, 2000).

19. Vittorio Taviani, quoted in Aldo Tassone, *Parla il cinema italiano* (Milano: Il Formichiere, 1980), 2:362. On *Saint Michael Had a Rooster*, see also Guido Aristarco, *Sotto il segno dello scorpione: Il cinema dei fratelli Taviani* (Messina: D'Anna, 1978), 101–52.

20. See Carlo Celli, *Gillo Pontecorvo: From Resistance to Terrorism* (Lanham, Md.: Scarecrow, 2005); and Irene Bignardi, *Memorie estorte a uno smemorato: Vita di Gillo Pontecorvo* (Milano: Feltrinelli, 1999).

21. Pauline Kael "The Battle of Algiers" (1966), in *5001 Nights at the Movies* (New York: Picador, 1991), 55.

22. Edward Said, "The Quest for Gillo Pontecorvo" (1988), in *Reflections on Exile, and Other Literary and Cultural Essays* (London: Granta Books, 2001), 284.

23. On the genesis of *Burn!*, see Celli, *Gillo Pontecorvo*, 69, who describes the film as a "colonial, postcolonial parable."

24. On this dialectical crossing of opposed trajectories, see Davis, *Slaves on Screen*, 51.

25. Frantz Fanon, "Racism and Culture" (1956), in *The Fanon Reader*, ed. Azzedine Haddour (London: Pluto, 2006), 19–31. On this Fanonian dimension of *Burn!*, see Michael T. Martin, "Podium for the Truth? Reading Slavery and the Neocolonial Project in the Historical Film: *Queimada* (*Burn!*) and Sankofa in Counterpoint," *Third Text* 23, no. 6 (2009): 723.

26. Said, "The Quest for Gillo Pontecorvo," 285.

27. Joan Mellen, "An Interview with Gillo Pontecorvo," *Film Quarterly* 26, no. 1 (1972): 2.

28. Frantz Fanon, *The Wretched of the Earth* (New York: Grove, 1963), 93. On the almost literal correspondence between the essay of Fanon and some dialogues in Pontecorvo's films, see Neelam Srivastava, "Anti-Colonial Violence and the 'Dictatorship of the Truth' in the Films of Gillo Pontecorvo," *Interventions: International Journal of Postcolonial Studies* 7, no. 1 (2005): 97–106.

29. Said, "The Quest for Gillo Pontecorvo," 289.

30. Pierre Nora, "Between Memory and History: Les *Lieux de Mémoire*," *Representations* 26 (1989): 7.

31. Ibid., 8–9. On the relationship between history and memory, see, in particular, Paul Ricœur, *Memory, History, Forgetting* (Chicago: University of Chicago Press, 2004); and Enzo Traverso, *Le Passé, mode d'emploi: Histoire, mémoire, politique* (Paris: La Fabrique, 2005).

32. Walter Benjamin, *The Origin of German Tragic Drama* (London: Verso, 1977), 140.

33. Cf. Michel Ciment, "Entretien avec Theo Angelopoulos," *Positif* 415 (1995): 26.

34. Quoted in Arthur J. Pomeroy, "The Sense of Epiphany in Theo Angelopoulos' Ulysses' Gaze," *Classical Receptions Journal* 3, no. 2 (2011): 220.

35. Ibid., 222.

36. Chris Marker, *Le fond de l'air est rouge: Scènes de la troisième guerre mondiale, 1967–1977* (Paris: François Maspero, 1978), 5. See also Michael Walsh, "Chris Marker's *A Grin Without a Cat*," *Moving Image* 3, no. 1 (2003): 168.

37. See Carlo Ginzburg, "Clues: Roots of an Evidential Paradigm," in *Clues, Myths, and the Historical Method* (Baltimore: Johns Hopkins University Press, 1989), 87–112.

38. Marker, *Le fond de l'air est rouge*, 6.

39. Ibid.

40. Ibid., 59–60.

41. Chris Marker, "Sixties," *Critical Quarterly* 50, no. 3 (2008): 30. Borrowed from Lewis Carroll's *Alice's Adventures in Wonderland*, the Cheshire cat became a totemic figure for Chris Marker (and gave the title to the English version of *Le fond de l'air est rouge*).

42. Ibid., 29. See Barry Langford, "'So Intensely Historical': Spectres of Theatre, Phantoms of Revolution in Marx and Marker," *Film Studies* 6 (2005): 64–72.

43. Marker, "Sixties," 32.

44. Marker, *Le fond de l'air est rouge*, 10.

45. Siegfried Kracauer, *Theory of Film*, ed. Miriam Bratu Hansen (Princeton: Princeton University Press, 1997), 226.

46. Ibid., 45.

47. Ibid., 226. In a review written in 1926 for the *Frankfurter Zeitung*, Kracauer already had presented *Battleship Potemkin* as a film that, "perhaps for the first time," had been able to "show the reality by the means of cinema." See Siegfried Kracauer, "Die Jupiterlampen brennen weiter," in *Kino* (Frankfurt: Suhrkamp, 1974), 75. On the affinities between Kracauer's theory of film and microhistory, see Carlo Ginzburg, "Details, Early Plans, Microanalysis: Thoughts on a Book by Siegfried Kracauer," in *Threads and Traces: True False Fictive* (Berkeley: University of California Press, 2012), 180–92.

48. Marker, *Le fond de l'air est rouge*, 6.

49. Ibid., 200.

50. This point is stressed by Sarah Cooper, *Chris Marker* (Manchester: Manchester University Press, 2008), 110.

51. Cf. David Foster, "'Thought Images' and Critical Lyricism: The *Debkbild* and Chris Marker's *Le Tombeau d'Alexandre*," *Images et Narratives* 10, no. 3 (2009): 12.

52. Javier Cercas, *Soldiers of Salamis* (New York: Bloomsbury, 2004). On the genesis of this movie, see Graham Fuller, *Loach on Loach* (London: Faber and Faber, 1998), 98–104; and Francis Rousselet, *Ken Loach, un rebelle* (Paris: Cerf-Corlet, 2002), 123–32.

53. Cf. Marcel Oms, *La Guerre d'Espagne au cinéma* (Paris: Cerf, 1986).

54. Jacques Rancière, "The Distribution of the Sensible: Politics and Aesthetic," in *The Politics of Aesthetics* (London: Bloomsbury, 2004), 7–14.

55. *The Collected Works of William Morris: Lover Is Enough; Poems by the Way*, ed. May Morris (London: Longmans, 1911), 9:181.

56. Interview with Ken Loach quoted in Philippe Pilard, *Land and Freedom: Ken Loach* (Paris: Nathan, 1997), 91.

57. The political positions of David Carr (POUM) and Gene Lawrence (Communist Party) in *Land and Freedom* have their historiographical equivalents in Pierre Broué, *The Revolution and the Civil War in Spain* (Cambridge: MIT Press, 1972); and Julian Casanova, *The Spanish Republic and Civil War* (New York: Cambridge University Press, 2010).

58. George Orwell, *Homage to Catalonia* (New York: Harcourt, 1952), 104–5.

59. On the controversies surrounding Capa's famous photograph, see H. Rosi Song, "Visual Fictions and the Archive of the Spanish Civil War," *MLN* 129, no. 2 (2014): 367–90.

60. Carmen Castillo had already depicted the death of Miguel Enriquez in *Un día de Octubre en Santiago* (Santiago: Editorial Sin Fronteras, 1986).

61. Ibid, 97–100.

62. Mónica Echeverria, Carmen Castillo, *Santiago—París: El vuelo de la memoria* (Santiago: LOM, 2002), 176.

63. Daniel Bensaïd, "Entretien avec Carmen Castillo," *Rouge* 2230 (2007).

64. In May 2010, a MIR Memorial was inaugurated in Villa Grimaldi, a former torture center of Santiago today transformed into a Peace Park, which contains the list of 580 MIR activists whose assassination had been proved.

65. Ibid.

66. Rancière, "The Distribution of the Sensible," 24.

67. Primo Levi, *Survival in Auschwitz* (New York: Simon and Schuster, 1996), 87.

68. Patricio Guzman, "Lo que debo a Chris Marker," in *Nuevo Texto Crítico* 47–48 (2011–12): 61–68.

69. Cf. Patrick Blaine, "Representing Absences in the Postdictatorial Documentary Cinema of Patricio Guzman," in *Latin American Perspectives* 40, no. 1 (2013): 114–30.

70. Cf. Patrick MacFadden, "Saturn's Feast: Loach's Spain: *Land and Freedom* as Filmed History," in *Agent of Challenge and Defiance: The Films of Ken Loach*, ed. George McKnight (Westport: Greenwood, 1997), 144–59.

71. Paul Celan, "The Meridian: Speech on the Occasion of the Award of the Georg Büchner Prize," in *Selected Poems and Prose*, ed. John Felstiner (New York: Norton, 2001), 410.

4. BOHEMIA

1. Henry Murger, *Latin Quarter: Scènes de la vie de Bohème* (New York: Mitchell, 1930).

2. Quoted by Helmut Kreuzer, *Die Boheme: Beiträge zur ihrer Beschreibung* (Stuttgart: J. B. Metzler, 1968), 7.

3. See Arno J. Mayer, *The Persistence of the Old Regime: Europe to the Great War* (New York: Pantheon, 1981).

4. Jerrold Seigel, *Bohemian Paris: Culture, Politics, and the Boundaries of Bourgeois Life, 1830–1930* (New York: Viking, 1986), 5.

5. Theodor Geiger, *Aufgaben und Stellung der Intelligenz in der Gesellschaft* (Stuttgart: F. Enke, 1949), 136.

6. On the English origins of dandyism, see Ellen Moers, *The Dandy: Brummell to Beerbohm* (London: Secker and Warburg, 1960); on Brummell, see also Jean Barbey d'Aurevilly, *Dandyism* (New York: PAJ, 1988). Other scholars, however, consider the dandy as a descendant of the Bohemian: see, for instance, Cesar Grana, *Bohemian Versus Bourgeois: French Society and the French Man of Letters in the Nineteenth Century* (New York: Basic, 1964), 151.

7. Walter Benjamin, "On Some Motifs in Baudelaire," in *Selected Writings*, ed. Howard Eiland and Michael W. Jennings, 4 vols. (Cambridge: Harvard University Press, 2003), 4:328.

8. Alexis de Tocqueville, *Souvenirs* (Paris: Bouquins-Laffont, 1985), 817–18.

9. Norbert Elias, *Mozart: Portrait of a Genius* (Berkeley: University of California Press, 1993).

10. Erich Mühsam, *Unpolitische Erinnerungen* (Berlin: Volk und Welt, 1958), 305 (quoted also by Kreuzer, *Die Bohème*, 360–61). The sociologist Lewis A. Coser defines Bohemians as a "community of uprooted," in *Men of Ideas: A Sociologist's View* (New York: Free Press, 1997), 8.

11. Jules Vallès, *Les réfractaires* (1865; Paris: Editeurs Français Réunis, 1955).

12. Max Weber, *The Protestant Ethic and the Spirit of Capitalism* (New York: Scribner, 1958). Paul Honigsheim underlines the deep connection Bohemia has with an original Catholic culture, counterreformist and hostile to capitalism. See Honigsheim, "Die Bohème," in *Kölner Vierteljahreshefte für Soziologie* 3 (1923): 67–69. On the lack of "elective affinities" between Catholicism and the spirit of capitalism, see Michael Löwy, *The War of Gods* (London: Verso, 1996), chap. 2.

13. Seigel, *Bohemian Paris*, 4.

14. Honigsheim, "Die Bohème," 60.

15. Ibid., 61.

16. Robert Michels, "Zur Soziologie der Bohème und ihrer Zusammenhänge mit dem geistigen Proletariat" (1932), in *Masse, Führer, Intellektuelle: Politisch-soziologische Aufsätze, 1906–1933*, ed. Joachim Milles (Frankfurt: Campus, 1988), 219.

17. Siegfried Kracauer, *Jacques Offenbach and the Paris of His Time* (New York: Zone Books, 2002), chap. 6.

18. Honigsheim, "Die Bohème," 70.

19. Michels, "Zur Soziologie der Bohème," 216.

20. Erich Mühsam, "Die Bohême," *Die Fackel* 8, no. 202 (1906): 10.

21. Jean Genet, *The Thief's Journal* (1949; New York: Grove, 1994).

22. Adolphe Chenu, *Les conspirateurs . . . Les sociétés secrètes, la préfecture de police sous Caussidière* (Paris: Garnier, 1850); Lucien De la Hodde, *Histoire des sociétés secrètes et du parti républicain de 1830 à 1848* (Paris: Lanier, 1850).

23. See the portrait of Hussonet by Jerrold Seigel, *Bohemian Paris*, 67.

24. Kreuzer, *Die Bohème*, 7.

25. Karl Marx, "Les conspirateurs" (1850), in *Collected Works*, by Karl Marx and Friedrich Engels, 50 vols. (New York: International, 1975–2005), 10:318.

26. Ibid.

27. Ibid.

28. Ibid., 317.

29. Ibid., 318.

30. Ibid.

31. Karl Marx, *The Eighteenth Brumaire of Louis Bonaparte*, in *Collected Works*, 11:110.

32. Ibid., 149.

33. Ibid.

34. Karl Marx, *The Civil War in France*, in Marx and Engels, *Collected Works*, 22:343.

35. Seigel, *Bohemian Paris*, 274.

36. Ibid., 183.

37. Max Nordau, *Degeneration* (Lincoln: University of Nebraska Press, 1993).

38. Pierre Birnbaum, *Un mythe politique: La "République juive"* (Paris: Fayard, 1988), 209–12.

39. Walter Benjamin, "Eduard Fuchs: Collector and Historian," in *Selected Writings*, 3:274.

40. On the relationship the young Marx had with Bohemia while stayed in Paris, during the July Monarchy, see Lloyd Kramer, *Threshold of a New World: Intellectuals and the Exile Experience in Paris, 1830–1848* (Ithaca: Cornell University Press, 1988). On the importance of the Parisian experience in Marx's intellectual formation, see Michael Löwy, *The Theory of Revolution in the Young Marx* (Leiden: Brill, 2003).

41. Cf. Friedrich Engels, "On the History of the Communist League," in *Collected Works*, 26:313.

42. Karl Marx, "Economic and Philosophic Manuscripts," in *Selected Writings*, ed. David McLellan (New York: Oxford University Press, 1977), 89.

43. Frédérique Desbuissons, "Le café: Scène de la vie de bohème," in *Bohèmes: De Léonard de Vinci à Picasso*, ed. Sylvain Amic (Paris: Rmn-Grand Palais, 2012), 66–73.

44. Quoted in T. J. Clark, *Image of the People: Gustave Courbet and the 1848 Revolution* (Berkeley: University of California Press, 1999), 113.

45. Petra ten-Doesschate, ed., *Correspondance de Courbet* (Paris: Flammarion, 1996), 97. Cf. Bertrand Tellier, "Courbet, un utopiste à l'épreuve de la politique," in *Gustave Courbet* (Paris: Éditions RMN-Grand Palais, 2007), 19–28.

46. Cf. Jonathan Beecher, "Courbet, Considérant et la Commune," in *Courbet, peinture et politique*, ed. Noël Barbe and Hervé Touboul (Ornans: Les Editions du Sekoya, 2013), 51–64.

47. Clark, *Image of the People*, 34.

48. ten-Doesschate, *Correspondance de Courbet*, 92.

49. Youssef Ishaghpour, *Le portrait de l'artiste dans son atelier* (Paris: Circé, 2011), 13–19.

50. On Millet, see T. J. Clark, *The Absolute Bourgeois: Artists and Politics in France, 1848–1851* (London: Thames and Hudson, 1973), chap. 3.

51. Quoted in Clark, *Image of the People*, 134.

52. Cf. Linda Nochlin, *Courbet* (New York: Thames and Hudson, 2007), chap. 2; Florence Hudowicz, "Bohème et modernité," in *Bohèmes*, 177.

53. Cf. Bertrand Tillier, "Courbet: Un utopiste à l'épreuve de la politique," 23.

54. Quoted by Dolf Oehler, *Le spleen contre l'oubli: Baudelaire, Flaubert, Heine, Herzen* (Paris: Payot, 1996), 31.

55. Ibid., 22.

56. Ishaghpour, *Courbet*, 28.

57. Laurence des Cars, "L'expérience de l'histoire: Courbet et la Commune," in *Gustave Courbet*, 425–26.

58. See, especially, extracts from the article by Marx and Engels on the Parisian conspirators quoted in Walter Benjamin, *The Arcades Project*, ed. Howard Eiland (Cambridge: Harvard University Press, 1999), 605–8.

59. Charles Baudelaire, *Oeuvres* (Paris: Gallimard, Bibliothèque de la Pléiade, 1932), 2:728. Quoted in Walter Benjamin, "The Paris of the Second Empire in Baudelaire," in *Selected Writings*, 4:4–5.

60. Ibid., 5.

61. See commentaries on theses Baudelaire passages in Oehler, *Le spleen contre l'oubli*, 212–13.

62. Zeev Sternhell, *La droite révolutionnaire: Les origines françaises du fascisme* (Paris: Seuil, 1978).

63. On the relationship between fascism and the cultural avant-garde, see George L. Mosse, *Masses and Man: Nationalist and Fascist Perceptions of Reality* (New York: Howard Fertig, 1980).

64. See Ian Kershaw, *Hitler, 1889–1936: Hubris* (London: Allen Lane, 1998), chaps. 2 and 3.

65. See Margaret Cohen, *Profane Illuminations: Walter Benjamin and the Paris of Surrealist Revolution* (Berkeley: University of California Press, 1993), 109.

66. Walter Benjamin, "The Work of Art in the Age of Its Technological Reproducibility," in *Selected Writings*, 3:122.

67. Walter Benjamin, "Surrealism," in *Selected Writings*, 2:1:215.

68. Ibid., 216. On this topic, see Michael Löwy, "Walter Benjamin et le surrealisme," in *L'etoile du matin: Marxisme et surrealisme* (Paris: Syllepse, 2000), 37–56.

69. Benjamin, "The Paris of the Second Empire in Baudelaire," 18–39; see also "The Return of the Flâneur" (1929), in *Selected Writings*, 2:1:262–67.

70. Lev Trockij, "Hanno sete di cultura" (1908), in *Letteratura e rivoluzione*, ed. Vittorio Strada (Turin: Einaudi, 1973), 274–75, 392.

71. Ibid., 276.

72. Leon Trotsky, *The Bolsheviks and World Peace* (New York: Boni and Liveright, 1918), 138.

73. Leon Trotsky, *Literature and Revolution*, ed. William Keach (Chicago: Haymarket, 2005), 115.

74. Ibid., 132.

75. Ibid., 128.

76. Baudelaire, *Oeuvres*, 711. See also Irving Wohlfarth, "*Perte d'auréole*: The Emergence of the Dandy," *Language Modern Studies* 85, no. 4 (1970): 529–71.

77. Jean-Paul Sartre, *Baudelaire* (Paris: Gallimard, 1970), 124. See also Marie-Christine Natta, *La grandeur sans convinction: Essai sur le dandysme* (Paris: Éditions du Félin, 1991), 32–33.

78. Honoré de Balzac, *Traité de la vie élégante*, quoted in Robert Kempf, *Dandies: Baudelaire and Cie* (Paris: Seuil, 1977), 20.

79. See Hannah Arendt, "The Jew as Pariah: A Hidden Tradition" (1944), in *The Jewish Writings*, ed. Jerome Kohn and Ron H. Feldman (New York: Schocken, 2007), 275–97.

80. See Kreuzer, *Die Boheme*, 37.

81. Letter to Julius Bab dated August 18, 1904, in Erich Mühsam, *Zur Psychologie der Erbtante: Satirisches Lesebuch, 1900–1933* (Berlin: Eulegenspiegel, 1984), 27.

82. Gustav Landauer, *Sein Lebensgang in Briefen* (Frankfurt: Rütten und Löning, 1929), 1:126; quoted also in Kreuzer, *Die Bohème*, 37. On the affinity of anarchism and Bohemia, see also Michels, "Zur Soziologie der Bohème," 224.

83. Quoted in Isaiah Berlin, *Karl Marx* (London: Fontana, 1995), 142–43.

84. See his letter to Friedrich Adolph Sorge dated September 27, 1877, in Marx and Engels, *Collected Works*, 45:278. A certain image of a revolutionary, Bohemian, and conspiring Marx is not alien to the workers movement if, in 1922, the leader of the Italian communist party, Antonio Gramsci, could describe him, in the pages of *Ordine Nuovo*, as "a man of science as well as a critic and a sectarian and partisan demagogue, God and the Devil, Apollo and the king of the Gypsies [*il re degli Zingari*]" who spent years in libraries to do his research as well as climb to an "attic room to organize conspiracies recruiting pimps as well." See Antonio Gramsci, "Classicismo, romanticismo, Baratono . . . " (1922), in *Socialismo e fascismo: L'Ordine Nuovo, 1921–1922* (Turin: Einaudi, 1974), 446.

85. Leone Trockij, "Eros e la morte," *Letteratura e rivoluzione*, 239; Leon Trotsky, "On Death and Eros" (1908), in *Revolutionary History* 7, no. 2 (1999).

86. Quoted in William Johnston, *Vienna: The Golden Age* (New York: Potter, 1981), chap. 7. For a portrait of Trotsky as intellectual Bohemian, see Hans Mayer, "Comrade Shylock," in *Outsiders: A Study in Life and Letters* (Cambridge: MIT Press, 1982).

87. Hendrik de Man, *Gegen den Ström: Memoiren eines europäischen Sozialisten* (Stuttgart: Deutsche Verlags-Anstalt, 1953), 130. Perhaps other witnesses experienced a similar astonishment discovering that Henrik de Man became a fascist during the Second World War.

88. On Trotsky's critique of Lenin for his "authoritarian" concept of the revolutionary party, see Pierre Broué, *Léon Trotsky* (Paris: Fayard, 1988), chap. 4.

89. Leon Trotsky, "Manifesto for an Independent Revolutionary Art," in *Art and Revolution: Writings in Literature, Politics and Culture* (New York: Pathfinder, 1972).

90. On the relations between Trotsky and surrealism, see Arturo Schwarz, *André Breton e Leon Trotsky: Storia di un'amicizia tra arte e rivoluzione* (Roma: Samonà e Savelli, 1974); and Maurice Nadeau, *History of Surrealism* (New York: MacMillan, 1965).

91. Victor Serge, *Memoirs of a Revolutionary* (New York: New York Review Books, 2012).

92. On Reed, see Robert Rosenstone, *Romantic Revolutionary: A Biography of John Reed* (New York: Knopf, 1975). On the atmosphere in Greenwich Village at the beginning of the century, when the first generation of American

social writers were formed, see Daniel Aaron, *Writers on the Left: Episodes in American Literary Communism* (New York: Columbia University Press, 1992), 10–11.

5. MARXISM AND THE WEST

1. Jürgen Osterhammel, *The Transformation of the World: A Global History of the Nineteenth Century* (Princeton: Princeton University Press, 2014), 86–87.
2. Karl Marx and Friedrich Engels, *The Communist Manifesto* (London: Verso, 2012), 40.
3. Karl Marx, "Vorwort: Zur Kritik der politischen Ökonomie," in *Werke*, by Karl Marx and Friedrich Engels, 43 vols. (Berlin: Dietz, 1956–90), 13:9; Karl Marx and Friedrich Engels, *A Contribution to the Critique to the Political Economy*, in *Collected Works*, 50 vols. (New York: International, 1975–2005), 29:263.
4. Karl Marx, *Das Kapital*, 3 vols. (Berlin: Dietz, 1975), 1:12; *Collected Works*, 35:9.
5. Karl Marx, "Brief an die Redaktion der *Otetschestwennyje Zapiski*" (1877), in Marx and Engels, *Werke*, 19:111; *Collected Works*, 24:200. See also Theodor Shanin, *Late Marx and the Russian Road: Marx and the Peripheries of Capitalism* (New York: Monthly Review Press, 1983), 136; and Harry Harootunian, *Marx After Marx: History and Time in the Expansion of Capitalism* (New York: Columbia University Press, 2015), 5.
6. Friedrich Engels, "Nachwort (1894) zu Soziales aus Russland," in *Werke*, 22:432.
7. Letter to Nikolai Danielson of March 15, 1892, in Karl Marx and Friedrich Engels, *Briefe über "Das Kapital"* (Berlin: Dietz, 1954), 341; *Collected Works*, 49:384.
8. Sheila Fitzpatrick, *The Russian Revolution* (New York: Oxford University Press, 1994), 9.
9. Kevin Anderson, *Marx at the Margins: On Nationalism, Ethnicity, and Non-Western Societies* (Chicago: University of Chicago Press, 2010), 237, 244.
10. G. W. F. Hegel, *Vorlesungen über die Philosophie der Geschichte*, ed. Eva Moldenhauer and Karl Markus Michel (Frankfurt: Suhrkamp, 1970), 12:133–34; Hegel, *The Philosophy of History*, ed. J. Sibree (New York: P. F. Collier, 1901), 163.
11. Hegel, *Vorlesungen über die Philosophie der Geschichte*, 135, 137; *The Philosophy of History*, 166.

12. Ranajit Guha, *History at the Limit of World-History* (New York: Columbia University Press, 2002), 7–23.

13. Robert Young, *White Mythologies: Writing History and the West* (London: Routledge, 1990), 3.

14. Sandro Mezzadra, *La condizione postcoloniale* (Verona: Ombre corte, 2008), 57.

15. Cf. Ellen Meiksins-Wood, *The Origin of Capitalism: A Longer View* (London: Verso, 2002).

16. Cf. Daniel Bensaïd, *Marx for Our Times: Adventures and Misadventures of a Critique* (London: Verso, 2002).

17. Michael Löwy and Robert Sayre, *Romanticism Against the Tide of Modernity* (Durham: Duke University Press, 2001), chap. 3.

18. Arno J. Mayer, *The Persistence of the Old Regime: Europe to the Great War* (New York: Pantheon, 1981).

19. Osterhammel, *The Transformation of the World*, 764–65.

20. Ibid., 754; see also Christopher A. Bayly, *The Birth of the Modern World, 1780–1914* (Oxford: Blackwell, 2004), 454.

21. Cf. Domenico Losurdo, *Il peccato originale del Novecento* (Rome: Laterza, 1998).

22. Karl Marx and Friedrich Engels, *The Civil War in the United States* (New York: International, 1974), 221. See Robin Blackburn, *An Unfinished Revolution: Karl Marx and Abraham Lincoln* (London: Verso, 2011).

23. Friedrich Engels, "Der magyarische Kampf," in Marx and Engels, *Werke*, 6:172. On the notion of "peoples without history," see the classical study Roman Rosdolsky, *Zur nationalen Frage: Friedrich Engels und das Problem der "geschichtslosen" Völker* (Berlin: Olle und Wolter, 1979).

24. Friedrich Engels, "Der Sozialismus in Deutschland," in Marx and Engels, *Werke*, 22:252.

25. Karl Marx, "The Future Results of British Rule in India" (1853), in Karl Marx and Friedrich Engels, *On Colonialism* (Moscow: Progress, 1960), 76.

26. Karl Marx, "The British Rule in India," in *On Colonialism*, 41.

27. Friedrich Engels, "Extraordinary Revelations, Abd-El-Kader, Guizot's Foreign Policy," in Marx and Engels, *Collected Works*, 6:471.

28. Karl August Wittfogel, *Oriental Despotism: A Comparative Study of Total Power* (New Haven: Yale University Press, 1957).

29. Perry Anderson, *Lineages of the Absolutist State* (London: New Left Books, 1974), 472. On this debate, see the studies gathered in Anne M. Bailey and Joseph R. Llobera, eds., *The Asiatic Mode of Production: Science and Politics* (London: Routledge, 1981).

30. Karl Marx, *Das Kapital*, 1:379; *Collected Works*, 35:364.

31. Harootunian, *Marx After Marx*, 156.

32. Mike Davis, *Late Victorian Holocausts: El Niño and the Making of the Third World* (London: Verso, 2001), 27.

33. David Landes, *The Wealth and Poverty of the Nations: Why Some Are So Rich and Some So Poor* (New York: Norton, 1998); Jack Goody, *The Theft of History* (New York: Cambridge University Press, 2006).

34. Bayly, *The Birth of the Modern World*, 62.

35. Marx, "The Future Results of British Rule in India," 82.

36. Marx, *Das Kapital*, 1:779; *Collected Works*, 35:739.

37. Osterhammel, *The Transformation of the World*, 125–26.

38. Davis, *Late Victorian Holocausts*, 9; Karl Polanyi, *The Great Transformation* (Boston: Beacon, 1944), 160.

39. Cf. Marcel Merle, "L'anticolonialisme," in *Le livre noir du colonialisme*, ed. Marc Ferro (Paris: Robert Laffont, 2003), 611–45.

40. Marx in a letter to Engels (February 14, 1858), Marx and Engels, *Collected Works*, 40:266. On this "missed encounter," see Bruno Bosteels, *Marx and Freud in Latin America: Politics, Psychoanalysis, and Religion in Times of Terror* (London: Verso, 2012).

41. Karl Marx, "The Indian Revolt" (1857), in *On Colonialism*, 130–34.

42. Karl Marx, "Persia and China" (1857), in *On Colonialism*, 111.

43. Anderson, *Marx at the Margins*, 31.

44. Marx, "Persia and China," 116.

45. Karl Marx and Friedrich Engels, *Ireland and the Irish Question* (London: Lawrence and Wishart, 1971).

46. Karl Marx, *Ethnological Notebooks* (Assen: Van Gorcum, 1972); Friedrich Engels, *The Origins of the Family, Private Property, and the State, in the Light of the Researches of Lewis H. Morgan* (New York: International, 1972).

47. John Stuart Mill, *On Liberty* (Oxford: Oxford University Press, 1991), 14–15.

48. Alexis de Tocqueville, *Democracy in America* (New York: Penguin, 2004), 1:29.

49. Edward Said, *Orientalism* (New York: Random House, 1979), 154.

50. See Vivek Chibber, *Postcolonial Theory and the Specter of Capital* (London: Verso, 2013). Among the Marxist critical assessments of Said's vision of orientalism, see Aijaz Ahmad, *In Theory: Classes, Nations, Literatures* (London: Verso, 1992); and Alex Callinicos, *Theories and Narratives: Reflections on the Philosophy of History* (Cambridge: Polity, 1995), 151–65.

51. Gilbert Achcar, *Marxism, Orientalism, Cosmopolitanism* (Chicago: Haymarket, 2013), 68–102.

52. Cf. Benedict Anderson, *Under Three Flags: Anarchism and Anti-Colonial Imagination* (London: Verso, 2005), 2, 72.

53. C. L. R. James, *The Black Jacobins: Toussaint L'Ouverture and San Domingo Revolution* (New York: Vintage, 1963).

54. Adolfo Gilly, *The Mexican Revolution* (1970; New York: New Press, 2006).
55. Peter Linebaugh and Markus Rediker, *The Many-Headed Hydra: Sailors, Slaves, Commoners, and the Hidden History of the Revolutionary Atlantic* (London: Verso, 2012).
56. Cf. Gesine Krüger, *Kriegsbewältigung und Geschichtsbewusstsein: Realität, Deutung und Verarbeitung des deutschen Kolonialkrieges in Namibia 1904 bis 1907* (Göttingen: Vandenhoeck und Ruprecht), 65–66.
57. Cf. Robert C. Young, *Postcolonialism: An Historical Introduction* (Oxford: Blackwell, 2001). On the Marxist debate after Marx on the national question, see Georges Haupt, Michael Löwy, and Claudie Weill, *Les marxistes et la question nationale, 1848–1914* (Paris: Maspero, 1974).
58. Dipesh Chakrabarty, *Provincializing Europe: Postcolonial Thought and Historical Difference* (Princeton: Princeton University Press, 2000), 16. According to Chakrabarty, Marx's writings "constitute one of the founding moments in the history of anti-imperial thought" (47).
59. Paul Buhle, *C. L. R. James: The Artist as Revolutionary* (London: Verso, 1988), 106; Andrew J. Douglas, *In the Spirit of Critique: Thinking Politically in the Dialectical Tradition* (Albany: State University of New York Press, 2013), 160.
60. Enzo Traverso, "To Brush Against the Grain: The Holocaust and the German-Jewish Culture in Exile," *Totalitarian Movements and Political Religions* 5, no. 2 (2004): 243–70; Paul Gilroy, *The Black Atlantic: Modernity and Double Consciousness* (London: Verso, 1993).
61. Edward Said, *Representations of the Intellectual* (New York: Vintage, 1994), 63.
62. Theodor W. Adorno, "Spengler After the Decline," in *Prisms* (Cambridge: MIT Press, 1982), 65. See Oswald Spengler, *The Decline of the West* (New York: Oxford University Press, 1991).
63. Adorno, "Spengler After the Decline," 71.
64. Alan J. MacKenzie, "Radical Pan-Africanism in the 1930s: A Discussion with C. L. R. James," *Radical History Review* 4 (1980), 74.
65. J. R. Johnson (C. L. R. James), "Trotsky's Place in History," in *C. L. R. James and Revolutionary Marxism: Selected Writings, 1939–1949*, ed. Scott McLemee and Paul Le Blanc (Atlantic Highlands: Humanities Books, 1993).
66. Adorno, "Spengler After the Decline," 72.
67. James, "Trotsky's Place in History."
68. C. L. R. James, "Foreword" (1980), in *The Black Jacobins* (London: Allison and Busby, 1980), v.
69. Max Horkheimer and Theodor W. Adorno, *Dialectic of Enlightenment: Philosophical Fragments* (Stanford: Stanford University Press, 2002), xvi.
70. Theodor W. Adorno, *Minima Moralia: Reflections on a Damaged Life* (London: Verso, 2005), 233.

71. C. L. R. James, *Mariners, Renegades, and Castaways: The Story of Herman Melville and the World We Live In* (Hanover: University Press of New England, 2001), 141.

72. Ernst Bloch, "Non-Contemporaneity and Obligation to Its Dialectics" (1932), in *Heritage of Our Time* (Berkeley: University of California Press, 1991), 104–16.

73. James, *Mariners, Renegades, and Castaways*, 30.

74. Ibid., 16.

75. Ibid., 45.

76. Ibid., 54. In 1952, James had probably read Hannah Arendt's book on totalitarianism, published in New York one year earlier, perhaps even Franz Neumann's interpretation of National Socialism—a book to which he could have been introduced by Herbert Marcuse—but these are only speculations. Written in prison, James's essay on Melville does not include a bibliography. See Hannah Arendt, The *Origins of Totalitarianism* (New York: Harcourt Brace, 1951); and Franz Neumann, *Behemoth: The Structure and Practice of National Socialism, 1933–1944* (New York: Oxford University Press, 1944).

77. James, *Mariners, Renegades, and Castaways*, 19. On James and Arendt, see Richard King, "The Odd Couple: C. L. R. James, Hannah Arendt and the Return of Politics in the Cold War," in *Beyond Boundaries: C. L. R. James and Postnational Studies*, ed. Christopher Gair (London: Pluto, 2006), 108–27.

78. Adorno, *Minima Moralia*, 55. See Hegel's famous letter to Niethammer of October 13, 1806: Hegel, *The Letters*, ed. Clark Butler and Christiane Seiler (Bloomington: Indiana University Press, 1984), 114.

79. Detlev Peukert evoked this allegory to describe the attitude of Weber in front of modernity: Peukert, *Max Webers Diagnose der Moderne* (Göttingen: Vabdenhoeck und Ruprecht, 1989), 27.

80. James, *Mariners, Renegades, and Castaways*, 40.

81. Ibid., 33.

82. Max Horkheimer, "The Revolt of Nature," in *Eclipse of Reason* (New York: Continuum, 2004), 92–127.

83. Theodor W. Adorno, *Negative Dialectics* (London: Routledge, 2003).

84. C. L. R. James, *Notes on Dialectic: Hegel, Marx, Lenin* (1948; London: Pluto, 2005). See Georg Lukács, *History and Class Consciousness* (London: Merlin, 1971); According to Raya Dunayevskaya, a close intellectual partner of James in the 1940s, the "real tragedy of Adorno (and the Frankfurt School)" was that of a "one-dimensionality of thought which results when you give up the Subject, when one does not listen to the voices from below." Dunayevskaya, *Philosophy and Revolution* (New York: Columbia University Press, 1989), 187.

85. C. L. R. James, *The Black Jacobins: Toussaint L'Ouverture and the San Domingo Revolution* (New York: Vintage, 1989), 3–4.

86. Frantz Fanon, *The Wretched of the Earth* (New York: Grove, 1963), 101.

87. Ibid., xi.

88. I borrow this definition to Antonio y Vazquez Arroyo, "Universal History Disavowed: On Critical Theory and Postcolonialism," *Postcolonial Studies* 11, no. 4 (2008): 464.

89. See Susan Buck-Morss, *Hegel, Haiti, and Universal History* (Pittsburgh: University of Pittsburgh Press, 2009), 106.

90. Buhle, *C. L. R. James*, 106.

91. C. L. R. James, *American Civilization* (Cambridge: Blackwell, 1993), 151. On this topics, see Bill Schwarz, "C. L. R. James's American Civilization," in Gair, *Beyond Boundaries*, 128–56; and Brian W. Alleyne, "Cultural Politics and Globalized Infomedia: C. L. R. James, Theodor W. Adorno and Mass Culture Criticism," *Interventions* 1, no. 3 (1999): 361–72.

92. Siegfried Kracauer, *Theory of Film: The Redemption of Physical Reality*, ed. Miriam Bratu Hansen (Princeton: Princeton University Press, 1997), 217–18.

93. C. L. R. James, *Beyond a Boundary* (London: Stanley Paul, 1968).

94. Walter Benjamin, *The Arcades Project* (Cambridge: Harvard University Press, 1999); Walter Benjamin, "The Work of Art in the Age of Its Mechanical Reproducibility," in *Selected Writings*, ed. Howard Eiland and Michael W. Jennings, 4 vols. (Cambridge: Harvard University Press, 2003–06), 3:133.

95. Walter Benjamin, "Surrealism," in *Selected Writings*, 1:207–21.

96. Walter Benjamin, "Marcel Brion, Bartolomé de Las Casas, Père des Indiens," in *Gesammelte Schriften*, ed. Rolf Tiedemann and Hermann Schweppenhäuser, 10 vols. (Frankfurt: Suhrkamp, 1991), 3:180–81.

97. Herbert Marcuse, *Eros and Civilization* (Boston: Beacon, 1974), xx.

98. See Young, *Postcolonialism*, 134–39.

99. See Perry Anderson, *Considerations on Western Marxism* (London: Verso, 1978).

100. See Cedric Robinson, *Black Marxism: The Making of the Black Radical Tradition* (London: Zed, 1983), 97.

101. W. E. B. Du Bois, *Black Reconstruction in America* (Rutgers: Transaction Books, 2012); and Eric Williams, *Capitalism and Slavery* (Bloomington: University of North Carolina Press, 2012). Their theses have been confirmed by the historical investigations of the last decades. See notably Robin Blackburn, *The Making of New World Slavery: From the Baroque to the Modern, 1492–1800* (London: Verso, 1997).

102. On Western Marxism's ambiguities on colonialism, see Edward Said, *Culture and Imperialism* (London: Vintage, 1994), 336.

103. See Timothy Brennan, "Subaltern Stakes," *New Left Review* 89 (2014): 67–88.

6. ADORNO AND BENJAMIN

1. Gershom Scholem, "Walter Benjamin and His Angel," in *On Walter Benjamin: Critical Essays and Recollections*, ed. Gary Smith (Cambridge: MIT Press, 1988), 54.

2. Theodor W. Adorno, "Introduction to Benjamin's *Schriften*," in *On Walter Benjamin*, 15.

3. Walter Benjamin, "Agesilaus Santander (First Version)," in *Selected Writings*, ed. Howard Eiland and Michael W. Jennings, 4 vols. (Cambridge: Harvard University Press, 2003–06), 2:2:713.

4. Theodor W. Adorno, *Minima Moralia: Reflections on a Damaged Life* (London: Verso, 2005), 15. This definition has become the title of a book that summarizes the philosophy of the German thinker: Gillian Rose, *The Melancholy Science: An Introduction to the Thought of Theodor W. Adorno* (New York: Columbia University Press, 1978).

5. Theodor W. Adorno and Walter Benjamin, *The Complete Correspondence, 1928–1940*, ed. Henri Lonitz (Cambridge: Harvard University Press, 1999).

6. Max Horkheimer and Theodor W. Adorno, *Dialectic of Enlightenment: Philosophical Fragments* (Stanford: Stanford University Press, 2002), 4.

7. Walter Benjamin, "On the Concept of History," in *Selected Writings*, 4:392.

8. On the relationship between Adorno and Benjamin, see Richard Wolin, *Walter Benjamin: An Aesthetic of Redemption* (Berkeley: University of California Press, 1994), chap. 6, 163–212; and Eugene Lunn, *Marxism and Modernism: An Historical Study of Lukács, Brecht, Benjamin, and Adorno* (London: Verso, 1985), 149–279.

9. Theodor W. Adorno, "Benjamin the Letter Writer," in *The Correspondence of Walter Benjamin, 1910–1940*, ed. Gershom Scholem and Theodor W. Adorno (Chicago: University of Chicago Press, 1994), xviii.

10. Ibid., xix.

11. See this picture in Hartmut Scheible, *Theodor W. Adorno* (Hamburg: Rowohlt, 1989), 135; it is curiously not included in Theodor W. Adorno Archiv, ed., *Adorno: Eine Bildmonographie* (Frankfurt: Suhrkamp, 2003).

12. Theodor W. Adorno, *Kierkegaard: Construction of the Aesthetic* (Minneapolis: University of Minnesota Press, 1989); Walter Benjamin, *The Origin of German Tragic* Drama (London: New Left Books, 1977).

13. Walter Benjamin, "Kierkegaard: The End of Philosophical Idealism," in *Selected Writings*, 2:2:703–5.

14. See Detlev Peukert, *The Weimar Republic: The Crisis of Classical Modernity* (New York: Hill and Wang, 1992), chap. 1. (Adorno was too young for participating in the conflict; Benjamin avoided the war by moving to Switzerland.)

15. Theodor W. Adorno, "Erinnerungen," in *Über Walter Benjamin: Aufsätze, Artikel, Briefe* (Frankfurt: Suhrkamp, 1990), 79.

16. Siegfried Kracauer, "Über die Freundschaft," in *Schriften*, vol. 5.1, *Aufsätze, 1915–1926* (Frankfurt: Suhrkamp, 1990), 37.

17. Cf. Leo Löwenthal, "Erinnerung an Theodor W. Adorno," in *Schriften*, vol. 4, *Judaica: Vorträge, Briefe* (Frankfurt: Suhrkamp, 1984), 78. On the passionate relationship between Kracauer and the young Adorno, see their letters of 1923–25, whose intimacy was never attained by Adorno's correspondence with Benjamin: Theodor W. Adorno and Siegfried Kracauer, *Briefwechsel, 1923–1966* (Frankfurt: Suhrkamp, 2008).

18. Gretel Adorno and Walter Benjamin, *Correspondence, 1930–1940* (Cambridge: Polity, 2008), 210.

19. Ibid., 230.

20. Adorno and Benjamin, *The Complete Correspondence*, 9.

21. For a biographical profile of both, see in particular Stefan Müller-Doohm, *Adorno: A Biography* (Cambridge: Polity, 2005); Howard Eiland and Michael W. Jennings, *Walter Benjamin: A Critical Life* (Cambridge: Harvard University Press, 2014).

22. Gershom Scholem, ed., *The Correspondence of Walter Benjamin and Gershom Scholem, 1932–1949* (New York: Schocken, 1989), 153.

23. Ibid., 248.

24. Hannah Arendt, "Walter Benjamin, 1892–1940," in *Men in Dark Times* (New York: Harcourt Brace and Jovanovich, 1968), 153–205. Arendt deeply disliked Adorno, who contributed to the failure of the academic career of her first husband, Günther Stern (Anders). After their first meeting, she said: "That one's not coming into our house!" See Elisabeth Young-Bruehl, *Hannah Arendt: For Love of the World* (New Haven: Yale University Press, 1982), 80. In spite of this antipathy, which probably influenced her judgment, her interpretation of the relationship between the two philosophers appears extremely pertinent.

25. See notably the letter of Scholem to Benjamin of April 13, 1933, in Scholem, *The Correspondence of Walter Benjamin and Gershom Scholem*, 39.

26. Ibid., 27.

27. Ibid., 39.

28. Ibid., 42.

29. Walter Benjamin, *Gesammelte Schriften,* ed. Rolf Tiedemann and Hermann Schweppenhäuser, 10 vols. (Frankfurt: Suhrkamp, 1972–89), 6:227. See Momme Brodersen, *Walter Benjamin: A Biography* (London: Verso, 1996), 204.

30. Scholem, *The Correspondence of Walter Benjamin and Gershom Scholem,* 93–94.

31. Ibid., 262.

32. Susan Buck-Morss, *The Origin of Negative Dialectics: Theodor W. Adorno, Walter Benjamin and the Frankfurt Institute* (New York: Free Press, 1977), 137.

33. Theodor W. Adorno and Walter Benjamin, *The Complete Correspondence,* 37.

34. See Rolf Wiggershaus, *The Frankfurt School: Its History, Theory, and Political Significance* (Cambridge: MIT Press, 1995), 153; Müller-Doohm, *Adorno,* 184.

35. Adorno and Benjamin, *The Complete Correspondence,* 183–84. Cf. Siegfried Kracauer, *Orpheus in Paris: Jacques Offenbach and the Paris of His Time* (New York: Knopf, 1938; New York: Zone, 2002).

36. Ibid., 150–51.

37. Arendt, "Walter Benjamin," 159.

38. Adorno and Benjamin, *The Complete Correspondence,* 252. See also Walter Benjamin, *Understanding Brecht* (London: New Left Books, 1973).

39. Scholem and Adorno, *The Correspondence,* 626.

40. Walter Benjamin, "On the Concept of History," 391. On the identification of the "Antichrist" with the ruling classes, see Rolf Tiedemann, *Dialektik im Stillstand: Versuche zum Spätwerk Walter Benjamins* (Frankfurt: Suhrkamp, 1983), 113.

41. Horkheimer and Adorno, *Dialectic of Enlightenment,* xvi.

42. Ibid., 172. See also Theodor W. Adorno, "Types and Syndromes," in *The Authoritarian Personality,* ed. Theodor W. Adorno (New York: Harper and Row, 1950), 747.

43. Scholem and Adorno, *The Correspondence,* 622. Gershom Scholem did not share this positive appreciation of the essay of Horkheimer: Scholem, *The Correspondence of Walter Benjamin and Gershom Scholem,* 264–65.

44. Walter Benjamin, "Central Park," in *Selected Writings,* 4:188.

45. Theodor W. Adorno, "Aldous Huxley and Utopia," in *Prisms* (Cambridge: MIT Press, 1982), 95–117.

46. Theodor W. Adorno, *Minima Moralia* (London: Verso, 2005), 33.

47. Georg Simmel, "The Stranger," in *The Sociology of Georg Simmel*, ed. Kurt H. Wolff (New York: Free Press, 1950), 402–8.

48. Quoted in Martin Jay, *Adorno* (Cambridge: Harvard University Press, 1984), 13.

49. Quoted in Rolf Wiggershaus, *The Frankfurt School*, 210.

50. Adorno and Benjamin, *The Complete Correspondence*, 55.

51. Cf. Martin Jay, "The Ungrateful Dead," *Salmagundi* 123 (1999): 25.

52. Cf. Martin Jay, "Adorno in America," *Permanent Exiles: Essays on the Intellectual Migration from Germany to America* (New York: Columbia University Press, 1986), 120–37.

53. Scholem, *The Correspondence of Walter Benjamin and Gershom Scholem*, 72.

54. Arendt, "Walter Benjamin," 160.

55. Walter Benjamin, "Eduard Fuchs: Collector and Historian," in *Selected Writings*, 3:274.

56. Adrienne Monnier, "Benjamin," in *Rue de l'Odéon* (Paris: Albin Michel, 1960), 171–84.

57. Adorno and Benjamin, *The Complete Correspondence*, 212.

58. Quoted in Denis Hollier, ed., *Le collège de sociologie, 1937–1939* (Paris: Folio-Gallimard, 1995), 504.

59. Ibid., 884.

60. Walter Benjamin, "Surrealism: The Last Snapshot of the European Intelligentsia," in *Selected Writings*, 2:1:215.

61. Ibid., 216.

62. Michael Löwy, "Walter Benjamin et le surréalisme: Histoire d'un enchantement révolutionnaire," in *L'étoile du matin* (Paris: Syllepse, 2000), 40–42. "Gothic Marxism" is the title of the first chapter of Margaret Cohen, *Profane Illuminations: Walter Benjamin and the Paris of Surrealist Revolution* (Berkeley: University of California Press, 1993). Her interesting interpretation is not convincing, however, when she describes Benjamin's Marxism as contaminated by irrationalism, 1–3. See also Jean-Marc Lachaud, "Walter Benjamin et le surréalisme," in *Présence(s) de Walter Benjamin*, ed. Jean-Marc Lachaud (Bordeaux: Publications du service culturel de l'université Michel de Montaigne, 1994), 83–96.

63. Walter Benjamin, *The Arcades Project* (Cambridge: Harvard University Press, 1999), 883.

64. Ibid., 831.

65. Walter Benjamin, "Central Park," in *Selected Writings*, 4:182.

66. Walter Benjamin, "The Storyteller: Observations on the Works of Nikolai Leskov," in *Selected Writings*, 3:144.

67. Adorno and Benjamin, *The Complete Correspondence*, 321.

68. Ibid., 104–14.

69. Ibid., 280–87. See also Wolin, *Walter Benjamin*, 173–79.

70. Walter Benjamin, "Central Park," in *Selected Writings*, 4:188; see also Lunn, *Marxism and Modernism*, 163–65.

71. Cf. Theodor W. Adorno, "Locking Back on Surrealism," in *Notes on Literature* (New York: Columbia University Press, 1991), 1:86–90.

72. Theodor W. Adorno, "Benjamin's *Einbahnstrasse*," in *Notes on Literature*, 2:322.

73. Theodor W. Adorno, "Portrait of Walter Benjamin," in *Prisms*, 236.

74. Cf. Max Horkheimer, *Gesammelte Schriften*, ed. Alfred Schmidt and Gunzelin Schmid Noerr, 19 vols. (Frankfurt: Fischer, 1985–96), 15:361, letter of Adorno of June 8, 1935. See also Brodersen, *Walter Benjamin*, 234–235; and Eiland and Jennings, *Walter Benjamin*, 493–95.

75. Adorno and Benjamin, *The Complete Correspondence*, 128.

76. Walter Benjamin, "The Work of Art in the Age of Its Technological Reproducibility," in *Selected Writings*, 3:106.

77. Adorno and Benjamin, *The Complete Correspondence*, 130.

78. See Siegfried Kracauer, "The Mass Ornament," in *The Mass Ornament: Weimar Essays* (Cambridge: Harvard University Press, 1995), 75–87.

79. Adorno, "Walter Benjamin the Letter Writer," xix.

80. Adorno and Benjamin, *The Complete Correspondence*, 132.

81. Cf. Max Horkheimer, "The Revolt of Nature," in *Eclipse of Reason* (New York: Oxford University Press, 1974), 65–89.

82. Theodor W. Adorno, "On Jazz," in *Essays on Music* (Berkeley: University of California Press, 2002), 470–95; on the "sado-masochistic elements" in jazz, see p. 478. See also Theodor W. Adorno, "Perennial Fashion: Jazz," in *Prisms*, 119–32.

83. Theodor W. Adorno, "On the Fetish-Character in Music and the Regression of Listening," in *Essays on Music*, 301.

84. See Theodor W. Adorno, "Arnold Schoenberg, 1874–1951," in *Prisms*, 147–72.

85. Adorno and Benjamin, *The Complete Correspondence*, 159.

86. Walter Benjamin, "The Work of Art in the Age of Its Technological Reproducibility," in *Selected Writings*, 3:122.

87. Adorno and Benjamin, *The Complete Correspondence*, 144. During their conversations in Paris in 1936, however, Benjamin advanced some critical observations on Adorno's essay on jazz, as he pointed out in a letter of May 5, 1940: see p. 326.

88. Adorno and Benjamin, *The Complete Correspondence*, 249.

89. Ibid.

90. Theodor W. Adorno, "A Portrait of Walter Benjamin," in *Prisms*, 234.

91. Bertolt Brecht, *Journals, 1934–1955* (New York: Routledge, 1996), 159.

92. Gershom Scholem, "Walter Benjamin," in *On Jews and Judaism in Crisis* (New York: Schocken, 1976), 187.

93. Michael Lowy, *Fire Alarm: Reading Walter Benjamin's "On the Concept of History"* (London: Verso, 2005), 68.

94. Susan Buck-Morss, *Dialectic of Seeing: Walter Benjamin and the Arcades Project* (Cambridge: MIT Press, 1991), 249.

95. Horkheimer and Adorno, *Dialectic of Enlightenment*, 148.

96. Walter Benjamin, "On the Concept of History," in *Selected Writings*, 4:397.

97. Walter Benjamin, "Paralipomena to 'On the Concept of History,'" in *Selected Writings*, 4:402. See also the aphorism titled "Fire Alarm" in Walter Benjamin, *One-Way Street: Reflections* (London: Verso, 1997), 84.

98. Walter Benjamin, "Paris: The Capital of the Nineteenth Century," in *Selected Writings*, 3:33–34.

99. See Miguel Abensour, "Walter Benjamin entre mélancolie et révolution: Passages-Blanqui," in *Walter Benjamin et Paris*, ed. Heinz Wismann (Paris: Editions du Cerf, 1986), 247.

100. Benjamin, "On the Concept of History," 394.

101. Adorno and Benjamin, *The Complete Correspondence*, 84.

102. Walter Benjamin, "The Author as Producer," in *Selected Writings*, 2:2:780.

103. Cf. Christoph Hering, *Die Rekonstruktion der Revolution: Walter Benjamins messianischer Materialismus in den Thesen "Über den Begriff der Geschichte"* (Frankfurt: Lang, 1983), 180.

104. Herbert Marcuse, "Revolution und Kritik der Gewalt," in *Materialen zu Benjamins Thesen "Über den Begriff der Geschichte,"* ed. Peter Bulthaup (Frankfurt: Suhrkamp, 1975), 23–27.

105. See Theodor W. Adorno and Herbert Marcuse, "Correspondence on the German Student Movement," *New Left Review* 233 (1999): 123–36.

106. Adorno and Benjamin, *The Complete Correspondence*, 342.

7. SYNCHRONIC TIMES

1. Lisa Fittko, *Escape Through the Pyrenees* (Evanston, Ill.: Northwestern University Press, 1991).

2. Ingrid Scheurmann, "Nouveaux documents sur la mort de Walter Benjamin," in *Pour Walter Benjamin*, ed. Ingrid Scheurmann and Konrad Scheurmann (Bonn: Inter Nationes, 1994), 276–315.

3. Walter Benjamin and Gershom Scholem, *Correspondence, 1932–1940* (New York: Schocken, 1989), 268.

4. Cf. Denis Peschanski, *La France des camps: L'internement, 1938–1946* (Paris: Gallimard, 2002).

5. Perry Anderson, *In the Tracks of Historical Materialism* (London: Verso, 1983), 32.

6. Daniel Bensaïd, *Jeanne de guerre lasse* (Paris: Gallimard, 1991), 34.

7. Daniel Bensaïd, *Une lente impatience* (Paris: Stock, 2004), 451; English translation: *An Impatient Life* (London: Verso, 2014).

8. Daniel Bensaïd, *Moi, la révolution* (Paris: Gallimard, 1989).

9. Bensaïd, *Jeanne de guerre lasse*. See the remarkable essay by Josep Maria Antentas, "Daniel Bensaid's Joan of Arc," *Science and Society* 79, no. 1 (2015): 63–89.

10. Daniel Bensaïd, *Les Trotskysmes* (Paris: Presses universitaires de France, 2002).

11. Perry Anderson, *Considerations on Western Marxism* (London: New Left Books, 1976).

12. Bensaïd, *Une lente impatience*, 361.

13. Ibid., 449.

14. Daniel Bensaïd, *Fragments mécréants I: Sur les mythes identitaires et la République imaginaire* (Paris: Lignes, 2005); Bensaïd, *Fragments mécréants II: Un nouveau théologien, Bernard-Henry Lévy* (Paris: Lignes, 2008).

15. Bensaid, *Une lente impatience*, 69.

16. Bensaid, *Jeanne de guerre lasse*, 263.

17. Bensaid, *Une lente impatience*, 449.

18. Daniel Bensaïd and Henri Weber, *Mai 68, une répétition générale* (Paris: Maspero, 1968).

19. Daniel Bensaïd, *Marx l'intempestif: Grandeur et misères d'une aventure critique XIXᵉ–XXᵉ siècles* (Paris: Fayard, 1995); Bensaid, *Marx for Our Times: Adventures and Misadventures of a Critique* (London: Verso, 2009).

20. Ibid., 110. See Antonio Gramsci, *Quaderni del Carcere*, ed. Valentino Gerratana, 4 vols. (Torino: Einaudi, 1975), 2:1403.

21. Daniel Bensaïd, *La discordance des temps* (Paris: Les Editions de la Passion, 1995), 187.

22. Daniel Bensaid, *Marx, mode d'emploi* (Paris: Zones, 2009), chap. 5.

23. Daniel Bensaïd, *Walter Benjamin: Sentinelle messianique* (Paris: Plon, 1990). According to the dates ending the book, it had been written in Paris between March and June 1990.

24. On Daniel Bensaïd, see the contributions gathered in a special issue of *Lignes* 32 (2010).

25. Bensaïd, *Walter Benjamin*, 7.

26. Walter Benjamin, "The Work of Art in the Age of its Mechanical Reproducibility," in *Selected Writings*, ed. Howard Eiland and Michael W. Jennings, 4 vols. (Cambridge: Harvard University Press, 1999), 3:122.

27. Among the authors who preceded Bensaïd's political reading of Benjamin, see Christoph Hering, *Die Rekonstruktion der Revolution: Walter Benjamins messianischer Materialismus in der Thesen "Über den Begriff der Geschichte"* (Frankfurt: Peter Lang, 1983); Terry Eagleton, *Walter Benjamin or Towards a Revolutionary Criticism* (London: New Left Books, 1981); Michael Löwy, *Redemption and Utopia: Jewish Libertarian Thought in Central Europe: A Study in Elective Affinity* (Stanford: Stanford University Press, 1992), chap. 6. Now, see also Esther Leslie, *Walter Benjamin: Overpowering Conformism* (London: Pluto, 2000); and Michael Löwy, *Fire Alarm: Reading Walter Benjamin's "On the Concept of History"* (London: Verso, 2005).

28. Hannah Arendt, "Walter Benjamin, 1892–1940," in *Men in Dark Times* (London: Penguin, 1973), 168.

29. Bensaïd, *Une lente impatience*, 278.

30. Cf. Gershom Scholem, *Walter Benjamin: The Story of a Friendship* (New York: Schocken, 1988), 255.

31. Bensaïd, *Une lente impatience*, 364. On Mandel, see Jan Willem Stutje, *Ernest Mandel: A Rebel's Dream Deferred* (London: Verso, 2009).

32. Bensaïd, *Walter Benjamin*, 124.

33. Ibid., 39.

34. Bensaïd, *Moi, la révolution*, 230.

35. Ibid., 231.

36. Ibid., 230. On the debates raised by this commemoration, see Steven L. Kaplan, *Farewell, Revolution: Disputed Legacies: France, 1789/1989* (Ithaca: Cornell University Press, 1995).

37. Walter Benjamin, "On the Concept of History," in *Selected Writings*, 4:391.

38. Ibid., 254.

39. Ibid., 261.

40. Ibid., 255.

41. Walter Benjamin, *The Arcades Project* (Cambridge: Belknap, 1999), 462.

42. Ibid., 463.

43. Benjamin, "On the Concept of History," 395.

44. Benjamin, *The Arcades Project*, 471.

45. Susan Buck-Morss, *Dialectic of Seeing: Walter Benjamin and the Arcades Project* (Cambridge: MIT Press, 1991), 249.

46. Benjamin published short texts under this title (*Denkbilder*) in different newspapers of the Weimar Republic; on the "dialectical image," see Benjamin, *The Arcades Project*, 462–63, as well as "On the Concept of History," 403.

47. Deniel Bensaïd, *Qui est le juge? Pour en finir avec le tribunal de l'histoire* (Paris: Fayard, 1999), 167.

48. François Furet, *The Passing of an Illusion: The Idea of Communism in the Twentieth Century* (Chicago: University of Chicago Press, 1999), 502.

49. Daniel Bensaïd, "L'inglorieux vertical: Péguy critique de la raison histo-rique," in *La Discordance des Temps: Essais sur les crises, les classes, l'histoire* (Paris: Les Editions de la Passion, 1995), 206.

50. Charles Péguy, "Un poète l'a dit," in *Œuvres en prose*, ed. Robert Burac, 2 vols. (Paris: Gallimard, 1968), 2:869.

51. Bensaïd, "L'inglorieux vertical," 191.

52. Ibid., 193.

53. Ibid., 190.

54. Walter Benjamin, *One-Way Street* (London: New Left Books, 1979), 80.

55. Benjamin, *The Arcades Project*, 460.

56. Daniel Bensaïd, *Résistances: Essai de taupologie générale* (Paris: Fayard, 2001), 15–16.

57. See Werner Fuld, *Walter Benjamin, zwischen den Stuhlen: Eine Biographie* (Munich: Hanser, 1979).

58. Bensaïd, *Walter Benjamin*, 16.

59. Walter Benjamin, *Moscow Diary* (Cambridge: Harvard University Press, 1986); Walter Benjamin, "Conversations with Brecht," in *Understanding Brecht* (London: Verso, 2003), 105–21.

60. Walter Benjamin, "Surrealism," in *Selected Writings*, 2:1:207–21. On Ben-jamin and Trotsky, see Werner Kraft, "Über Benjamin," in *Zur Aktualität Walter Benjamins*, ed. Siegfried Unseld (Frankfurt: Suhrkamp, 1972), 69; Enzo Traverso, "Benjamin und Trotzki," *Das Argument* 5, no. 222 (1997): 697–704; and Esther Leslie, *Walter Benjamin: Overpowering Conformism* (London: Pluto, 2000), 228–34.

61. Gershom Scholem, "Toward an Understanding of the Messianic Idea in Ju-daism," in *The Messianic Idea in Judaism, and Other Essays on Jewish Spiri-tuality* (New York: Schocken, 1971), 12.

62. Herbert Marcuse, "Revolution und Kritik der Gewalt: Zur Geschichtsphilo-sophie Walter Benjamins," in *Materialen zu Walter Benjamins Thesen "Über den Begriff der Geschichte,"* ed. Peter Bulthaup (Frankfurt: Suhrkamp, 1975), 26–27.

63. Benjamin, "On the Concept of History," 391.

64. Ibid., 392.

65. Walter Benjamin, "Theories of German Fascism," in *Selected Writings*, 2:1: 312–21.

66. Bensaïd, *Marx l'intempestif*, 13.

67. Bensaïd, *Walter Beniamin*, 158.

68. Ibid., 158. More lucidly, Terry Eagleton highlights the fact that strategic re-flection does not belong to Benjamin's thought: Eagleton, *Walter Benjamin or Towards a Revolutionary Criticism*, 176–78.

69. Bensaïd, *Walter Benjamin*, 169; Benjamin, *The Arcades Project*, 388–89.

70. Benjamin, "On the Concept of History," 397.

71. Benjamin implicitly refers to Schmitt in thesis 8, where he mentions the "state of emergency" that has become the rule (ibid., 392). Bensaïd analyses this passage (47, 49), without establishing any link to Schmitt. On the aborted dialogue between Benjamin and Schmitt, the theoretician of the "state of exception" (*Ausnahmezustand*), during the Weimar Republic, see Susanne Heil, *"Gefährliche Beziehungen": Walter Benjamin und Carl Schmitt* (Stuttgart: J. B. Metzler, 1996). See also Enzo Traverso, *Fire and Blood: The European Civil War, 1914–1945* (London: Verso, 2016), 236–45. Bensaïd will later come back to Schmitt (and Agamben) in *Éloge de la politique profane* (Paris: Albin Michel, 2008), chap. 2.

72. Walter Benjamin, "Critique of Violence," in *Selected Writings*, 1:236–52.

73. Walter Benjamin, "Theological-Political Fragment," in *Selected Writings*, 3:305–6.

74. Stéphane Moses, *The Angel of History: Rosenzweig, Benjamin, Scholem* (Stanford: Stanford University Press, 2009).

75. Isaac Deutscher, *The Non-Jewish Jew* (London: Oxford University Press, 1968).

76. Bensaïd, *Walter Benjamin*, 155.

77. Ibid., 249.

78. Ibid., 230.

79. Ibid., 229.

80. Daniel Bensaïd, "Utopie et messianisme: Bloch, Benjamin et le sens du virtuel," in *La discordance des temps*, 208.

81. Scholem, "Toward an Understanding of the Messianic Idea in Judaism," 13–14.

82. Walter Benjamin, "Paris, Capital of the Nineteenth Century," in *Selected Writings*, 3:33–34.

83. Benjamin, "On the Concept of History," 390.

84. Moses, *The Angel of History*, 108.

85. Karl Marx and Friedrich Engels, *The Communist Manifesto* (London: Verso, 2012), 74.

86. Bensaïd, *Moi, la révolution*, 199.

87. Bensaïd, *Walter Benjamin*, 97.

88. Benjamin, "On the Concept of History," 394.

89. Daniel Bensaïd, *Le pari mélancolique: Métamorphoses de la politique, politique des métamorphoses* (Paris: Fayard, 1997). Cf. Lucien Goldmann, *The Hidden God: A Study of Tragic Vision in the Pensées of Pascal and the Tragedies of Racine* (New York: Humanities Press, 1964).

90. Bensaïd, *Le pari mélancolique*, 290.

INDEX

Abd el-Kader, El Djezairi, 159, 162
Abensour, Miguel, 28; *Les Passages Blanqui*, 240*n*25; *Walter Benjamin et Paris*, 270*n*99
Achcar, Gilbert, *Marxism, Orientalism, Cosmopolitanism*, 164, 261*n*51
Act Up, 21
Adler, Friedrich, 126
Adorno, Theodor W. xvi, 19, 27, 166–77, 178–203, 219, 229; *Aesthetic Theory*, 184; and Benjamin (hierarchical relationship with), 183–86; (and Benjamin), *Correspondence*, 265*nn*5, 9, 266*n*20, 267*nn*33, 35, 38, 268*nn*50, 57, 67, 269*nn*75, 77, 80, 87, 88, 270*nn*101, 106; (and Horkheimer), *Dialectics of Enlightenment*, 169, 174, 177, 184, 201; exile, 179, 186–89, 191–92;

on jazz, 173, 199, 269; and C. L. R. James, 166–74; *Kierkegaard: Construction of the Aesthetic*, 181, 184, 266*nn*12, 13; letters' writer, 180–83; and mass culture, 198–200; "The Meaning of Working Through the Past," 238*n*48; *Minima Moralia*, 169, 171; *Negative Dialectics*, 184; "Spengler After the Decline," 262*nn*62, 63, 66
Agamben, Giorgio, 19, 86; 249*n*2, 274*n*71; "On the Uses and Advantages of Living Among Specters," 19, 238*n*49
AIDS, 20, 213–14
Alembert, Jean d', 122
Algeria, 18, 96, 159, 225
Allende, Salvador, 38, 111
American Civil War, 158

275

Lightning Source UK Ltd.
Milton Keynes UK
UKHW011810190822
407559UK00001B/5